BY THE EDITORS OF
CONSUMER GUIDE®

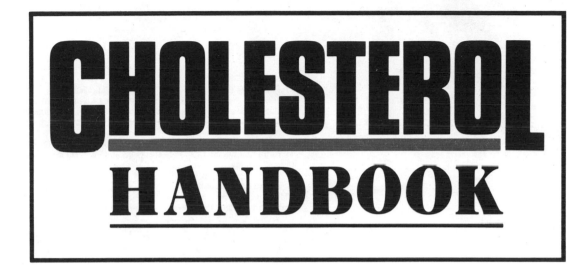

CHOLESTEROL HANDBOOK

Contributing Authors:

Neil Stone, M.D.

Arline McDonald, Ph.D.

With assistance from the National Heart, Lung, and Blood Institute of the National Institutes of Health

Beekman House

Notice:
The Editors of CONSUMER GUIDE® and Publications International, Ltd., the contributors, the consultants, and the publisher take no responsibility for any possible consequences from the use of the material in this publication. The publisher advises the reader to check with a physician before beginning any dietary program or therapy. This publication does not take the place of your physician's recommendations for diet modification. Every effort has been made to assure that the information in this publication is accurate and current at the time of printing.

Acknowledgment:
This publication was prepared with assistance from the National Heart, Lung, and Blood Institute, the federal health agency responsible for coordinating and administering the National Cholesterol Education Program, a national partnership effort involving 35 national medical, public health, and voluntary health organizations and agencies. Although the contents are the responsibility of the authors and editors, appreciation is extended to the following for reviewing manuscript and recommending modifications or revisions: Dr. James Cleeman, Dr. Basil Rifkind, Dr. Barbara Dennis, Ms. Karen Donato, and Mr. Michael White.

Contributing Authors:
Neil Stone, M.D., is an associate professor of medicine at Northwestern University Medical School in Chicago. He is an internist, cardiologist, and lipid specialist who served on the Adult Treatment Panel of the National Cholesterol Education Program. He has written over 40 publications on cardiovascular disease and has been involved in the field for 18 years.

Arline McDonald, Ph.D., is a nutritionist in the Department of Community Health and Preventive Medicine at Northwestern University Medical School in Chicago. She served as chairman of the nutrition program committee of the Chicago Heart Association in 1987 and 1988.

Contents

Introduction

News about cholesterol seems to be popping up everywhere—on television, in newspapers and magazines, even in casual conversation. Sometimes the news is difficult to understand, sometimes it contradicts something else you've heard, and sometimes it's simply inaccurate.

If you're tired of struggling to make sense of it all, you've come to the right place. Our experts in nutrition and heart disease have sorted through the confusing data, claims, and controversies for you and placed the accurate information you need right at your fingertips. And you *do* need accurate, timely information about cholesterol because understanding and taking control of your cholesterol levels can help you protect the health of your heart.

In 1985, cardiovascular disease (disease of the heart and blood vessels, including heart disease and stroke) killed close to one million Americans—that's nearly as many as cancer, accidents, and all other causes of death *combined*. Almost one in two Americans dies of cardiovascular disease. Heart disease is the leading cause of death in the United States. The leading kind of heart disease is coronary heart disease, which occurs when the arteries that supply the heart with blood become narrowed by fatty deposits and blood clots. When these clogs completely block the blood supply to a portion of the heart, a heart attack occurs and that part of the heart dies. Heart attacks strike 1.5 million Americans each year and kill more than half a million of them.

These are frightening statistics, but they're statistics that you can't afford to ignore. Coronary heart disease is not an unavoidable part of growing older, nor is it something that you don't need to think about until you're over 65. Indeed, almost half of all heart attacks occur in people *under* the age of 65. You can make changes now that will decrease your risk of ever having a heart attack.

One of the three major controllable risk factors for coronary heart disease is an elevated level of cholesterol in the blood. (Smoking and high blood pressure are the other two major controllable risk factors for coronary heart disease.) A high level of blood cholesterol plays a role in the narrowing of arteries. The amount of cholesterol in your blood and the way that your body handles that cholesterol is greatly affected by your diet. The food choices you make and the cooking methods you use can either help to elevate your blood cholesterol levels or help to bring them into a desirable range. By taking the time to learn what cholesterol is, where it comes from, how it affects your heart, and what you can do about it, you can control this risk factor and decrease your chances of becoming a heart disease statistic.

We've made understanding cholesterol easy with this thorough, authoritative guide to cholesterol and your heart. To ensure that the information presented in this book is the most accurate and up-to-date, we've enlisted the assistance of the National Heart, Lung, and Blood Institute (NHLBI) of the National Institutes of Health. NHLBI is responsible for coordinating and administering the National Cholesterol Education Program (NCEP), which is a national joint effort that strives to help educate people about the importance of reducing high blood cholesterol. The NCEP includes representatives from more than 35 national medical, public health, and voluntary health organizations and agencies.

The book is divided into three parts. In Part I, you'll find the basics—the ABCs of cholesterol. We explain what cholesterol is and what role it plays in the body. We explore how the cholesterol and fat in the foods you eat affect the cholesterol in your blood. You'll learn why certain types of dietary fat tend to raise blood cholesterol levels while other types of dietary fat can help to decrease them. You'll discover how cholesterol is transported through your body and how the way it is transported affects the health of your heart and blood vessels. We explain the differences between "saturated fat" and "unsaturated fat," so-called "good cholesterol" and "bad cholesterol," and "HDLs" and "LDLs"—all those terms that everyone seems to be talking about.

Part I also discusses the latest scientific research linking a diet high in saturated fat and cholesterol to coronary heart disease. We explain what the research means and how you can use it to make heart-smart changes in your life. You'll also find guidelines for when and how to have your blood cholesterol levels checked, how you can help ensure that your test results are accurate, what your results mean, and what you can do about them.

In Part II, you'll find the type of analysis that CONSUMER GUIDE® is known for. We look at the various methods for controlling cholesterol and explain the pros and cons, benefits and risks based on scientific evidence. We analyze the most popular diet programs, therapies, and supplements, including oat bran, fish oils, yogurt, and lecithin. We also look at the roles that drugs, like lovastatin and niacin, and surgery can play in treating high blood cholesterol. You'll also find information about how your entire lifestyle can affect your blood cholesterol levels and your risk of coronary heart disease. We discuss how you can use weight control, exercise, and stress management in an overall program to prevent or reduce high blood cholesterol.

In Part III, you'll find tools to help you adopt a heart-healthy diet. We help you to analyze your current diet, decide what changes need to be made, and set up goals for a lifelong heart-smart diet. You'll find practical tips on choosing foods that are low in saturated fat and cholesterol, reading food labels, and planning and preparing meals that will help you lower blood cholesterol.

To get you started down the path of healthful eating, we've included a variety of low-fat, low-cholesterol recipes, complete with nutrient information. Since limiting the amount of salt or sodium in your diet may help you prevent or control high blood pressure, we've also included sodium values and tips for reducing the sodium content of the recipes. Following the recipe section, you'll find a cholesterol and fat counter that lists the calorie, fat, and cholesterol contents of hundreds of generic, brand name, and fast foods.

You *can* make changes to lower blood cholesterol and decrease your risk of heart disease. You're holding in your hands the information you need to make those changes. So start making them today. Your heart will thank you for it.

PART I:

Cholesterol & Your Health

CHAPTER 1:

Cholesterol's Role in the Body

What is Cholesterol?

Cholesterol is a white, odorless, fat-like substance that is a basic ingredient of the human body. It is one of a group of substances known as **lipids** (fats), which do not dissolve in water. Every cell in the body is wrapped in a protective covering (membrane) composed partly of cholesterol. Indeed, cholesterol is so essential to our health and well-being that our bodies have the ability to manufacture it, guaranteeing that we always have a readily available supply.

Cholesterol is also found in many foods, although you can't taste it or see it on your plate. All animals have the ability to produce cholesterol, so all foods from animal sources, like milk, eggs, cheese, butter, and meat, contain cholesterol. Plants, on the other hand, do not manufacture cholesterol, so plant foods, like cereal grains, nuts, fruits, vegetables, and vegetable oils, do not contain cholesterol.

How Does Your Body Use Cholesterol?

As a vital part of the body's chemistry, cholesterol is used to produce the steroid hormones required for normal development and functioning. These include the sex hormones **estrogen** and **progesterone** in women and **testosterone** in men. These hormones give women and men the physical traits that are characteristic of their sexes; they also play a role in reproduction. Other steroid hormones produced from cholesterol are **cortisol,** which is involved in regulating blood sugar levels and defending the body against infection, and **aldosterone**, which is important for retaining salt and water in the body. The body can even use cholesterol to make a significant amount of **vitamin D**, the vitamin responsible for strong bones and teeth, when the skin is exposed to sunlight.

Cholesterol is also used to make bile, a greenish fluid that is produced by the liver and stored in the gallbladder. The body needs bile to digest foods that contain fat. Bile acts as an **emulsifier**—it breaks down large globules of fat into smaller particles so they can mix better with the enzymes that digest fat. Once the fat is digested, bile helps the body to absorb it. The presence of bile in the intestines is required before cholesterol can be absorbed from foods. The body also needs bile in order to absorb vitamins A, D, E, and K, called **fat-soluble** vitamins, from food or supplements.

Balancing Cholesterol in the Body

Your body has the ability to make all the cholesterol it needs for these various functions. A diet that contains animal products, however, also supplies cholesterol to the body. In an effort to balance these two sources of cholesterol, your body adjusts the amount it produces each day. For example, when most of the foods you eat come from animal sources, your body gets a substantial dose of **dietary cholesterol**, so your body slows down its own production of cholesterol. On the other hand, when most of the foods you eat come from plant sources, your body manufactures more cholesterol in order to meet its needs. Another vital factor in how your body handles cholesterol is the amount of saturated fat in your diet, which will be discussed in more detail later in this section.

Your body can also eliminate some excess cholesterol through bile. Whenever bile is released into the intestine, a portion of it is absorbed back into the body to be used again. The remaining bile, however, is excreted in the feces. To keep the cholesterol balance, the body can dissolve excess cholesterol in the bile and can also convert more cholesterol into bile acids so that the cholesterol will be excreted with the feces.

As you'll see later in this chapter, several factors —most notably the amount of saturated fat you eat —can greatly affect the way your body handles cholesterol.

Cholesterol in the Blood

Some cholesterol is always present in the blood because blood helps to transport cholesterol through the body. As mentioned earlier, cholesterol is a lipid, so it doesn't mix with water. Blood, however, is made up of a substantial amount of water. Therefore, in order to move the cholesterol through the bloodstream, the body wraps the cholesterol in proteins, forming **lipoproteins**. Lipoproteins work by surrounding cholesterol and preventing it from coming in contact with the blood. The lipoproteins glide through the bloodstream like boats carrying cholesterol to its destinations in the body.

Two types of lipoproteins play a major role in transporting cholesterol. **Low-density lipoproteins** or **LDLs** carry cholesterol to the body's cells, where it can be woven into the covering or membrane of the cell, used to make vitamin D or steroid hormones, or stored. **High-density lipoproteins** or **HDLs** are thought to carry cholesterol from the cells back to the liver so it can be removed from the body in the bile. A third type of lipoprotein, called a **chylomicron,** is responsible for picking up dietary cholesterol from the intestines after it has been absorbed from food.

The amount of cholesterol in the blood can be referred to as either **serum cholesterol** or **plasma cholesterol**. The plasma is the watery part of the blood remaining after the blood cells have been removed. The serum is the watery part of the blood remaining after both the blood cells and the clotting factors have been removed. For simplicity's

sake, in this book we will refer to cholesterol in the blood simply as **blood cholesterol**. The level of cholesterol in your blood is expressed in "milligrams per deciliter (mg/dl)," which indicates the weight of the cholesterol found in one deciliter of blood (see Chapter 3 for more information on cholesterol values).

Usually, blood cholesterol tests measure the **total** amount of cholesterol in your blood. However, your blood can also be tested to see how much of that cholesterol is contained in the form of HDLs and how much is in LDLs. In the future, something called an **apolipoprotein** may also be routinely measured. Apolipoproteins are the protein portions of lipoproteins; they are alphabetically designated as A, B, C or E. Scientists are currently studying these subunits of lipoproteins to see what additional information they can provide about the body's blood cholesterol levels.

The Importance of Blood Cholesterol Levels

If cholesterol is normally present in your blood, why should you worry about it? The reason is that the total amount of cholesterol in your blood reveals how efficiently your body is using and managing cholesterol. Excessive cholesterol in your blood may mean that something is going wrong with your body's balancing mechanism.

The way that your cholesterol is divided between HDLs and LDLs provides even more information. When more of the cholesterol in your blood is being carried by HDLs, there is less danger of cholesterol accumulating in the body; the HDLs, after all, are responsible for taking that excess cholesterol to the liver so that it can be excreted. That's why HDLs are often referred to as "good" cholesterol. If, however, LDLs are carrying more of the cholesterol, the balance is tipped in favor of cholesterol remaining in the body. LDLs, therefore, are often referred to as "bad" cholesterol.

In 1985, Joseph Goldstein and Michael Brown won the Nobel Prize for Medicine and Physiology for their pioneering work with LDL-cholesterol. Their research explained how LDLs exchange cholesterol with the cells of the body. The researchers found that only certain types of cells could accept cholesterol from LDLs. These cells have special structures called **receptors**, located on the surface of their membranes, that are responsible for pulling in the cholesterol from the LDLs. A large number of these receptors are found on the surface cells of the liver; the rest are found on a variety of other cells in the body. When these cells have taken up all the cholesterol that they can manage, the number of receptors shrinks to decrease the amount of cholesterol entering the cell. Any extra LDL-cholesterol then remains in the blood.

This is where the danger to your heart lies. The LDLs take the unused cholesterol and deposit it in the walls of your arteries (the vessels that carry oxygen-rich blood to the cells of the body). As you'll see in the next section of this book, this excess cholesterol can accumulate to such an extent that it completely blocks the flow of blood. Once the artery is blocked, the cells that depend on that blood flow for oxygen will die. If the blockage occurs in the arteries that supply the heart, called the **coronary arteries**, some of the heart's cells die and a heart attack occurs.

How Do Blood Cholesterol Levels Get Too High?

You may be wondering how blood cholesterol levels get high enough to cause all that damage. After all, we've told you that the body has a mechanism to balance cholesterol levels. If too much dietary cholesterol is consumed, the body decreases the amount it produces. Plus, the body can dump some excess cholesterol into the bile that leaves the body.

The answer lies partly in nature and partly in nurture. Heredity plays a role in how efficiently the body handles its cholesterol. Despite how naturally well-equipped we might be, however, the way we live our lives—particularly our dietary habits—can eventually lead to this problem.

When Biology is Destiny

Some people with high levels of blood cholesterol have inherited a disorder in their ability to handle cholesterol called **familial hypercholesterolemia**. As Goldstein and Brown discovered, this disorder affects the receptors on the cells that are responsible for accepting cholesterol from LDLs. These people either have too few receptors, no receptors, or receptors that do not work properly, which allows cholesterol to accumulate in the blood. This disorder can be detected early in childhood. If untreated, people with familial hypercholesterolemia often die of heart disease before the age of 50. Familial hypercholesterolemia, however, accounts for less than one percent of all cases of high blood cholesterol.

How Diet Affects Blood Cholesterol

In the United States, blood cholesterol levels tend to rise progressively with age. For many Americans, this is probably due to dietary and lifestyle habits acquired over time. The body's mechanism for balancing cholesterol—passed down from our ancestors over a period of hundreds of thousands of years—is simply not designed to handle the challenge of our modern lifestyles.

Unhealthy habits, such as overeating, a lack of regular exercise, and smoking, all take a toll on the delicate balance of cholesterol in our bodies. The three dietary factors that are chiefly responsible for the mild to moderately elevated blood cholesterol levels seen in the United States are saturated fats, dietary cholesterol, and excessive total calories.

Fat and cholesterol are a big part of the modern American diet. In fact, 37 percent of the calories we eat daily come from dietary fat. Most of this fat is derived from animal products, outweighing the fat derived from plant products by almost two to one. The large number of animal products we eat also contributes about 400 to 500 milligrams (mg) of dietary cholesterol daily. Compared with many countries around the world where heart disease is much less common, the consumption of this much fat and cholesterol is unusual.

We have not always eaten like this. For many hundreds of thousands of years, our ancestors survived by eating diets that were rich in roots, nuts, and berries. Later, the bountiful lakes and streams provided early humans with plenty of fish. The only meat that was eaten came from game animals that were hunted or smaller animals that were caught by hand. This meat was much lower in fat than the meat that we eat today, which comes from domesticated grain-fattened animals.

It has only been in modern times, however, that the fat content of our diets has increased most substantially. Dating back to the eighteenth century, Americans have prized fried foods, meat, and dairy products. And long before the advent of fast foods, animals were bred to have a high ratio of fat to lean. Milk cows were also bred to give high-fat milk.

Technology has also brought about food processing, creating many new food products rich in saturated fat and cholesterol, such as commercially prepared baked goods, snack foods, and candy. Fast-food restaurants have also become commonplace. A single meal at one of these ablishments can easily provide half the amount of dietary fat usually eaten daily. Given how recently in human history these new food choices and eating habits have developed, it is no wonder that our bodies have difficulty managing the high fat content of the modern diet. We simply have not subsisted long enough on this fare to be well adapted to it.

No other substance has as great an impact on the cholesterol balance within the body as saturated fat. To understand how fat affects blood cholesterol levels, however, we must first understand what fat is and what role it plays in the body.

What is Fat?

Fat is nature's storehouse of energy-yielding fuel. Most fats are made up primarily of **triglycerides**—three fatty-acid chains attached to a glycerol molecule. To use the energy stored in fat, the body breaks down triglycerides into fatty acids. Individual cells then oxidize or burn the fatty acids for energy. Protein and carbohydrates such as sugars and starches also provide energy, but fat, with over two times as much energy available per gram, is a denser and thus far more economical source of energy for the body.

All living things—including plants—have the ability to manufacture fatty acids and assemble them into molecules of fat to store energy. Different species tend to manufacture different types of fat. As a general rule, animals manufacture a fat composed mainly of **saturated** fatty acids and plants manufacture a fat that is rich in **polyunsaturated** fatty acids. Some plants also manufacture **monounsaturated** fatty acids, which are similar to polyunsaturated fatty acids but are much less complex. The terms saturated and unsaturated refer to the number of hydrogen atoms found in the fatty acids that make up dietary fat—saturated fats have the maximum number of hydrogen atoms, polyunsaturated have the fewest. The degree of saturation determines which form (solid or liquid) the fat takes at room temperature, how useful it is in cooking and baking, and as you'll see later, how it affects your blood cholesterol levels.

Fats that consist primarily of saturated fatty acids are called **saturated fats**. They are typically solid at room temperature. Butter, lard, and the marbling and visible fat in meats are saturated fats. Much of the fat in milk is also saturated and solid at room temperature, but the process of **homogenization** breaks the fat into fine particles and scatters it throughout the liquid portion of the milk.

Polyunsaturated fats, on the other hand, are usually liquid at room temperature. These liquid oils are found mostly in the seeds of plants. The oils from safflowers, sunflowers, corn, soybeans, and cotton are polyunsaturated fats made up primarily of polyunsaturated fatty acids.

Like polyunsaturated fats, **monounsaturated fats** are also liquid at room temperature. Examples of fats rich in monounsaturated fatty acids are olive oil and rapeseed or canola oil.

Sometimes vegetable oils are chemically modified to change some of their polyunsaturated fatty acids to saturated ones. This process, called **hydrogenation**, is useful commercially because it improves the shelf life of the oils and allows the less expensive vegetable oils to acquire important baking properties that are normally found in the more costly animal fats. **Hydrogenated** or **partially hydrogenated** vegetable oils are more saturated than the original oils from which they're made. Margarine and vegetable shortening are examples of hydrogenated or partially hydrogenated vegetable oils.

Although most animal fats are usually saturated and most vegetable fats unsaturated, there are some noteworthy exceptions. Fish and chicken fats have fewer saturated fatty acids and more polyunsaturated fatty acids than do red meats such as beef, veal, lamb, and pork. The fat from fish is actually so rich in polyunsaturated fatty acids that it takes the form of an oil at room temperature just like fats usually found only in vegetables.

By the same token, a few vegetable fats are so rich in saturated fats that they are solid at room temperature. Palm oil, coconut oil, and palm kernel oil contain between 50 and 80 percent saturated fat. Coconut oil and palm oil are widely used in the commercial production of nondairy creamers, snacks such as popcorn or chips, baked goods, and candy. Cocoa butter, the fat found in expensive chocolates, is also rich in saturated fatty acids.

Foods rich in fat are usually those prepared by frying, basting, or marinating in butter, margarine, oil, or drippings from meats and poultry. Fat-rich foods can also be detected by their greasy textures. Sometimes fat can be seen as a solid whitish substance found around the perimeter of a cut of meat or running through it. The fat in poultry comes from the skin. Dairy products including whole milk, ice cream, and most cheeses are also rich sources of saturated fat. Sometimes, however, it's hard to spot the fat in foods. For example, commercially prepared baked goods, like pies, cakes, and cookies, are common sources of "hidden fats." Although we may think of them only as "sweets," they are often prepared with oils that provide hefty doses of saturated fatty acids as well.

The Importance of Fat in the Body

Humans also have the ability to manufacture fat. When you provide your body with more energy than it can use right away, it packages that energy into fat and stores it. The energy that your body uses and stores comes from fuels in the foods you eat. Carbohydrate and fat are the primary energy-yielding fuels, but under some limited circumstances, protein can also be used for energy. Alcohol is another fuel available to the body.

The amount of energy that can be obtained from a particular food is represented by the number of **calories** it produces when it is burned in the body. Foods that are high in calories will provide more energy than low-calorie foods. When you consume excess energy from food, that extra energy is stored in the body as fat, regardless of whether the calories came from fat or whether they came from carbohydrate or protein.

We all need some stored fat to provide our bodies with energy at times when we're not eating. Body fat is especially important as a source of energy during the night, because vital functions such as breathing and circulation require energy even while you're asleep. During pregnancy, women acquire additional fat to support the products of conception and to provide adequate energy for milk production following delivery.

Besides serving as stored energy, body fat also has several practical purposes. A cushion of fat distributed at strategic places throughout the body protects the heart, lungs, kidneys, and other organs from injury. And a layer of fat found just below the skin helps insulate us from heat loss.

Women have more body fat than men. A certain degree of fatness in women is necessary to initiate and maintain menstruation. The increase in body fat appears in adolescence and is a natural physical consequence of maturation.

The amount of fat in your body varies, depending on how much energy your body has stored. Only when an adult continually consumes more calories than the body needs for daily activities and vital functions does body fat begin to accumulate, causing weight gain. Besides detracting from physi-

cal appearance and causing psychological distress, excessive body fat is also harmful to your health. Diabetes, high blood pressure, and heart disease are but a few of the negative health risks of being overweight.

Fat in the Blood

Like cholesterol, some fat is normally found in the blood; it travels through the blood to get from its food sources and body stores to the cells that use it. Fat also needs lipoproteins to carry it through the bloodstream. To illustrate how important these lipoproteins are for fat transport, drop a tablespoon of oil or a pat of butter into a glass of water and watch what happens. The fat and water repel each other. This reaction makes transport of fat through blood difficult. When fat is encased in a lipoprotein that prevents it from contacting the blood, however, it can move effortlessly through the bloodstream.

Although all lipoproteins carry some triglycerides (fat molecules), the **chylomicrons** and the **very-low-density lipoproteins (VLDLs)** are the primary movers of triglyceride. Each transports triglycerides from a particular source.

When dietary fat is digested in the body, the fatty acids are released and then packaged into triglycerides in the intestines. The chylomicrons pick up these triglycerides, along with dietary cholesterol, and transport them through the blood to the muscle cells and fat cells. An **enzyme** residing on these cells breaks down the chylomicrons so that the fatty acids can enter the cells. The dietary cholesterol is left behind in the **remnant**, which makes its way to the liver. The enzyme works quickly; it can clear from the blood half the triglycerides absorbed from a meal within five minutes. Within a few hours after a meal, the enzyme has removed all the chylomicrons from the blood.

When your body makes its own fat in order to store extra calories from food, a different lipoprotein takes care of transportation. The VLDLs carry the fat that is made in the liver, along with cholesterol, to the cells where the fat is stored. Once the VLDLs have dropped off their triglycerides, they contain mostly cholesterol and become LDL molecules.

In order to have your blood triglyceride level measured, you have to fast for 12 hours. This allows enough time for the chylomicrons to be cleared from the blood. Once the chylomicrons are cleared, a blood test will show how much triglyceride is circulating in your blood. A simple formula can then be used to determine how much of that triglyceride is being carried in VLDLs. The level of triglycerides carried in VLDLs is important because, as we mentioned, once the VLDLs drop off their triglycerides, they become cholesterol-laden LDLs. High levels of triglycerides in blood measured after an overnight fast are especially significant if blood cholesterol levels are also high.

How Dietary Fat Affects Blood Cholesterol

The relationship between dietary fat and blood cholesterol is a close one. Not all sources of fat, however, have the same impact on blood cholesterol. Saturated fat is more of a culprit in disturbing the body's cholesterol balance than unsaturated fat. For reasons that are not well understood, saturated fats suppress the production of LDL receptors, which are responsible for pulling cholesterol out of the bloodstream. As a result, less LDL is bound and degraded, so the total amount of cholesterol in the blood rises.

Polyunsaturated fats, on the other hand, tend to lower total cholesterol levels *when they replace saturated fats in the diet.* This is an important qualifier to keep in mind. Adding large amounts of polyunsaturated fats to your diet without removing saturated fats will increase your total fat intake, and consequently your total calorie intake. What's more, scientific experiments in which people were given formulas containing different proportions of saturated and unsaturated fats in carefully measured amounts have shown that polyunsaturated fats are only half as effective at lowering cholesterol levels as saturated fats are at raising it. In other words, you can't eat all the saturated fats you want and then expect to make up for it by piling on the polyunsaturated fat. Another reason to eat polyunsaturated fats in moderation is that while polyunsaturated fats lower levels of LDL, they also lower levels of HDL—although to a much lesser extent.

Early experiments concluded that monounsaturated fats had no effect at all on blood cholesterol. More recent evidence, however, has challenged this contention. For example, a diet that is high in monounsaturated fats from olive oil is now believed to be responsible for the lower blood cholesterol levels found in people living in Mediterranean countries. The new evidence indicates that monounsaturated fats lower total blood cholesterol levels by lowering LDLs *without* lowering HDLs.

The total amount of fat in your diet can also be important in terms of how your body handles cho-

lesterol. Since a gram of fat provides over twice the number of calories as a gram of protein or carbohydrate, a high-fat diet is likely to be a high-calorie diet as well. As you'll see in Chapter 7, excessive calorie intake leading to obesity tends to raise total blood cholesterol. In addition, a high-fat diet is likely to be high in saturated fats, which further disturbs the body's cholesterol balance.

What About Dietary Cholesterol?

Dietary cholesterol also affects blood cholesterol levels by suppressing the production of LDL receptors. Dietary cholesterol's impact is less than that of fat, however, because of the body's feedback mechanism, which slows cholesterol production when amounts in the diet are large. The degree to which dietary cholesterol affects blood cholesterol seems to depend on how much total fat and saturated fat are eaten along with it. An important point to emphasize, however, is that there is much variability among individuals in terms of how a change in dietary cholesterol will affect blood cholesterol levels.

The balance between dietary cholesterol and cholesterol manufactured by the body is best when moderate amounts of fat are consumed. Unfortunately, it is difficult to separate a diet high in saturated fat from one that is high in cholesterol. Foods that are rich in cholesterol are typically rich in saturated fat as well. The only foods that contradict this rule are shellfish, like lobster and shrimp, which are rich in cholesterol but have a high content of polyunsaturated rather than saturated fat.

The richest sources of dietary cholesterol are egg yolks. They contribute more than 35 percent of the cholesterol in the American diet. A single egg yolk can provide 250 mg of cholesterol. Additional sources of cholesterol that are also rich in saturated fat include beef, pork, veal, lamb, butter, whole milk, cheese, cream, and ice cream. Sausages, luncheon meats, and frankfurters contain large amounts of fat, saturated fat, and cholesterol.

Commercially prepared baked goods, candy, and processed snack foods are frequently overlooked sources of considerable fat, saturated fat, and cholesterol. These "sweets" are often made with palm oil, coconut oil, or partially hydrogenated vegetable oils because these oils add flavor and are often cheaper than less saturated oils. Many of these products are prepared with eggs. When they contain chocolate, these products can also provide a hefty dose of cocoa butter.

CHAPTER 2:

Cholesterol & Coronary Heart Disease

Why Worry About Your Diet?

These days it seems as though everywhere you turn, someone is telling you to change your diet. One manufacturer after another claims that by switching and swapping the foods you eat for the products they manufacture, you can live a healthier life. Newspapers, magazines, and television continually run stories about the dangers of a poor diet. Much of this news has to do with how you can help your heart by watching what you eat. But do you really need to worry about heart disease? More importantly, do your food and lifestyle choices really have that much to do with the health of your heart?

The answer to both of these questions is a resounding "YES." Cardiovascular disease—disease of the heart and blood vessels—continues to be *the* major health problem in the United States today. In 1985, the most recent year for which such statistics are available, nearly half of all deaths in this country were due to cardiovascular disease. Heart disease continues to be the leading cause of death in the United States.

The leading kind of heart disease is **coronary heart disease**. It occurs when the arteries that supply blood to the heart muscle are either critically narrowed or clogged by fatty deposits and blood clots. When these clogs completely cut off the blood supply to the heart, a heart attack occurs and part of the heart muscle dies. Heart attacks strike 1.5 million Americans each year and kill more than half a million of them. What's more, nearly half of all heart attacks occur in persons who are *under* the age of 65.

The good news is that coronary heart disease can be prevented and controlled through changes in lifestyle. Until the mid-1960s, the death rate from coronary heart disease increased steadily. Since the late 1960s, however, that rate has taken a downward turn. Indeed, from 1976 to 1985, the death rate from coronary heart disease fell nearly 24 percent. According to one researcher's estimates, about 40 percent of that decline may have been due to striking medical advances, such as coronary care units, coronary bypass surgery, use of new cardiac drugs, and reductions in blood pressure. A nationwide reduction in blood cholesterol levels, however, may have accounted for about 30 percent of the decline, and a decrease in cigarette smoking may have accounted for about 24 percent. So, more than 50 percent of the reduction in coronary heart disease may have been due to lifestyle changes. While it is difficult to determine precisely how much of the decrease is due to each factor, it is clear lifestyle changes can affect risk.

Although Americans have steadily changed their dietary habits, this effort has only recently received national attention. Part of the delay in spreading the word was that doctors didn't agree on whether cholesterol really plays a role in coronary heart disease. It's not surprising then that as late as the mid-1980s neither physicians nor their patients knew much about the cholesterol issue.

In 1983 and again in 1986, the National Heart, Lung, and Blood Institute sponsored telephone surveys of adult Americans to find out how aware they were of cholesterol's role in heart disease. In 1983, 61 percent of the participants said that they believed dietary factors were a major cause of high blood cholesterol. That number rose to 65 percent in 1986. Yet only 35 percent of the participants in 1983 and 46 percent in 1986 said they had had their blood cholesterol levels checked. What's more, only 14 percent in 1983 and 23 percent in 1986 had made any changes in their diet to lower their blood cholesterol levels.

Patients weren't the only ones in the dark, however. In 1983, only 39 percent of the physicians surveyed believed that reducing a high blood cholesterol level would have a large effect on coronary heart disease. It's no wonder that so few patients were taking steps to control cholesterol through diet. Fortunately, 64 percent of the physicians surveyed in 1986 believed that lowering high cholesterol would have a large effect on coronary heart disease. This change in attitude may have come about, at least in part, because of the results of some of the research we'll be discussing in this chapter. On a less encouraging note, only 15 percent of the physicians in the 1986 survey felt that they had been successful in helping patients make changes in their diets to lower blood cholesterol levels.

Still, word does appear to be getting out. Largely due to the efforts of the American Heart Association (AHA) and the National Cholesterol Education Program (NCEP) under the auspices of the National Heart, Lung, and Blood Institute (NHLBI), an increasing number of Americans are becoming aware of their cholesterol level and the dietary factors that influence it. This book will help you join their ranks.

What is Atherosclerosis?

Atherosclerosis is the condition in which the inner layers of the artery wall, known as the **intima**, become thick and irregular due to deposits of fats (mainly in the form of cholesterol and another fat called a phospholipid) and other substances. When these deposits occur in the arteries that supply blood to the heart, the condition is called **coronary atherosclerosis**. As the buildup grows, the artery narrows and the flow of blood to the heart muscle is reduced. Like any other muscle, the heart needs blood to provide it with oxygen. When that blood

flow is reduced or completely blocked, some of the cells in the heart muscle can suffocate and die.

Atherosclerosis does not occur overnight. In most cases, the fatty buildups that can clog the artery develop "silently" over decades. Pathologists divide the telltale signs of atherosclerosis into two major types—the earliest deposits, called **fatty streaks,** and the advanced deposits, called **plaques**.

Fatty streaks, which contain about 25 percent fat, can be seen in the arteries of children. During fatty streak development, the cells that line the arteries are stimulated to take in more cholesterol than they can handle. Although this process is not completely understood, it may begin when the **endothelium**, the thin layer of cells lining the inside of the artery, is damaged. Several factors are suspected of causing this damage, including cigarette smoking and high blood pressure. Once the endothelium is damaged, blood cells called *monocytes*, which play a role in the body's healing process, may penetrate the endothelium. Once inside, the monocytes are transformed into scavenger cells. When the cholesterol level in the blood is high, these scavengers begin collecting cholesterol, forming a fatty streak. Some of these fatty streaks can grow into plaques as other cells begin accumulating and growing around the site of injury. Several types of cells appear to play important roles in this process, including smooth muscle cells, which are normally found in the middle layers of the blood vessel wall; platelets, which are elements of the blood-clotting process; and endothelial cells themselves, which release chemicals called growth factors that hasten the formation of fatty plaques.

Plaque is the hallmark of coronary atherosclerosis. It forms as more and more cholesterol is deposited at the site of the fatty streak. A simple plaque can also grow into a more complicated one when calcium accumulates and hardens the plaque, and when blood clots develop.

As the plaque grows, it narrows the artery and restricts blood flow to the heart, causing **coronary heart disease**. Often the first sign that the arteries are becoming critically blocked is **angina**. Angina is a pain or discomfort in the chest. It usually occurs during exertion, when the heart needs more oxygen. Unfortunately, sometimes the first symptom is a fatal heart attack. A heart attack occurs when blood flow to part of the heart is completely cut off and the cells in that area of the heart die. If enough of the heart is affected, the victim dies.

Fatty streaks, however, do not always grow into cholesterol-laden plaques. They *do* tend to progress to plaques in people who have high blood cholesterol caused either by genetic factors or diet. There is strong evidence based on animal experiments that cholesterol plays a key role in both the startup and the ongoing process of plaque formation called atherosclerosis.

Does Blood Cholesterol Level Identify Those at Risk?

There is wide agreement that the higher the level of blood cholesterol, the greater the risk of coronary heart disease. This relationship was first underscored by the pioneering Framingham Heart Study. Since 1948, the study has monitored 5,209 men and women for the development of coronary heart disease. Data from this and other studies was joined in a report, which showed that the risk for coronary heart disease increases as blood cholesterol level rises, especially as it rises past 200 mg/dl. One important finding was that with advancing age, there was less of a difference in the likelihood of heart attack between those with the highest blood cholesterol levels and those with the lowest. A likely explanation for this is that since blood cholesterol levels rise with age, there are simply more people who have a high level of blood cholesterol. Therefore, even the lowest levels were high enough to put those individuals at risk for coronary heart disease.

Recent follow-up data from a study of 361,662 men, called the Multiple Risk Factor Intervention Trial (MRFIT), has expanded our understanding of the link between blood cholesterol levels and heart disease. This very large study demonstrated clearly that there is no minimum level of blood cholesterol at which heart disease risk begins. Certainly, those at highest risk appeared to have levels above 240 mg/dl, while those at lowest risk had values below 200 mg/dl. Yet even those subjects with the lowest levels were not completely without risk. The data also emphasized that higher values for blood cholesterol compound the risk of coronary heart disease at an ever increasing rate (similar to the way interest is compounded in a checking account). Indeed, half of the deaths due to elevated blood cholesterol occurred in subjects whose blood cholesterol was above 253 mg/dl.

A closer look at the results of the study also appeared to show that certain habits could greatly increase a person's overall risk. For example, a smoker whose cholesterol level is under 181 mg/dl appears to have the same risk of coronary heart disease as a nonsmoker with a cholesterol level almost 60 points higher! The same holds true for an individual who has high blood pressure, another known risk factor for coronary heart disease. What's more, a person who has a low cholesterol level (under 182 mg/dl) but who smokes and has high blood pressure actually has the same risk for coronary heart disease as does a non-smoker with normal blood pressure and a high blood cholesterol level (246 mg/dl or more). In other words, other risk factors can turn a low-risk cholesterol level into a high-risk condition.

The effect of these other risk factors is particularly important if your blood cholesterol level is in the 200 to 239 mg/dl range, known as the "borderline-high" range, or higher. When two or more risk factors are present and the cholesterol level is in the borderline range, the risk for heart disease doubles. However, *in the complete absence of other risk factors, such as cigarette smoking, high blood pressure, and diabetes, the MRFIT results show that the overall risk of coronary heart disease for men is not increased markedly even at cholesterol levels as high as 200 to 239 mg/dl.*

So, in order to understand a person's risk of coronary heart disease, you have to look at more than blood cholesterol. You need to take into account other risk factors that could turn a seemingly innocent cholesterol level into a killer. The Adult Treatment Panel of the NCEP considers the following to be risk factors for coronary heart disease:

- male gender;
- high blood pressure;
- cigarette smoking;
- low HDL-cholesterol level (below 35 mg/dl);
- diabetes;
- obesity;
- family (parent, sibling, or child) history of coronary heart disease before the age of 56;
- vascular (blood vessel) disease of the extremities or brain.

See the section on cholesterol screening for more on how these factors can affect your risk.

What Do HDL and LDL Measurements Tell Us?

Lipoprotein measurements can also provide useful information about a person's risk of coronary heart disease. For instance, a person who has a high total blood cholesterol level usually has a high level of LDLs. Several studies, including Framingham, have shown that a high level of LDLs is an independent risk factor (a habit, trait, or condition that is associated with an increased chance of developing a disease, regardless of whether other predisposing traits or conditions are present) for coronary heart disease. When scientists looked at the arteries of young people who had died from causes other than heart disease, they found that the victims who had had high levels of LDL-cholesterol also had more fatty buildup in their arteries.

Further evidence of the role of LDLs comes from studies of the Pima Indians. Although obesity and diabetes (two risk factors for coronary heart disease) are common among the members of this group, they have low total cholesterol levels, low LDL-cholesterol levels, *and* low rates of coronary heart disease.

Studies of families with an inherited defect that causes high LDL levels also incriminate LDLs as the key to coronary heart disease risk. In a study of 116 families with familial hypercholesterolemia (inherited high cholesterol) conducted by the National Institutes of Health, family members who had the defect not only had a higher risk of coronary heart disease than unaffected family members, their coronary heart disease occurred an average of 20 years earlier.

Finally, studies of both diet and drug therapy have shown that lowering LDL-cholesterol levels decreases the risk of coronary heart disease. You'll learn more about the effects of diet and drugs in upcoming sections. For now, it's wise to remember that if you want to lower your risk of heart disease, lowering your level of LDLs is the place to start.

Measurement of your HDL-cholesterol level is another powerful tool in assessing your risk of coronary heart disease. In the early 1950s, scientists realized that patients with coronary heart disease had low levels of HDLs. A study done in 1966 found that men with low levels of HDL-2, a cholesterol-rich portion of HDL, were more likely to develop coronary heart disease. (The test used to measure HDL-2 is a specialized laboratory test that isn't available commercially.)

Beginning in 1968, as part of the Framingham study, 2,815 men and women ages 49 through 82 had both their lipoproteins and fasting lipids measured. The men and women who had low levels of HDL-cholesterol (less than 35 mg/dl) had eight times the risk of coronary heart disease as did those who had HDL-cholesterol levels above 65 mg/dl. A 12-year follow-up showed that the group that had HDL levels below 53 mg/dl experienced 60 to 70 percent more heart attacks than the group with higher HDL levels. In addition, the researchers found that low HDLs could predict the risk of heart attack in people who had the lowest total cholesterol levels.

These studies highlight the importance of HDL levels in understanding your risk of heart disease. Yet the link between HDLs and coronary heart disease is not as consistent as that between LDLs and coronary heart disease. For example, vegetarians in the United States tend to have low levels of HDL, along with low total cholesterol levels and low blood pressure, yet they have low rates of coronary heart disease. Unlike the large number of animal experiments that confirm the link between coronary heart disease and high LDL levels, there isn't enough animal research to confirm the link with low HDL levels.

In addition, scientists still haven't been able to prove that a low level of HDLs actually causes increased risk. It may simply be that a low HDL level occurs when some other unknown factor is also present—a factor that *does* increase your risk of coronary heart disease.

Scientific research appears to show that blood triglyceride level, unlike blood cholesterol level, does not independently predict risk of heart disease in the general population, although it did have predictive value for older women in the Framingham study. Doctors do not find large amounts of triglycerides in the plaques that clog arteries. On the other hand, people who have survived heart attacks often do have high blood triglyceride levels. A high triglyceride level, therefore, may indicate that you have another trait that increases your risk of coronary heart disease or it may simply tend to occur when proven risk factors, such as high LDLs, are present.

You may also hear about tests that measure the specific types of proteins that your HDLs and LDLs contain (called apoproteins). Some recent data has linked apoproteins B and A1 to coronary heart disease. So measuring these proteins may give doctors a clearer idea of a patient's risk. For example, some people who have normal levels of LDL may have higher than normal levels of apoprotein B (usually there's only one apo B molecule on each LDL). This higher level may indicate greater risk, which would

Likewise, low levels of apo A1, the apoprotein found on HDL molecules, seem to indicate a greater risk of coronary heart disease in some patients whose HDL-cholesterol levels alone don't indicate greater risk.

Preliminary research also appears to indicate that genetic differences in apoprotein E, a key protein in the metabolism of LDLs, may predict a person's risk for coronary heart disease. For example, people who have one form of apo E appear to have higher LDL levels and develop coronary heart disease earlier than those with other forms. On the other hand, those who have a different form of apo E may have some protection from heart disease.

Researchers have also found a way to measure Lp (a), a cholesterol-rich lipoprotein that makes up less than 15 percent of blood cholesterol. A high level of this lipoprotein is considered to be a major coronary risk factor.

Measurements of Lp (a) and apoproteins are providing researchers with more and more tools for predicting an individual's risk of coronary heart disease. Some of these tests are becoming available at labs. As a consumer, however, you'd be wise to avoid spending extra money for these tests until more research has been done and until the tests have been standardized.

Does Diet Identify Those at Risk?

Animal studies have provided us with a good deal of information about diet and coronary heart disease. For example, diets that are rich in saturated fats and cholesterol have caused atherosclerosis in many animal species, including primates. In addition, when attempts have been made to lower cholesterol, the plaques have grown smaller (regressed). Yet these studies need to be viewed carefully. For one thing, animals have a different range of lipoproteins than humans. Also, unlike blood cholesterol in animals, there's a limit to how high a human's blood cholesterol can go due to dietary excess. In other words, in order to get really high blood cholesterol levels, a human requires a bad diet and faulty genes. Despite these differences, the animal studies have provided useful information. Studies in humans seem to support the link between a diet that is high in cholesterol and saturated fat and an increased risk of coronary heart disease.

Studies of coronary heart disease in different populations with different diets have generally shown that those with the most extensive heart disease have elevated blood cholesterol levels *and* often eat diets rich in cholesterol and saturated fats. The Seven Countries Study, for example, was a landmark study of over 12,000 men ages 40 through 59 from 18 diverse populations. In the study, the researchers found a strong correlation between dietary saturated fat, blood cholesterol levels, and coronary heart disease. The results showed that western countries, such as Finland, the Netherlands, and the United States, had the highest saturated fat intake and the highest cholesterol levels on average. The Finns, who ate the most saturated fat, had the highest average blood cholesterol levels and the highest rates of coronary heart disease. The Japanese, on the other hand, consumed the least amount of saturated fat, had the lowest levels of blood cholesterol, and had the lowest rates of coronary heart disease.

These results are supported by studies such as the International Atherosclerosis Project, which looked at autopsy results from over 23,000 persons from 14 countries. This study showed that those individuals who had consumed more fat had more severe atherosclerosis. The researchers also noted that those individuals with the most advanced plaques came from populations with the highest average blood cholesterol levels.

A more recent study compared the plaques in the arteries of men from Tokyo and New Orleans. The results showed that in New Orleans, white men had approximately three times as much plaque in their coronary blood vessels as did their Japanese counterparts.

You may be wondering whether the differences between populations are caused by heredity. After all, maybe the Japanese have a low risk of coronary heart disease because of their genes. An eye-opening study explored this link. The Ni-Hon-San Study examined the dietary habits of Japanese living in Japan, Hawaii, and San Francisco in relation to their history of coronary heart disease. This allowed the researchers to see whether the Japanese diet or the Japanese genetic makeup was most important in determining their cholesterol levels. The Japanese who lived in Japan, where the traditional diet is low in saturated fat, had the lowest death rates from coronary heart disease. The Japanese who lived in Hawaii, where their diet consisted of traditional Japanese as well as western fare, had higher death rates from coronary heart disease. The Japanese who lived in San Francisco, however, ate a mostly western diet—meaning one that is high in fat and cholesterol—and had the highest death rates from coronary heart disease.

Population studies like these have also provided us with information about dietary factors other than saturated fat. For example, studies of the diet of people living in Mediterannean countries like Crete suggest that a high intake of monounsaturated oil may have a protective effect. The average blood cholesterol level in this area—while somewhat lower than the averages in countries like the United States—is not as low as would be expected considering the lower rate of heart disease found there. It's possible, therefore, that the high intake of olive oil—a monounsaturated fat—in this region may play a role in warding off heart disease.

A study in the village of Zutphen, Netherlands, gave us two more lessons about diet and coronary heart disease. First, regular fish intake was found to provide some protection against coronary heart disease in the men of this village (see Chapter 6 for more information on fish oils). In addition, the men's dietary cholesterol intake predicted their rates of coronary heart disease in a 20-year follow-up study.

Further support for the link between diet and heart disease comes from studies in which some of the participants were placed on special diets (this type of study is called a clinical trial). The Oslo study, for example, looked at 1,232 men ages 40 through 49 with normal blood pressure, no symptoms of coronary heart disease, and cholesterol levels of 290 to 380 mg/dl. The men were randomly selected to receive either diet and smoking advice or no advice (control group) over a five-year period. The group who received the advice showed a 13 percent decrease in blood cholesterol, a decline in smoking, and a 47 percent decline in incidence of sudden death and heart attack. What's more, it appeared that the dietary-induced decline in blood cholesterol, not the decrease in cigarette smoking, played the major role in reducing the number of heart attacks.

The Leiden study looked at the effects of a vegetarian diet on 39 men who had both high blood cholesterol levels and angina (chest pain). Before beginning the diet, and then two years later, the men underwent **coronary angiography**. A coronary angiogram is an X ray of the coronary arteries obtained after a cardiologist injects a dye into the coronary arteries. The vegetarian diet resulted in lower body weight, lower blood pressure, lower to-

tal cholesterol, and a healthier ratio of HDL to total cholesterol. The angiograms showed that in almost half of the subjects, the atherosclerosis had not progressed and that the size of the blockages correlated with the total cholesterol to HDL-cholesterol ratio. In other words, the plaques had not grown in the patients whose ratio of total cholesterol to HDL-cholesterol was in the desirable range (less than 6.9). On the other hand, those who had unfavorable total cholesterol to HDL ratios showed significant progression of their coronary heart disease.

Despite this impressive array of information about the effects of diet on coronary heart disease, some skeptics don't seem to be impressed with the benefits of a cholesterol-lowering diet for the general population. Researchers in Boston, for example, looked at Framingham and other studies and calculated how much extra life persons aged 20 to 60 could gain by adhering to a cholesterol-lowering diet. They found that for persons who are already at low risk, the gain in life expectancy was just three days to three months for a lifelong program of cholesterol reduction. For persons who are at high risk, the gain from such a program ranges from 18 days to 13 months. These estimates, however, have in fact been disputed by researchers at the NHLBI. And even the authors recognized that their calculations didn't take into account the other benefits that can accrue from a change to a healthier diet. For instance, diet modification may delay or prevent angina and nonfatal heart attacks. So even if these calculations are correct, the chance to live healthier in your later years without the discomforts, restrictions, and costs of coronary heart disease seems well worth any minor disadvantages of adopting a healthier diet.

Has Lowering Blood Cholesterol Helped?

Several studies have taken up the question of whether lowering blood cholesterol levels actually reduces a person's risk of coronary heart disease. All of the subjects in these studies were placed on cholesterol-lowering diets, but some of the subjects in each study were also given drugs designed to reduce cholesterol levels (those who didn't receive drugs were given a placebo—a "fake drug"—so that none of the subjects could tell who was getting the real thing).

The first and probably most influential of these studies was the carefully planned Lipid Research Clinics Coronary Primary Prevention Trial (LRC-CPPT) reported in January of 1984. In this study, 12

Lipid Research Clinics (11 in the United States and one in Canada) recruited 3,806 men ages 35 through 59 who had no symptoms of coronary heart disease. The subjects did, however, have plasma cholesterol levels above 265 mg/dl that remained high even after the men attempted a cholesterol-lowering diet. Each subject was followed for a minimum of seven years. All of the men received a modest cholesterol-lowering diet that limited their daily cholesterol intake to 400 mg and their polyunsaturated to saturated fat ratio to 0.8. This was designed to lower their blood cholesterol levels by just three to four percent. Each man was randomly assigned to either the drug group or the placebo group. The groups were comparable in terms of average age (47), average cholesterol level (291 mg/dl), and the presence of other risk factors for coronary heart disease. The drug chosen was cholestyramine, an effective lipid-lowering drug.

The results were impressive. The placebo group suffered 187 nonfatal heart attacks and fatal coronary deaths, while the drug group suffered 155 such events. The drug group had 24 percent fewer cardiac deaths and 19 percent fewer fatal heart attacks than the placebo group. The drug group also reported 20 percent less angina and 21 percent fewer referrals for coronary bypass operations from their doctors than did the placebo group. In this study, it also appeared that for every one percent lowering of blood cholesterol there was a two percent reduction in the risk of coronary heart disease. Thus, those men who were able to take the full dose of the drug experienced a marked decline in coronary heart disease compared to their counterparts in the placebo group. Those who took the drug experienced no significant side effects other than nonspecific gastrointestinal symptoms, which were expected since the drug can cause constipation.

Those minimal side effects are an important consideration. In a European study called the WHO Clofibrate Trial, for instance, a drug called clofibrate reduced the number of nonfatal heart attacks in the male subjects, although it didn't reduce the overall number of cardiac deaths. Unfortunately, the decline was accompanied by an increase in gallstones and in deaths related to disorders of the intestines, liver, and biliary systems. Obviously, not all cholesterol lowering is beneficial if the treatments are as deadly as the disease being treated. (You'll find more about this in the section on drugs.)

Other clinical trials, however, have supported the benefits from cholesterol lowering seen in the LRC-CPPT. One such study, called the Coronary Drug Project, looked at the influence of several lipid-lowering drugs in heart attack survivors. During the study, the drugs niacin and clofibrate both reduced the rate of nonfatal heart attack, but they did not lower the total number of heart-related deaths. In a 15-year follow-up, however, the group that took niacin showed significantly fewer deaths. This was a somewhat surprising result because most of the men had not continued to take the niacin after the original trial period ended.

Another major clinical study was the Helsinki Heart Study, which used a different lipid-lowering drug, called gemfibrozil. The study recruited 4,081 men ages 40 through 55 who, at the start of the trial, had a total cholesterol level of 289 mg/dl on average. Half of the men were randomly selected to receive the drug twice a day, the other half were given a placebo. Although the drug had been approved only for lowering triglycerides, it ended up lowering LDLs and raising HDLs in the study. As in the LRC-CPPT trial, differences between the two groups appeared after about two years. After five years, the drug group experienced a 34 percent reduction in new events of coronary heart disease. When the researchers took into account other risk factors, it appeared that the changes in HDL and LDL levels were strongly associated with the decrease in coronary heart disease.

Thus, research has shown that lowering LDL-cholesterol is of proven benefit in cutting your risk of coronary heart disease. This is especially true when other healthy changes, such as quitting smoking, maintaining ideal weight, and exercising, are also made. The final word is still out, however, on whether or not raising your HDL-cholesterol level can decrease your risk of coronary heart disease.

In the Helsinki Heart Study, as in the LRC-CPPT, there was no difference in total death rates or in cancer rates between the groups that received treatment and those that didn't. While you may wonder whether it's worth the time and trouble of taking drugs to lower your cholesterol if you're not going to live longer, you need to keep a couple things in mind. There's a good chance that lowering your cholesterol will improve the quality, if not the length, of your life by helping to ward off heart attacks. In addition, remember that it took 13 years before a difference in death rates appeared between the treatment and control groups in the Coronary Drug Project. The same kind of delay may be occuring in studies like the Helsinki Heart Study.

These drug trials looked at the ability of cholesterol-lowering treatment to delay or reduce heart attacks. Other studies, however, have actually looked at the plaques to see if treatment could delay their growth and perhaps even reverse them. These studies used coronary angiography (X rays of the arteries) to detect changes in the plaques.

One such study, called the Cholesterol Lowering Atherosclerosis Study, looked at men ages 40 through 59 who did not smoke and who had average blood cholesterol values in the mid-240 mg/dl range. The subjects were studied after they had gone through coronary bypass surgery, in which the surgeon removes a blood vessel from the leg or chest and uses it to reroute blood around a blocked coronary artery. The treatment group was given a cholesterol-lowering diet, niacin, and colestipol, which, on average, lowered their total cholesterol levels to 180 mg/dl, lowered their LDL levels to 97 mg/dl, and raised their HDL levels to 61 mg/dl. Two years after surgery, the men underwent a second angiogram. The results showed that those in the treatment group had significantly fewer plaques that had progressed and had fewer new plaques in arteries that had not been bypassed. Overall, artherosclerosis had actually regressed in 16.2 percent of the treatment group versus only 2.4 percent in the placebo group.

When taken as a whole, there does seem to be conclusive evidence that lowering high blood cholesterol reduces the risk of coronary heart disease. Cholesterol lowering also appears to be beneficial for people who already have coronary heart disease as well as for those who do not have the disease but are at high risk of getting it by virtue of moderately to severely elevated cholesterol levels.

CHAPTER 3:

Cholesterol Testing

What is a Cholesterol Test?

Getting your blood cholesterol level checked is the first step in keeping it under control. It is estimated that more than 100 million cholesterol tests are done annually. That number is expected to increase, thanks to the National Cholesterol Education Program (NCEP), which has launched a massive campaign to educate both patients and physicians about the importance of keeping tabs on blood cholesterol.

From the consumer standpoint, a cholesterol test is a simple blood test that's nearly painless and fairly inexpensive. In a doctor's office or at a hospital laboratory, a small amount of blood is drawn into a test tube and sent to a laboratory for analysis. The test result is then sent back to your doctor, who informs you of the numerical value and explains what it means. The numerical value indicates the weight, in milligrams, of the cholesterol contained in one deciliter of your blood (mg/dl).

New technology has also made large-scale cholesterol screening possible. Cholesterol screening programs use portable machines that deliver results in less than ten minutes, using blood drawn by pricking the patient's finger. The programs offer many Americans the convenience of having their cholesterol checked in such places as shopping malls and workplaces.

Most often, a blood cholesterol test will measure the total amount of cholesterol in your blood. Your blood cholesterol level, however, is not the only factor that you need to take into account when considering your risk of heart disease. So it's best to discuss all your risk factors with your doctor. We'll explain more about test results and risk factors in the section entitled "What Do My Results Mean?" at the end of this chapter.

Sometimes your doctor may request that your blood also be analyzed for specific fractions of cholesterol. As mentioned earlier, LDL is the fraction that raises your risk of coronary heart disease, so you want your LDL-cholesterol level to be low. HDL is the fraction that lowers your risk of coronary heart disease, on the other hand, so you want your HDL-cholesterol level to be high. LDLs, HDLs, and another fraction called VLDLs, which are rich in triglycerides (fat), all carry cholesterol in the blood. The sum of the cholesterols on each of these lipoproteins, LDL + HDL + VLDL, equals the total cholesterol. Your total cholesterol, HDL-cholesterol, and triglyceride levels can be measured directly. To figure out the level of VLDL-cholesterol, the total amount of triglyceride is divided by five, since a VLDL carries roughly five times as much triglyceride as it does cholesterol. To figure out the LDL level, the amounts of HDL and VLDL are subtracted from the total amount of cholesterol. We will discuss these in more detail in the following section, but measurement of these specific cholesterol fractions often requested by your doctor when a previous test showed that you had a total cholesterol level above the desirable range.

What are Cholesterol Ratios?

Many patients find it hard to keep the various fractions of cholesterol straight in their minds. LDL values easily get confused with HDL values. Thus, many physicians find it easier to provide their patients with a simple ratio of total blood cholesterol to HDL or of LDL to HDL.

These ratios are strong predictors of coronary heart disease. In the Framingham study, for instance, the ratio of total cholesterol to HDL and the ratio of LDL to HDL were found to have the strongest associations with coronary heart disease. The researchers suggested that a total cholesterol to HDL ratio greater than six and an LDL to HDL ratio greater than four indicated a high risk for coronary heart disease.

Although these ratios are simple ways of summarizing a lot of confusing data, the specific values that make up the ratios need to be looked at individually. The fractions that make up the ratio give you important information that is lost if they are not considered separately. *Indeed, the NCEP does not use ratios in its recommendations specifically because it considers the fractions to be independent risk factors for coronary heart disease.* Therefore, you need to ask for the individual values if they are not provided to you.

It is useful to know which of the components (or both) of the ratio are abnormal in order to provide appropriate treatment. The factors that affect LDL-cholesterol are often very different from the ones that affect HDL-cholesterol. For instance, experienced physicians know that in some patients, a high level of LDLs responds very well to a low-cholesterol, low-fat diet, while a low HDL level may be improved when the patient quits smoking, starts aerobic exercise training, or loses weight. LDLs and HDLs are both affected by medications, but often differing ones. In addition, ratios appear to be of little value in individuals who have extremely low HDL or very high LDL levels.

Finally, measurements of HDL-cholesterol can vary three times as much as total cholesterol measurements, even when they're performed at the best labs. This can cause potentially serious problems if these measurements are used to predict risk and prescribe treatment. For instance, consider the patient whose HDL level falls in the 30 to 40 mg/dl range; a ten percent testing error in one direction can put that person in the high-risk group, while a ten percent error in the other direction can put that same individual in the low-risk group.

Who Should Undergo Cholesterol Testing?

The recent NCEP Adult Treatment Panel Report suggests that all adults age 20 and over have a non-fasting cholesterol test to see if they have a blood cholesterol level that is high enough to warrant further evaluation. The new guidelines advise that the test be performed again at least once every five years. How often you should have your level checked, however, depends on the results of that first test, so be sure to read the section entitled "What Do My Results Mean?"

Ensuring Accurate Test Results

New technology and increasing awareness of cholesterol's role in heart disease may soon make cholesterol testing in your doctor's office as common as blood pressure measurements. Yet there's still some concern over how accurately the test results reflect a person's true cholesterol level.

A variety of factors can influence the accuracy of your test results, ranging from the effectiveness of the machine used in analyzing your blood to the time of year that you have the test performed. Some of the factors that you and your physician should keep in mind when interpreting the results of your test are discussed in the following paragraphs.

Until very recently, most blood samples were analyzed by large clinical laboratories staffed with certified technicians. Due to a lack of uniform standards, however, the results from these labs have been shown to vary considerably. For example, in 1985, the College of American Pathologists sent a sample blood specimen to more than 5,000 laboratories in the United States to have it analyzed for blood cholesterol. The answers that came back ranged from 193 to 379 mg/dl. According to the Centers for Disease Control (CDC), the correct value was 263 mg/dl. Fortunately, this undesirable situation is being remedied by the NCEP's Laboratory Standardization Panel. The panel's recommendations, when in place, should allow greater confidence in the cholesterol values obtained. In the meantime, a good first step is to ask your doctor if the lab doing your analysis is standardized to ensure quality results.

Most physicians are now aware of the new desktop cholesterol analyzers. Each one employs a different technology to analyze blood cholesterol. These machines make widespread cholesterol screening possible, but they also increase the likelihood that results will vary. For example, unskilled operators may report results that are less accurate and precise than those reported by more-skilled operators.

Besides these mechanical sources of variability, other factors can affect the accuracy of your test results. These factors need to be kept in mind so that your test results can be interpreted correctly. *Biologic factors* that must be taken into account include age, sex, seasonal variation, recent diet, recent alcohol intake, exercise, family history of cholesterol disorders, other systemic illnesses that affect blood fat levels, pregnancy, recent change in weight, and medications.

Your age and sex influence your blood cholesterol level. In childhood, females have higher cholesterol values. Males actually show a significant decline during adolescence, when testosterone starts flooding their bodies. Adult males over the age of 20, however, generally have higher levels of cholesterol than females. Once women reach menopause, though, they have higher cholesterol levels than their male counterparts.

Seasonal variation has been shown to affect cholesterol values. In one study, for example, the cholesterol levels of subjects who were not receiving treatment were an average of 7.4 mg/dl higher in December than in June. The reasons for this are still unknown.

Your cholesterol levels are also clearly affected when you eat excessive calories or increase your intake of saturated fat and cholesterol. Excess alcohol intake raises your triglyceride levels and HDL levels. To ensure that your test results are consistent, therefore, you need to have the test performed after you've maintained your usual diet and weight for at least two weeks. In other words, you don't want to have your cholesterol tested the day after Thanksgiving or the day after you quit a diet.

Engaging in vigorous exercise just before your blood test can temporarily lower your cholesterol and triglyceride values. It's wise, therefore, to take a day off from intense workouts just before you take the test. (On the other hand, *regular*, vigorous exercise can have a longer-lasting effect by raising HDL and lowering triglyceride levels. This is discussed in greater detail in the section on exercise.)

A personal or family history of certain diseases can also affect your results and your treatment. For example, a family history of elevated lipids is important because genetic forms of high cholesterol often do not respond fully to diet therapy. Yet these disorders increase your risk of heart disease by ex-

posing you to lifelong elevated cholesterol levels. These two points need to be considered when your doctor is deciding how to interpret your test results. Likewise, a severely elevated cholesterol level (more than 280 mg/dl) that suddenly appears later in life may be caused by a disease that needs to be detected and treated before the cholesterol levels can be lowered. Hypothyroidism (due to insufficient amounts of thyroid hormone) is a common secondary cause of elevated cholesterol levels. This disease can be diagnosed by a blood test. People with poorly controlled diabetes also tend to have high cholesterol levels. Other less commonly found causes include nephrotic syndrome (a kidney disease), obstructive liver disease, and in rare instances, dysgammaglobulinemia (a disorder of the immune system) and porphyria (a group of metabolic disorders).

Some medications used to treat other medical problems can also affect cholesterol levels. They include medications used to lower blood pressure (hydrochlorothiazide, chlorthalidone, non-selective beta blockers such as propranolol), estrogen preparations, and anabolic steroids.

Cholesterol values also rise progressively in pregnancy and often take several months to a year to return to pre-pregnancy levels. It's important for your doctor to know if you could be pregnant, since high cholesterol caused by pregnancy is only temporary and does not warrant treatment—especially drug therapy—to get it under control.

In addition to these biologic factors, situational factors must also be considered when your cholesterol values are interpreted. *Situational factors* that can affect lipid testing include fasting, your posture for the 30 minutes before the blood is drawn, recent surgery, and recent illnesses such as heart attack and infection.

If you're having your blood screened to see if your total blood cholesterol level is high, you don't need to fast before you have the test done. Recent food intake has a very small effect on these results. On the other hand, if you're going to have your HDL and triglyceride levels measured and your LDL level calculated, you need to fast for 12 to 16 hours before the test is performed.

Even your posture before the blood test can affect the values obtained. A blood sample drawn after you've been sitting for 30 minutes will show a higher cholesterol level than a sample drawn when you're lying down. This difference comes into play if you have one test done in a screening program (where you may have been standing or sitting) and a follow-up test performed in a hospital (where you may have been laying down).

Finally, it's widely recognized that cholesterol values fall and triglyceride values rise after a heart attack, major surgery, or extensive burns. After a major vascular event such as a heart attack or stroke, physicians should wait at least eight weeks before performing cholesterol measurements. This allows the patient to be on a steady diet and at a stable weight when the measurements are made.

Practically speaking, there are a few steps you can take to help reduce non-laboratory errors. Before you have the test done, ask yourself "Have my diet, exercise patterns, medications, and health been stable for the past two or three weeks? If the answer is yes, then proceed with checking your cholesterol. If not, it may be best to delay the test until these factors have been consistent for at least two weeks. If you're unsure, a wise practice is to average the results of two separate tests for cholesterol and triglycerides taken within a one- to six-week period (the NCEP recommends a second test in any case if the result of the first test is over 200 mg/dl). This average can then be used in deciding whether further tests and treatment are in order. Using two measurements, there's a 90 percent chance that the average is within 9.3 percent of your true cholesterol level; for three tests this falls to 7.6 percent. The NCEP Adult Treatment Panel cautions that if the results of two tests for either total cholesterol or LDL level are not within 30 mg/dl of each other, you should have a third test done and use the average of the three. These precautions help to ensure that the results of your tests accurately reflect your actual cholesterol level. An accurate cholesterol value allows your doctor to prescribe adequate dietary or drug treatment.

What Do My Results Mean?

The NCEP has established guidelines to help you and your doctor interpret your cholesterol test results and decide how to handle them. As we said before, all adults 20 years of age or older should undergo a blood test to check total cholesterol levels. According to the NCEP, a total blood cholesterol level below 200 mg/dl is considered "desirable," a total between 200 and 239 mg/dl is considered "borderline-high," and a total of 240 or above is considered "high."

If your test results show that you have a high blood cholesterol level or a borderline-high blood cholesterol level (over 200 mg/dl), you must undergo a second test to confirm it. This is especially important if your cholesterol falls in the borderline 200 to 239 mg/dl range. This is the cut-off range used to decide whether an individual needs to be evaluated further. If the results of the two tests differ by more than 30 mg/dl, you should have a third test done. The average of the test results can then be used as your initial "baseline" cholesterol value. In between the tests, make an effort not to change your eating habits. After all, you want the results of the tests to reflect your cholesterol values when you're on your usual diet.

Research has shown that at a blood cholesterol level of 240 mg/dl, the risk of coronary heart disease begins to rise sharply. Yet the daily experience of physicians and the decades-long experience of researchers is that your risk of coronary heart disease at *any* level of cholesterol depends on your clinical risk profile as well. This profile takes into account:

- age (*the older you are, the greater your total risk*);
- sex (*men in our society have two to three times the risk of coronary heart disease as women; they also develop the disease an average of ten years earlier than women*);
- high blood pressure (*greater than 140/90*);
- cigarette smoking (*more than ten a day*);
- diabetes mellitus;
- family history of premature coronary heart disease (*a parent or sibling who had a heart attack or died suddenly before the age of 56*);
- low HDL level (*below 35 mg/dl confirmed by repeat testing*);
- history of definite cerebrovascular disease (*impaired blood flow to the brain due to atherosclerosis*) or peripheral vascular disease (*impaired blood flow to the extremities due to atherosclerosis*);
- severe obesity (*30 percent or more overweight*).

According to the NCEP, you have a high-risk clinical profile if you have definite coronary heart disease (you've had a heart attack or there's evidence of impaired blood flow to your heart, as in angina) *or* two or more of the risk factors just described. It's important to remember that if you're a male, you already have one risk factor, so you only need one more risk factor to be placed in the high-risk category.

If you have a "desirable" blood cholesterol level below 200 mg/dl, you'll be given general information on diet and other risk factors. In addition, you should have another blood cholesterol test within five years. Of course, if you change your diet, gain weight, experience changes in general health, start new medications, or alter your level of physical activity, you may need to be screened more frequently. Although coronary heart disease can occur in persons with cholesterol values in this desirable range, studies suggest that rates of coronary heart disease for this group are low and if the disease does occur, it does so at a much later age than in people with higher blood cholesterol (some researchers believe that males whose total blood cholesterol is under 200 mg/dl but who have low HDLs and a family history of heart disease may be at higher risk for coronary heart disease). This is true, however, only if your blood cholesterol level continues to remain in the desirable range.

If you have a "borderline-high" blood cholesterol level, but have no evidence of coronary heart disease and less than two other risk factors, you are also considered to require no further evaluation. You should be given general dietary information. You should also have another test done in one year. If you are young and have only one other risk factor, your doctor may decide to test your lipoproteins. The NCEP makes it clear that doctors need to make an individual judgment about testing and follow-up for young persons.

If you have a "borderline-high" blood cholesterol level and have coronary heart disease or at least two other risk factors, you need to be evaluated further. The same is true if you have a blood cholesterol level of 240 mg/dl or more. Since your LDL level can provide more specific information about your risk of coronary heart disease, and since the goals of your treatment will depend on your level of LDL, you need to have your lipoproteins measured. The results of this test will be the key to deciding how your cholesterol levels should be treated.

Since there can be both biologic and laboratory variations in LDL measurements just as in total cholesterol measurements, the test must be performed twice. If the two LDL values obtained differ by less than 30 mg/dl, then the average of the two is used as the baseline. If the difference is greater than 30 mg/dl, you need to make an effort to keep your diet, activity level, and weight stable and then have your LDL level tested again.

Levels of LDL below 130 mg/dl are considered "desirable." If your LDL level is below 130 mg/dl, you'll probably receive general information about diet and risk factors and be instructed to have your total cholesterol measured again within five years.

If your LDL level is in the 130 to 159 mg/dl range, you are considered to have a "borderline-high risk" of coronary heart disease. If your LDL level is 160 mg/dl or more, you are in the "high-risk" group. The NCEP recommends that those with "borderline" LDL values who do not have coronary heart disease and who have less than two other risk factors should be given information on the Step 1 cholesterol-lowering diet (see the section called "The Dietary Approach" in Part II) and should have their cholesterol levels checked on a yearly basis.

The NCEP recommends further clinical evaluation and dietary treatment for those with LDL values of 160 mg/dl or more and for those with LDL values of 130 to 159 mg/dl who have definite coronary heart disease or at least two other risk factors. An HDL level of 35 mg/dl or more is considered acceptable. If your HDL level falls below 35 mg/dl, you should receive information on quitting smoking, losing weight, and increasing physical activity (all factors that appear to affect HDL levels).

Clinical evaluation is performed to see if your elevated LDL level is due solely to genetic causes or whether it is due, at least in part, to secondary causes such as diet, medications, or diseases. In order to do this, your doctor will review your medical history and family history and perform a physical examination. Your doctor will also review any medications you take to see if they could be causing your cholesterol problem. In addition, your doctor will determine whether or not you have inherited a form of high blood cholesterol.

Before treatment is begun, your doctor will decide whether laboratory studies should be performed to rule out secondary causes of high blood cholesterol.

The evaluation and tests will help your doctor understand what's causing your high blood cholesterol level and determine how to go about treating it. As you'll see in Part II of this book, *diet therapy is considered the cornerstone of cholesterol-controlling therapy.* Drug therapy should be considered only when diet therapy has failed to lower your blood cholesterol to an acceptable level (or in rare cases when a quicker and more drastic lowering is essential). Even then, however, diet therapy *must* be continued.

PART II:

Methods For Controlling Cholesterol

CHAPTER 4:

The Dietary Approach

First and Foremost

For years, researchers and doctors have been searching for a culprit behind the heart disease epidemic in the United States. Unfortunately, the American diet has long been a prime suspect. As you learned in Part I of this book, scientific evidence continues to highlight the role of diet in elevated blood cholesterol and consequently in the development and progression of coronary heart disease. That evidence also shows that perhaps no other dietary substances have as great an effect on your blood cholesterol level—and your risk of coronary heart disease—as saturated fat and cholesterol.

It's not surprising, then, that doctors consider diet therapy to be the first line of defense against high blood cholesterol levels. Indeed, even with the advent of more effective lipid-lowering drugs, diet modification holds center stage. Drug therapy is considered only when diet therapy has failed to achieve sufficient lowering of blood cholesterol. What's more, even when drugs are prescribed, diet therapy must be continued.

In light of the importance of diet in both the development and treatment of high blood cholesterol, goals and guidelines have been established over the years to improve the American diet. The earliest of these guidelines were established by the American Heart Association (AHA). As you'll see, other organizations have since joined the fight for a heart-healthy American diet. Their work has resulted in

sound guidelines for controlling cholesterol through diet.

Not a Passing Fancy

As early as 1957, a group of scientists presented evidence to the AHA that implicated an excess of calories, total fat, and saturated fat in the development of coronary heart disease. The AHA responded in 1961 by publishing their first set of dietary recommendations. These early recommendations encouraged Americans to modify their diet by decreasing calories, total fat, and cholesterol, and by substituting polyunsaturated for saturated fats. Although details have since been added, the basic recommendations for lowering blood cholesterol have remained unchanged for over 25 years.

In response to the growing concern over the role of the American diet in a number of major diseases, the Senate Select Committee on Nutrition and Human Needs was convened in the mid-1970s. After hearing months of expert testimony, the committee issued recommendations called the "Dietary Goals for the United States." These goals were broader in scope than those put forth by the AHA; they addressed starch, refined sugars, and sodium, as well as calories, fat, and cholesterol. The Senate committee's recommendations for lowering total fat, saturated fat, and cholesterol, however, were identical to those of the AHA.

A second edition of the Dietary Goals was published shortly after the first. The revised goals adjusted the recommendation for sodium (to about 5 grams per day) and added a recommendation for calories and weight. In 1978, the AHA also added a recommendation for sodium intake amid the growing body of evidence that the sodium content of the American diet encourages high blood pressure (another risk factor for coronary heart disease).

At about the same time, the Department of Agriculture released its "Dietary Guidelines for the United States." These recommendations were generally more lenient than the Dietary Goals. Nonetheless, the Dietary Guidelines also recommended changes in dietary fat, saturated fat, and cholesterol consumption that were consistent with those originally proposed by the AHA.

The point of this brief history is that the basic points of the original AHA dietary recommendations have stood the test of time. Their endurance over the years despite new scientific findings is testimony to their credibility. The push for a lower-fat diet for Americans is not a passing fancy; it is a serious attempt to stop the disability and the premature loss of millions of lives caused by heart disease. The AHA has been at the forefront of this movement to protect the hearts and lives of Americans and has set an example for other health and scientific organizations. It emphasizes a comprehensive approach to cutting heart disease risk by controlling all risk factors for the disease, including high blood cholesterol.

The original AHA dietary plan consisted of three phases. The Phase I diet recommended reducing the average dietary fat intake in the United States from its current level of between 35 and 40 percent of total calories to a moderate level of 30 percent of calories. In this phase, saturated fat, polyunsaturated fat, and monounsaturated fat would each provide a third of the fat calories (or ten percent of the total calories) in the diet. Dietary cholesterol would be lowered from its current level of about 500 mg to less than 300 mg. The Phase I diet was recommended as a first step for patients who needed to lower their blood cholesterol, as well as for anyone who wanted to adopt healthier eating habits.

Phase II of the AHA diet was intended for patients with high blood cholesterol who did not have success in lowering their blood cholesterol with the Phase I diet. Phase III was prescribed for those who could not lower their blood cholesterol level enough using the first two phases. Neither Phase II nor Phase III was recommended for healthy people because these diets would be needlessly strict for healthy individuals. Phase II and Phase III would lower total fat intake stepwise, first to 25 percent of total calories and then to 20 percent. Cholesterol intake would be reduced to between 200 and 250 mg in Phase II and to less than 100 mg in Phase I. The distribution of fat calories in both these phases would lower saturated fat intake to about six percent of calories and polyunsaturated fat to between six and eight percent, leaving monounsaturated fat to make up the difference.

All three phases restricted polyunsaturated fat intake to a maximum of ten percent of calories because of questions about the possible toxic effects of high levels of this type of fat. All three phases also emphasized consumption of enough calories to maintain optimal weight.

The momentum for dietary change was accelerated further in 1984 with the *Consensus Development Conference on Lowering Blood Cholesterol to Prevent Heart Disease*. From this conference, the Expert Panel on Detection, Evaluation, and Treatment of High Blood Cholesterol in Adults was established. Based on its review of all the evidence on hand, the panel stressed the central role of diet in treating patients with high blood cholesterol— whether or not drugs were also being used. As part of the National Cholesterol Education Program (NCEP), the panel developed a set of dietary guidelines that simplified the original AHA approach. The three phases of the AHA diet were condensed into two steps. In its latest recommendations, the AHA has abandoned its three-phase approach in favor of the same Step One and Step Two approach of the NCEP.

Step-By-Step Reduction

Since excess calories and two non-essential nutrients—namely saturated fat and dietary cholesterol—are the chief culprits in raising blood cholesterol, the Step One and Step Two diets focus on reducing them in the American diet. The minimum goals of diet therapy are to lower LDL-cholesterol levels below 160 mg/dl in most people and below 130 mg/dl in those who have definite coronary heart disease or two or more risk factors for the disease.

The Step One diet is the initial dietary approach to lowering elevated blood cholesterol levels. It is nutritionally adequate yet it restricts total fat intake to less than 30 percent of total calories, saturated fat intake to less than ten percent of total calories, and dietary cholesterol intake to less than 300 mg per day. Since the typical American diet contains 35 to 40 percent of calories as fat, this translates into a 14 to 25 percent reduction in total fat. This diet plan can be followed without the aid of a dietitian.

In the Step Two diet, saturated fat is further reduced to less than seven percent of total calories and dietary cholesterol is reduced to less than 200 mg per day. There is no further reduction in total fat intake in this diet because a diet that is much lower in fat would feel less filling and might, therefore, decrease the patient's willingness to adhere to the program in the long term. In addition, a recent study has shown that lower total fat intakes (that is, lower than the level prescribed in the Step One diet) are not necessary to adequately lower LDL-cholesterol in the blood. The Step Two diet is more intensive than the Step One diet, however, so it's highly recommended that those people on the Step Two diet seek the help of a registered dietitian.

STEP ONE DIET
- Restrict *total fat* to less than 30 percent of total calories
- Restrict *saturated fat* to less than ten percent of total calories
- Restrict *dietary cholesterol* to less than 300 mg per day

STEP TWO DIET
- Restrict *total fat* to less than 30 percent of total calories
- Restrict *saturated fat* to less than seven percent of total calories
- Restrict *dietary cholesterol* to less than 200 mg per day

Keeping Tabs on Your Progress

During dietary therapy, your doctor will periodically check your blood cholesterol level. To simplify this monitoring, your doctor may use your total blood cholesterol level for the majority of checks; your LDL level may only need to be checked periodically. The aim is to get total choles-

terol levels under 240 mg/dl in most people and under 200 mg/dl in those who have definite coronary heart disease or at least two risk factors for it. By reducing total cholesterol in this way, the LDL level should also decrease. Once the goal for total cholesterol has been reached, the LDL level must be checked again to confirm that the LDL goal has also been met.

During the first year of dietary therapy, your doctor may want to check your total cholesterol level every three months. After that, you'll probably be tested every six months. If your levels show that you're not meeting your goal through dietary therapy, you may be referred to a registered dietitian who can provide specific, individualized dietary counseling.

If, despite this two-step diet and dietary counseling, your LDL goal is not met, your doctor may consider placing you on a cholesterol-lowering drug. For most patients, a minimum of six months of dietary therapy is required before drugs are prescribed to lower stubbornly high levels. There are some exceptions, however. Some patients may require a year or more of dietary therapy and counseling before drugs are considered, while others may not be able to take the drugs at all. For example, some elderly patients are considered poor candidates for drug therapy and so must continue with intensive diet therapy. On the other hand, in patients with severely elevated LDL levels (more than 225 mg/dl) indicating an underlying genetic disorder or those who have active coronary heart disease, shorter periods of dietary therapy may be tried before drug therapy is added.

It's important to note, however, that even when a cholesterol-lowering drug is prescribed, the patient must still follow a cholesterol-lowering diet. The NCEP report emphasized that "drug therapy should be added to dietary therapy, and not substituted for it."

You'll find practical guidelines for meeting the goals of diet therapy in Part III of this book. In the next two chapters, we'll take a look at some popular cholesterol-controlling diet programs and some foods, fads, and supplements that have been advocated for lowering blood cholesterol.

CHAPTER 5

Popular Diet Programs

The Choice is Yours

The push for a healthier lifestyle has spawned a variety of books promoting diet programs to control blood cholesterol. Some of these programs take up where the American Heart Association (AHA) and National Cholesterol Education Program (NCEP) guidelines leave off by showing you specific methods and providing structured plans for cutting down on saturated fat and cholesterol and replacing them with healthier alternatives. Others emphasize specific foods or supplements to lower blood cholesterol. Cholesterol-lowering programs like these have the potential to make heart-healthy eating more convenient and enjoyable. As in any other aspect of your health, however, you have to look at your choices carefully.

To help you find a program that's safe and effective for you, our heart and nutrition experts have reviewed several of the most popular diet programs that make claims for controlling cholesterol. Before we look at the individual programs, however, we'll explain what the reviewers were looking for as they critiqued the programs.

Asking the Right Questions

To guide them in their reviews, our experts used a list of questions. This list is a handy guide not only for the reviews in this book, but for future reference. Since the campaign against high blood cholesterol and heart disease is not simply a fad, chances are you'll see more diet programs appearing in the future. To evaluate them, you and your doctor can use the approach outlined here.

Who is the author? Who is the audience?
Answering these questions involves more than reading the title and credit line. It entails looking at the author's qualifications and motivations for developing the program.
Questions to ask:
—Is this an acknowledged expert sharing his or her years of experience in the field?
—Is this book derived from the personal experience of a heart attack victim?
—Is this a person with a mission?
—What kind of audience is the book designed for?
—Is the book designed for the general population, which has been advised to lower its total fat intake?
—Is this program just for the heart attack victim?
—Is there advice for readers who are overweight, have high blood pressure, or are diabetic?
—Does it address the problems of people with different kinds of lipid problems, such as high triglycerides?

What is the dietary approach?
You need to take a close look at the contents of the program.
Questions to ask:
—What type of dietary therapy is recommended?
—How is it explained?
—Are there enough details given so that the aver-

age person can actually begin the diet without outside help?

Is it believable?
Good diets are credible as well as edible.
Questions to ask:
—Is the diet based on proven, nutritionally sound concepts?
—Is there a tendency toward anecdotal or personal accounts? These make for delightful reading but may also present a biased or inaccurate picture of the true value of the diet.
—Is the dietary advice flexible and feasible? That is, is there enough variety here so that a long-term approach is possible? Some diets, for instance, can be adhered to only by those with an extreme level of motivation. Clearly, dietary supplements or a marked focus on a single food or food group may be very effective in the short term for weight loss and improvement in blood cholesterol levels. However, if the dieter doesn't learn healthier eating habits, or as so often happens, tires of the one-sided nature of the diet, the chance of a backslide over the long run is great.
—Is the dietary plan comprehensive? That is, does it deal with the other risk factors for heart and metabolic disorders, such as overweight, high blood pressure, diabetes, and other kinds of blood fat problems? Highly focused diets that lower cholesterol at the expense of increasing blood pressure, for example, make no sense in the long run.
—Is the dietary plan safe? You can't assume that simply because a diet program is popular it is also safe. Poor-quality liquid protein diets that were popular in the 1970s, for example, proved fatal for some dieters. Diet plans endorsed by leading health organizations such as the AHA, on the other hand, are checked carefully to be sure that they are nutritionally adequate. It is essential that you consult your personal physician before you begin any diet program or therapy.
—Is the dietary plan affordable? A lower fat diet should—considering the high price of many high-fat foods—be cheaper. If the program calls for too many special foods or gadgets, however, the cost could become prohibitive.

What's new? What's good?
Questions to ask:
—Does this program have advantages over the traditional cholesterol-lowering diets recommended by the AHA and NCEP? For instance, some pro-

grams offer new insights into how to rate foods and recipes; others offer practical and innovative plans for achieving a lower intake of saturated fat and cholesterol.

Reviewing the Programs

The 8-Week Cholesterol Cure
by Robert E. Kowalski
Who is the author? Who is the audience?
The author is a free-lance medical writer who had a heart attack and two coronary bypass operations by the time he was 41 years old. The book is one of several written by patients who have been frightened into changing their lifestyles by their bouts with heart disease. Because these books are based on personal experience, they are often both inspiring and believable.

Kowalski's program is the one he himself used to lower his high blood cholesterol after diet and exercise therapy failed to get it down to a desirable level. While the book is addressed to the general population and contains some useful information for the health-conscious consumer, the program is really appropriate only for those individuals with high blood cholesterol for whom diet and exercise therapy has failed to lower blood cholesterol to desirable levels.

What is the dietary approach?
The author promotes the combination of diet, oat bran, and niacin to control elevated blood cholesterol and heart disease risk. The diet plan promoted by this book is comparable to the former AHA Phase III diet, with only 20 percent of the calories coming from fat (the AHA, however, recommended its Phase III diet only for those with high blood cholesterol levels that were resistant to a more moderate 25 percent reduction in fat intake). Attention is given to weight control by reviewing the most common weight-reduction diets. Lowering sodium in the diet is advocated and practical suggestions are provided for achieving this. The book teaches the reader how to use information on package labels in order to select foods appropriate for this diet. It also offers advice for shopping and dining out.

Oat bran is promoted as a supplement to increase the amount of fiber in the diet. Recipes are included to enable the reader to incorporate the 1/2 cup of oat bran the author recommends each day into the diet plan. As much as three grams of niacin are recommended daily to further decrease cholesterol levels. The importance of managing stress is also addressed.

Is the diet believable?

Kowalski states that the program he developed for himself—which uses the combination of diet, oat bran, and niacin—is the most effective way to control blood cholesterol and heart disease risk in the "general population." Kowalski, however, is one of a small number of patients whose blood cholesterol levels do not respond to dietary therapy. The appropriateness and safety of this program for the majority of patients, whose blood cholesterol would respond to more moderate diet therapy, is questionable. While there is certainly nothing dangerous about the Phase III diet for adults, it is really a serious attempt at lowering blood cholesterol and not merely the "reasonable" diet that the author calls it. There is question as to whether this type of very-low-fat diet is practical or necessary for everyone.

The author also claims that his program lowers cholesterol without the use of drugs, which is misleading given the dose of niacin recommended. The recommended dose of three grams is more than several thousand times the normal dietary requirement for this vitamin. At levels needed to effectively lower cholesterol, niacin can no longer be considered simply a *vitamin supplement*; it behaves more like a cholesterol-lowering drug, with effects very different from the vitamin.

To complicate matters, Kowalski overstates the safety of the use of niacin. He wisely cautions readers to inform their doctors about taking the supplement, but by providing a dosage schedule, he seems to imply that self-dosing of niacin is safe. There is no mention of abnormal liver function tests that may result from high doses of niacin. Nor does the book discuss the possibility that this amount of niacin may push blood sugar levels into the diabetic range in people who already have high values.

Increasing consumption of dietary fiber by eating more oat bran is a responsible suggestion since fiber has cholesterol-lowering properties. At the level of oat bran recommended, however, some people may find it difficult to continue this supplement over the long term, no matter how delicious the recipes are. The number of foods that have to be prepared from scratch (to incorporate the level of oat bran recommended) may make this program less than practical for busy people or those who often eat away from home.

What's new? What's good?

The use of niacin supplements in patients with diet-resistant high blood cholesterol is not a new approach. It is, in fact, a conventional medical treatment for patients with high blood cholesterol that is resistant to dietary treatment. The safety of its use by the general population in the large doses advocated by this program is questionable, especially without medical supervision. The book does highlight the beneficial role of oat bran and provides useful suggestions and some tempting recipes for incorporating more oat bran into the diet.

Cholesterol & Children
by Robert E. Kowalski

Who is the author? Who is the audience?

Robert Kowalski, the author of **The 8-Week Cholesterol Cure**, adapts his approach to one he feels is suitable for children. It is aimed at the parents of children two years of age or older who are concerned about their children's blood cholesterol.

What is the dietary approach?

The diet is low in fat and rich in oat bran. It is promoted as a means for controlling cholesterol and is part of a comprehensive approach to a heart-healthy lifestyle that includes weight control, lower sodium intake, exercise, and stress management.

The level of fat intake advocated for this diet— 25 percent of total calories—would be difficult enough for adults, let alone children, to achieve. The author attempts to make it easier by showing readers how to calculate grams of fat from calories in order to monitor fat intake. He also offers tips for shopping with the kids and supplies recipes for low-fat versions of foods popular with kids. Many of the recipes, however, provide too much fat to be compatible with fat intake of 25 percent.

The book talks about the importance of reducing sodium, but the sodium content of most of the recipes is not greatly reduced. The amount of oat bran recommended is not stated; instead, recipes are provided that would add some oat bran to the diet. Information about vegetarian diets, vegetable oils, and fish oils is offered for parents to use if they wish. There is an attempt to make the diet flexible enough to be acceptable to children by offering advice on parties, holidays, and choices for snacks.

Is the diet believable?

The author recommends a level of dietary fat that is not appropriate for children based on current knowledge of the nutritional needs for growth and development in children. The safety of a diet that provides children with less than 30 percent of total calories as fat is currently being investigated. Many recipes in the book are misleading because they are not as low in fat as they present themselves to be. Also, if the author truly believes that overweight in children is as important a problem as he seems to imply, then the frequent use of corn syrup (a refined sweetener that contains the same number of calories as sugar) should also not be encouraged as it often is in the recipes in this book.

What's new? What's good?

Although we agree with the author's contention that children need to be aware of good dietary habits, we disagree with the significant dietary restrictions advocated in this book. The safety of a diet that provides children with less than 30 percent of total calories as fat has not been proven. The avoidance of excess calories in junk food is certainly to be commended, but a balanced, nutritionally sound dietary plan is more likely to meet with the approval of pediatricians and their patients alike. It is also important to emphasize that for children under two years of age, there is good reason to believe that dietary fat should not be restricted at all because such restriction may be harmful.

The Pritikin Program for Diet & Exercise
by Nathan Pritikin
Who is the author? Who is the audience?

The author was a man on a mission. A victim of heart disease, Nathan Pritikin popularized a strict, very-low-fat diet. This book is not for everyone. Only the most highly motivated people will find it useful. Those who are themselves victims of heart disease or have undergone coronary bypass surgery will get the most from this book.

What is the dietary approach?

When Nathan Pritikin first introduced his diet ten years ago, it was almost revolutionary in its challenge of the American dietary tradition of fat-rich foods. Even by today's standards, however, the consumption of only five to ten percent of total calories as fat is considered stringent. To get there, almost no fat or oil can be used. Even the few plant foods that contribute some fat, such as olives, nuts, and avocados, are excluded, although soybeans can be used as a substitute for meat, fish, or poultry. In addition to being very low in fat, the diet is also low in cholesterol, sodium, and sugar. A 600-calorie diet is also recommended for weight reduction. The book presents details to help with shopping and food preparation, as well as a number of recipes to get you started.

Is the diet believable?

Despite his history of heart disease as a younger man, autopsies after Pritikin's death showed that his coronary arteries were free of any blockage. Without evidence that his arteries were ever clogged, however, this cannot be taken as concrete proof that his dietary approach works. Nonetheless, populations that regularly eat a diet as low in fat as Pritikin's have low blood cholesterol levels and little risk of coronary heart disease.

Although a low-fat diet is desirable, recent studies question whether an extremely low fat intake (like the one recommended by Pritikin) is better than a moderately low fat intake. There are also some worries about the safety of the diet. It is definitely too low in fat to be adequate for children. The recommended level of fat intake (ten percent of total calories) is barely enough to meet the minimum adult requirement for dietary fat. Getting enough protein on this diet may also be a problem. Also, those who follow this program may not get enough iron, zinc, calcium, or vitamin B-12 from the diet unless they are knowledgeable about which foods can provide these nutrients and still fit within the diet plan. The diet for weight control advocates a dangerously low level of 600 calories daily and is not advisable without medical supervision. Pritikin did cover himself by allowing an additional 400 calories to be added to the diet "if needed," which would bring the total calorie intake up to a more reasonable level of 1000 calories.

The diet is supposed to save up to 25 percent on the food budget once the initial investment in nonstick utensils and equipment is made. Its major drawback is its rigid structure. Most people need more flexibility in a diet plan before they can incorporate it into their lives. Today's dependence on convenience foods and eating out make following Pritikin's recommendations very difficult. Suggestions for dining out are given, but they are probably not realistic enough to be followed successfully. The diet's reliance on home-prepared recipes demands more time than most people are able or willing to give.

Pritikin's philosophy is presented with scientific detail, including references at the end of the book.

Although some of the information in the book is sound, much of it is outdated. For example, in his attempt to almost completely eliminate fat from the diet, Pritikin suggested avoiding fatty fish. We now know that fish—even fatty types—can be beneficial for achieving what Pritikin intended with his low-fat diet. The book downplays the importance of behavior modification for establishing healthier eating habits. It also spends a good deal of time on the harmful effects of sugar with misleading and unsubstantiated claims about sugar's relationship to diabetes and blood cholesterol. Pritikin's views on sugar, alcohol, caffeine, and salt reflect his own bias and not the contemporary scientific literature.

What's new? What's good?

The Pritikin diet plan is commendable in what it did to draw attention to the important problem of excessive fat in the American diet. It is a comprehensive approach that deals not only with blood cholesterol, but also with obesity, high blood pressure, and a sedentary lifestyle. It is an acceptable program for diabetics to use as well.

The Living Heart Diet

by Michael E. DeBakey, Antonio M. Gotto, Jr., Lynne W. Scott, and John P. Foreyt

Who is the author? Who is the audience?

This is an impressive team. Dr. DeBakey is best known as the pioneering vascular surgeon who did the first successful coronary artery bypass operation in the United States. Dr. Gotto is a highly regarded medical scientist who has headed numerous studies in the area of heart disease and is a former president of the AHA. As a dietitian who has a number of publications to her name, Lynne Scott contributes the practical dietary advice. And Dr. Foreyt is a psychologist with extensive experience in studying behavior.

This book assembles a group of experts who are knowledgeable about blood cholesterol, diet, behavior, and heart disease. The detailed nature of the material, presented in a textbook format, makes this book a good choice for adults who are familiar with scientific writing. Not only people with high blood cholesterol, but any reader interested in warding off heart disease can benefit from this book.

What is the dietary approach?

The Living Heart Diet is identical to the former AHA Phase I diet and the current NCEP Step One diet, with fat intake limited to 30 percent of total calories and cholesterol intake limited to 300 mg or less per day. The program also offers low-sodium and low-calorie modifications of the basic diet. In addition, it presents the more restrictive low-fat Phase II and very-low-fat Phase III AHA diets for people with inherited **hyperlipidemias** (elevated blood cholesterol and triglycerides). The authors also discuss the various types of fat, fiber, and protein.

The program introduces simple techniques to help the reader follow these diets. One of these is the well-tested **Food Exchange System** used by diabetics to control the calorie, carbohydrate, and fat contents of their diets. This system not only helps you judge how much you are eating, it helps you keep track of calories and fat without requiring you to know the values for individual foods. Another technique is a point system to help you keep tabs on sodium.

The book is replete with recipes that show breakdowns of calories, fat, saturated fat, polyunsaturated fat, monounsaturated fat, cholesterol, and sodium in each serving. The values for these nutrients in common foods are listed in the appendix. Advice on eating out, food preparation, and reading package labels is provided. The book also includes brief discussions of secondary risk factors for heart disease, such as high blood pressure, smoking, and obesity.

Is the diet believable?

The book makes an excellent case for changing diet to promote heart health. The background material is impressively presented with detailed charts and illustrations. This is a well-balanced diet using sound nutritional principles. The low-calorie diet is reasonable for a healthy, weekly weight loss of one or two pounds. The exchange system allows the basic diet to be adapted to eating away from home and on the road. It does not advocate special foods or food products, so it should be no more expensive than your usual diet.

What's new? What's good?

The diet presented by the book is not new, but it is laid out in superb detail. The behavioral material is especially good. The recipes and menus carry out the charge of the diet—they allow you to decrease fat, saturated fat, cholesterol, and sodium intake. The nutrient breakdowns, meanwhile, let you know how you are doing in each of these areas.

Eater's Choice

by Dr. Ron Goor and Nancy Goor

Who is the author? Who is the audience?

Ron Goor comes from a family with a history of heart disease. His success in using diet to lower his blood cholesterol from a dangerously high 311 mg/dl to 200 mg/dl is the basis for this program. His experience in major research studies on blood cholesterol and his work as coordinator of the NCEP make him well-suited to the task. His wife adds the practical aspects of applying the dietary principles in the kitchen. The book is written simply and should appeal to most adults.

What is the dietary approach?

The emphasis in this book is on reducing saturated fat. The author feels that given their mutual dietary sources, dietary cholesterol will automatically be reduced when the saturated fat in the diet is decreased. Two levels of saturated fat are emphasized: ten percent of total calories and a more restrictive six percent of calories. The idea is that food choices aimed at lowering saturated fat will raise polyunsaturated and monounsaturated fat and lower dietary cholesterol at the same time. Eating more dietary fiber and drinking less alcohol are also stressed. Weight, exercise, smoking, and blood pressure are also discussed, providing a comprehensive approach to heart disease prevention.

To help you meet the goals of the book, the authors show you how to calculate the number of calories you consume as saturated fat, how to read food labels, and how to prepare foods. Sample two-week meal plans give you an idea of how to put the diet into practice. Plenty of recipes are provided to get you started on the program. Tips on eating out are offered. The importance of getting the whole family to adopt this eating style is also discussed.

Is the diet believable?

The program prescribes a well-balanced, low-fat diet. Nothing unorthodox is promoted. The weak link in the dietary approach is the lack of attention to dietary sodium. Because the program is based on making choices, the reader should find it affordable, fairly easy to follow, and adaptable to many different dining circumstances.

What's new? What's good?

This program was one of the first to put an emphasis on calculating saturated fat calories before making dietary choices. You're shown how to set a daily "saturated fat budget" and allowed to choose the individual foods that will fill it. This approach gives you flexibility and control over the foods you eat, while you lower cholesterol. There is a possibe drawback; this approach requires considerable background information and may be tedious for those who do not like numbers.

Controlling Cholesterol

by Kenneth H. Cooper, M.D., M.P.H.

Who is the author? Who is the audience?

The author is a leader in the health and fitness movement. He is responsible for coining the term "aerobics," and is director of the Aerobics Center in Dallas, Texas. His fitness program is used by many military organizations around the world. The book is written for motivated adults and provides advice that is also useful for children.

What is the dietary approach?

The former AHA Phase I, II, and III diets are promoted as "basic," "moderate," and "strict" low-fat diets. The step-wise approach to gradually lowering fat intake from Phase I to Phase III is given. Menus are provided to illustrate each of these diet steps in practice. The exchange system is explained as a way to monitor fat, carbohydrate, and protein composition of the diet. Weight control is stressed. The relationship of alcohol and coffee consumption to blood cholesterol is discussed. There are also chapters on the usefulness of fish oils, monounsaturated fats, oats, vitamins, and drug therapy for lowering blood cholesterol.

Is the diet believable?

The book provides massive documentation of the link between diet and blood cholesterol. What is missing is the detail necessary to make the diet really work. Presenting menus is fine up to a point; they give you an idea of how the diet works but they do not allow enough flexibility. Once the menus run out, what do you do next? How long can you keep repeating the same menus without causing the boredom that makes a diet fail? Despite this limitation, the diet is a safe and scientifically endorsed approach to lowering blood cholesterol. It is also affordable because it requires making wise food choices in the market rather than purchasing expensive supplements. The book offers a comprehensive approach to controlling cholesterol, using diet as the cornerstone of a program that also includes weight control, smoking cessation, and stress management. One important piece of the heart disease picture is missing, however: Nothing is said about blood pressure and dietary sodium.

What's new? What's good?

The book presents up-to-date information about current studies on diet, exercise, and blood cholesterol. As might be expected from the author's background, it is stronger on exercise than most other diet books and provides detailed exercise advice for children as well as adults.

The New American Diet
by Sonja L. Connor, M.S., R.D., and William E. Connor, M.D.
Who is the author? Who is the audience?

This is a husband and wife team; he's a skilled and noted researcher on cholesterol and she's a dietitian. Together they provide the balance that comes from combining scientific background with practical dietary advice. Adults who are highly motivated and disciplined are likely to find this approach satisfying.

What is the dietary approach?

The New American Diet presents a step-wise approach to lowering fat in the diet that represents the three phases of the AHA diet. The goal is to get dietary fat down to between 20 and 25 percent of total calories and dietary cholesterol down to less than 100 mg per day. The recommended saturated fat intake is no more than six percent of fat calories. The authors also discuss life-long weight control.

The program emphasizes healthier food selection and preparation as a way to shift the composition of the diet from reliance on foods from animal origin toward more foods of plant origin. A useful quiz is given to help readers evaluate their current diets. The reader will also find a helpful table that outlines the changes needed to phase in the dietary recommendations over one year. The diet goals are vividly illustrated by describing the food choices needed to meet them. New recipes and methods for modifying standard recipes are also included to get the reader started on the diet.

Is the diet believable?

The book makes an excellent case for its dietary approach by providing a rationale justifying a low-fat diet for a variety of maladies, not just high blood cholesterol. It is a safe and nutritionally sound approach to improving overall health

through lowering fat, saturated fat, and cholesterol and increasing dietary fiber. Attention is also given to dietary sodium intake. The book brims with practical advice on making the diet work for pregnant women, children, and vegetarians. An effort to integrate ethnic foods into the diet plan also broadens its appeal. The section on dealing with special situations, like holidays and breast feeding, without straying from the dietary goals is superb.

What's new? What's good?

The book presents a new way of classifying foods called the cholesterol-saturated fat index. This system takes into account the effect that the saturated fat content of foods has on the way dietary cholesterol will affect blood cholesterol levels. Using this index, the reader will be able to allow some foods in the diet that might be ruled out if cholesterol content alone were considered. The overall dietary approach is not new, but its emphasis on the very-low-fat Phase III of the AHA diet plan limits its broad application. It is questionable as to whether achieving this final phase is practical or even necessary for everyone.

Choices for a Healthy Heart
by Joseph C. Piscatella
Who is the author? Who is the audience?

Using his own experience with coronary bypass surgery at age 32 to motivate and inspire him, Joseph Piscatella presents a comprehensive approach to controlling life-threatening coronary heart disease. The easy-to-read writing style and well-founded recommendations should have broad appeal to all adults interested in good health, whether or not they suffer from heart disease or have a family history of the disease.

What is the dietary approach?

The dietary focus of the book is the "500-calorie solution," a simple but sound approach to weight control that calls for eating 500 fewer calories than you normally do each day. Dietary changes are also recommended to lower fat intake to 25 percent of total calories. This level of fat intake is slightly more restrictive than the 30 percent level of fat usually suggested as a first step in lowering fat in the diet, but it is consistent with the former AHA Phase II diet. The book incorporates ways to make the diet low in sodium as well. By addressing calories, fat, and sodium, this dietary approach tackles the major diet-related problems underlying heart disease, overweight, high blood cholesterol, and high blood pressure.

A strong point of this book is the clear and understandable manner in which the diet is explained. The reader is first taught how to calculate daily calorie needs and then shown dietary changes that will lower the daily calorie intake by 500 calories. The book is loaded with practical advice to help keep anyone interested in making these dietary changes on track. Tips on using package labels to identify fat-rich foods and on making wise choices while dining out or traveling are provided. The way fast foods and processed foods can sabotage the diet is also explained. Recipes for putting the dietary recommendations into practice abound. One of the most useful aspects of the book is the way it shows how to turn common recipes into healthier alternatives by using substitutions for ingredients that normally add fat and sodium. Most of the modified recipes would be acceptable; some, like the salad dressing in which water is substituted for all of the oil, are questionable.

Is the diet believable?

This diet is based on nutritionally sound principles for lowering calories and sodium in the diet. It has been researched thoroughly and is backed by excellent references. By including discussions on stress management, smoking, and exercise, the book responsibly avoids the implication that dietary change is all you need for a healthy heart. Balanced views on fat, sugar, salt, and caffeine are presented, although the recommendations to avoid food additives and soft drinks might be considered extreme by some. The diet is useful in that it can be readily adapted to a variety of lifestyles and pocketbooks. Following this dietary plan will not jeopardize overall health in any way, although a total fat intake of 25 percent is currently considered questionable for children. Research is currently underway to answer this question, but until it is resolved, most experts would recommend that children get 30 percent of their calories from fat.

What's new? What's good?

The book is an excellent instructional manual that takes a complicated set of dietary changes and simplifies them enough for most people to comprehend. The recipe modifications are a unique contribution and one of the best features of the book. They are described well and presented in an easy-to-follow format.

The Low-Cholesterol Oat Plan
by Barbara Earnest and Sarah Schlesinger
Who is the author? Who is the audience?

Authors Barbara Earnest and Sarah Schlesinger are knowlegeable about fiber and its importance in the diet, and they use this book to present this information to the public. Anyone who is interested in increasing fiber in their diet can benefit from this book, but it was written specifically for the person with high blood cholesterol in mind.

What is the dietary approach?

This is a comprehensive low-fat, low-salt, low-sugar diet that is rich in fiber (obtained by cooking with oats). The AHA dietary guidelines are promoted and background information explaining the relationship of diet to blood cholesterol and heart disease is included. The importance of weight control, exercise, and smoking cessation in the overall approach is also stressed. The program includes over 300 recipes for incorporating oat bran into the diet. The amounts of oat bran provided by each serving of the various recipes are given so you can keep track of how much oat bran you eat daily. An interesting, informative, and scientifically sound discussion of the different types of fiber found in foods is also presented.

Is the diet believable?

The oat diet promoted by this book is nutritionally sound. At the level of intake recommended, this type of fiber should not interfere with the absorption of minerals like calcium, magnesium, iron, and zinc. Once again, however, the program's focus on a single food may make it difficult to follow in the long run. How practical it is for average consumers depends on how much time and effort they are willing to spend in preparing foods at home.

What's new? What's good?

It is one of the first comprehensive guides to cooking with oats that also promotes a balanced approach to controlling blood cholesterol and heart disease through weight control and moderate intakes of fat and sodium.

Good Fat, Bad Fat: How to Lower Your Cholesterol & Beat the Odds of a Heart Attack
by Glen C. Griffin, M.D. and William P. Castelli, M.D.
Who is the author? Who is the audience?

The authors are two respected physicians. Dr. Griffin is the editor-in-chief of a popular medical magazine for practicing physicians. He has also had a coronary bypass operation and his personal experience adds an emotional flavor to the text. Dr. Castelli is the medical director of the famous Framingham Heart Study. The book is written for the average reader who is not necessarily well-versed in nutritional concepts. The style is motivational and easy to read. The book is loaded with practical suggestions for reducing the total fat and saturated fat in the diet.

What is the dietary approach?

Like many of the new books on diet and cholesterol, the emphasis in this book is on reducing the grams of saturated fat in the diet. The authors provide flexible guidelines for determining just how much saturated fat you should consume each day. In addition, they discuss the variables that must be considered when setting a calorie limit.

The recommendations for saturated fat and cholesterol are based on the NCEP Step One and Step Two diets. The less restrictive diet limits saturated fat to less than ten percent of total calories and daily cholesterol to less than 300 mg; the more restrictive phase limits saturated fat to less than seven percent of total calories and daily cholesterol to less than 200 mg. Advice is given on dealing with other risk factors, including overweight, cigarette smoking, and sedentary habits. Advice on eating out and modifying recipes is also included.

Is the diet believable?

The dietary program is really a straightforward presentation of the NCEP dietary guidelines, but in a simplified, practical format. Little is mentioned about dietary sodium, however, for patients with high blood pressure or fluid-retention problems. The numerical information is handled in a simple way so that the reader is not overwhelmed with tables and statistics. Most readers should have no trouble incorporating many of the practical suggestions into their dietary habits.

What's new? What's good?

Calculating grams of saturated fat is no longer a "new" idea. The aspects that make this book special are its readability, the ease with which it guides you from old high-fat habits to new low-fat habits, and the considerable information about heart disease that it packs into its small size. The large print and clear figures and graphs also greatly enhance the book's readability.

Count Out Cholesterol
by Dr. Art Ulene
Who is the author? Who is the audience?

The author, Dr. Art Ulene, is the spokesperson for the American Medical Association's Campaign Against Cholesterol and is also the health adviser on a network television program. The book is a comprehensive review of saturated fat, cholesterol, and fiber. It is written for the reader who desires an understandable and practical system for lowering blood cholesterol through diet.

What is the dietary approach?

The heart of the dietary approach is a clever system using values called SF1 and SF2. The SF1, which is based on gender, activity level, and weight, refers to the maximum amount of saturated fat you should consume in one day. Your SF2, which you determine by consulting a table in the book, refers to the number of grams of fiber you should consume each day. With this system, the author and his staff have removed the calculations usually needed in determining dietary goals. Another useful item in the book is a 30-day diary that gives you a chance to calculate your SF1 and SF2 and is also packed with helpful suggestions for lowering cholesterol.

Is the diet believable?

This is a unique presentation of the NCEP Step One and Step Two diets. A useful food table at the back of the book lists the SF1, SF2, and cholesterol content of a variety of foods. For foods not listed, readers may be able to calculate SF1 values using saturated fat information on food labels. Current labeling practices, however, may not provide the information needed to calculate the SF2 or soluble fiber value for some foods not listed in the book. Nonetheless, for the less compulsive reader who needs a workable system that covers most situations, this is a highly attractive idea.

What's new? What's good?

This is another book that helps the reader determine his or her daily saturated fat intake in order to put the NCEP guidelines into practice. While many books advise readers to eat more fiber, the SF2 system is unique and should encourage more variety and flexibility in high-fiber menus. The book also discusses important medical studies that have influenced the guidelines for lowering cholesterol through diet, thus giving the reader an understanding of the "whys" behind the recommendations.

CHAPTER 6:

Foods, Fads, & Supplements

Cholesterol "Cures?"

In addition to the diet programs that have been appearing on the shelves lately, a variety of individual foods, supplements, and therapies have been touted as having cholesterol-controlling powers. Some of these do indeed appear to play a role in reducing the level of cholesterol in the blood—when they are used wisely. Others, however, are merely fads that sap more money from your wallet than cholesterol from your bloodstream.

In this chapter, you'll find straightforward information about the benefits, risks, and reality behind the claims for the most popular cholesterol-lowering foods, fads, and supplements. There are some things you should keep in mind, however, as you review these products. For starters, there is no single food, beverage, or supplement that can cure you of a cholesterol problem on its own. If there were, we wouldn't have an epidemic of elevated blood cholesterol levels in this country.

As we said before, a healthy, balanced diet that's low in total fat, saturated fat, and cholesterol is the first line of defense against high blood cholesterol. It's not only the best way to lower elevated levels for the vast majority of Americans, it's a way to keep those levels in a healthy range for life. So even those supplements or dietary helpers that can have a beneficial effect on cholesterol need to be incorporated into a heart-smart diet. They cannot replace it. If you focus on a single supplement or food without paying attention to your other eating habits, you won't be solving your problem. Indeed, you may be creating new ones by depriving your body of the balanced nutrition it needs.

In addition, relying on a single food or supplement can make for a very boring diet. And that's the opposite of what you need. To control cholesterol, you need a varied, nutritionally adequate diet that you can stick with for life. So choose your foods wisely by selecting those that are lowest in saturated fat and cholesterol. If a particular food or supplement does appear to help, be sure to include it. But remember, moderation is the key. And if you have any doubts or questions, see your doctor.

Alcohol

For many people, the ritual evening cocktail is a sure cure for the day's troubles. These same individuals might not be surprised to learn that when consumed in moderation, alcohol may also offer some protection against heart disease. A psychological explanation for this is inescapable, but more tangible evidence seems to come from the higher HDL levels of drinkers as opposed to nondrinkers.

A closer look at HDL-cholesterol in drinkers confirms that alcohol consumption can raise HDL-cholesterol and that abstinence from alcohol for two weeks can lower it. This could be good news for those who imbibe in moderation. But experts raise a red flag at the idea of encouraging alcohol consumption as a means for raising HDL-cholesterol. For one thing, until we know more about how alcohol affects the different types of HDL-cholesterol, we cannot be sure that there is an advantage to raising HDL through alcohol consumption. For instance, alcohol may have more of an effect on the HDL_3 fraction than on the HDL_2 fraction. Unfortunately, a high level of HDL_3 does not appear to offer the protection that a high level of HDL_2 does.

In any case, encouraging consumption of alcohol as a way to raise HDL-cholesterol does not make good sense. Consuming large amounts of alcohol may raise blood pressure and thereby offset the protection against heart disease afforded by a higher HDL level. Heavy alcohol intake also increases blood triglycerides. In addition, heavy drinking is associated with liver damage, birth defects (when alcohol is consumed during pregnancy), psychosocial problems, serious accidents, and an increased risk of developing some forms of cancers, such as those of the breast and throat. So it's no wonder that moderate drinkers live longer than heavy drinkers. And it's no wonder that increasing your alcohol intake is not an acceptable—or wise—way to control blood cholesterol.

Chelation Therapy

Chelation therapy for atherosclerosis refers to the use of a **chelating agent** called ethylenediaminetetraacetate (EDTA) to remove calcium buildup from plaques in blood vessel walls. By removing calcium from plaques, chelation therapy is supposed to help ward off or reverse atherosclerosis. Despite studies claiming benefit from this therapy, however, critical analysis by respected medical journals has shown that chelation therapy is not an effective treatment for atherosclerosis.

The major flaw with studies claiming benefit from chelation therapy was that there were no suitable control groups (people who are like the treatment group in every way except that they did not receive the treatment in question) used. Without a control group, you don't know if any improvement seen in the treatment group was due to the therapy, the doctor's reassuring manner, or just chance. During the Revolutionary War, for example, physicians thought that bleeding a patient was an acceptable therapy for serious infectious diseases because prominent doctors reported that some patients recovered with this treatment. If a control group had been looked at, however, the physicians would have realized that bleeding not only didn't help, it hurt.

There is also a good deal of question about the safety of chelation therapy. Although life-threatening side effects can supposedly be avoided by limiting the dose to less than three grams daily, cases of kidney damage have been reported with lower doses. EDTA is excreted by the kidney, so it is particularly toxic to those with impaired kidney function. This medication can also cause problems with blood pressure, calcium levels, and blood clotting. In diabetics, this therapy may increase the need for insulin. Milder side effects associated with this drug include vomiting and rash.

Since there are no data from clinical trials that prove that EDTA is an effective treatment for atherosclerosis, and because of the potential for serious side effects, chelation therapy is definitely not recommended for the prevention or treatment of atherosclerosis.

Fish Oils

A group of Eskimos in Greenland provided the first indication that fish oils could play a beneficial role in controlling cholesterol and preventing heart disease. It seems that although these Eskimos consumed a diet rich in fat, they had low blood cholesterol levels and rarely suffered from heart disease. Closer scrutiny of the Eskimo diet uncovered fish as the source of most of the fat. The fat in these fish, however, was different from the fat found in other animals. It was rich in two polyunsaturated fatty acids, **docosahexaenoic acid** (DHA) and **eicosapentaenoic acid** (EPA). These **omega-3 fatty acids**, as they are called, are found in marine vegetation called phytoplankton. Fish obtain these fatty acids by feeding on phytoplankton and then store them in their fat. Fish consume different amounts of these fatty acids depending upon where they feed and how much fat they store; therefore some fish are better sources of these fatty acids than are others.

Research shows that a diet rich in fish oils may lower blood cholesterol. Fish oils in very high doses may also lower LDL and may increase HDL in some people. On the other hand, some studies show that lower doses of fish oils may raise LDL-cholesterol. Blood pressure also tends to decrease when fish oil consumption is increased.

Of course, you can also achieve all of these benefits by increasing your consumption of vegetable oil. Fish oils, however, appear to have added advantages. For instance, fish oils are more effective at lowering blood triglycerides than are vegetable oils. Unlike vegetable oils, fish oils may reduce the risk that dangerous blood clots will form and block partially clogged blood vessels. Fish oils also inhibit the action of **monocytes**, the cells in blood that play a role in the accumulation of fat and cholesterol in the blood vessel walls (plaque). Preliminary data also suggest that fish oils may be helpful in patients undergoing **balloon angioplasty**. Balloon angioplasty is a procedure in which a balloon attached to a catheter is inserted into a clogged artery. The balloon is then inflated, pushing the plaque against the artery walls and opening up blood flow. Early research seems to suggest that the artery is more likely to stay open if the patient is treated with a combination of fish oils and aspirin, as opposed to the standard treatment of aspirin alone.

Much of what we know about the benefits of fish oils is based on studies of people who, like the Eskimos, consume fish, not fish oil supplements. In a Dutch study, for instance, men who ate as little as seven ounces of fish a week, on average, over a 20-year period had some protection from heart disease. All other things being equal, twice as many men who ate less than an average of seven ounces of fish a week died from heart disease.

The type of fish and the way it is prepared may influence the cholesterol-lowering benefits that fish oils provide. Fatty fish, like white tuna, mackerel, herring, and salmon, are richer in the omega-3 fatty acids than are leaner fish, like halibut, cod, and flounder. But you don't have to pile on the fatty fish to get the benefits from the oils found in the fish. In the Dutch study, a full two-thirds of the fish in the diets of those men who were protected from heart disease was of the lean variety.

The benefits of eating fish can also be canceled out by preparing it with fat. For instance, the unexpected finding that heart disease was more common in the fish-eating provinces of Canada compared with the provinces where fish eating is less common was traced to the popular custom of frying cod in lard or other fats.

Foods absorb some of the fat used in cooking, especially when they are breaded. As a result, a fish that is fried, or breaded and then fried, will have a higher fat content than it would have if it were baked or broiled. Using vegetable oils will not solve the problem, even though these oils are rich in polyunsaturated fatty acids; the high temperatures required for frying will destroy many of these fatty acids and their beneficial properties. Using butter or lard is even worse because these fats add both saturated fats and cholesterol to the fish. Commercially prepared or processed fish are often made with coconut oil or palm oil.

The most obvious source of fish oils is fish. Fish oils, however, are now also available in capsule and liquid forms and are being promoted as a dietary supplement for lowering blood cholesterol. The use of supplements to achieve the benefits of fish oils is unnecessary, however, if you include more fish in your diet. Fish consumption is a safer and more economical way to increase EPA and DHA in the diet.

Fish oil supplements contain such small amounts of EPA and DHA that large quantities have to be taken to get the desired effects. Since there is concern over possible chemical contamination of fish, consuming such large concentrations of fish oils may increase the risk of a toxic reaction. Fish oil is also made up entirely of fat, so such large quantities would add unwanted calories to the diet. In high doses, fish oils may also increase the tendency of some people to bleed and may raise blood sugar in some diabetics. In addition, fish oils may depress the immune system and thereby increase vulnerability to infection. Vitamin balance in the body can also be upset by fish oils. A vitamin E deficiency may develop and, if cod liver oil is the supplement used, there is a danger of toxicity from too much vitamin A and vitamin D.

Therefore, eating fish is a better way to increase your intake of EPA and DHA than using fish oil supplements. There is no solid scientific evidence to support the use of fish oil supplements to lower blood cholesterol. The medical community considers the use of fish oil supplements to lower cholesterol as experimental and cautions against their use without a doctor's supervision. Even then, however, fish oil supplements are prescribed only for people with high blood triglycerides who have not responded to diet or drug therapy. Until a purified, concentrated preparation is available and tested in the United States, fish oils should be obtained from fish rather than from supplements. Remember: Better out of the stream than out of the bottle.

Garlic

The use of garlic as an aid to improving health is older than its use as a food. In ancient times, the garlic bulb was considered a common treatment for deafness, dropsy (abnormal accumulation of fluid in the body), intestinal parasites, leprosy, respiratory illnesses, and loss of appetite. Today, however, garlic is more commonly used as a food or food seasoning. It is available not only in its natural bulb form, but as a tablet, with or without parsley to neutralize its odor. It can also be purchased as an odorless capsule, syrup, tincture, or essential oil. Garlic does possess some germ-killing powers because of a substance it contains called **allicin**. By today's standards, however, garlic falls short of the effectiveness we have come to expect from a "medicine."

Garlic has received some recent attention as a means for lowering blood cholesterol. In one small study, for instance, blood cholesterol levels were reduced by 17 percent in a group of people who took 15 mg of garlic oil a day. Some of these people had high blood cholesterol to begin with, but others did not. The change in lipoproteins was also favorable. The garlic raised HDL-cholesterol and lowered LDL-cholesterol. Blood triglyceride levels were also lowered. Other research indicates that garlic may have the ability to slightly lower blood sugar levels and may function as a mild diuretic in relieving bloatedness from water retention. There are still questions, however, about whether garlic can prevent the formation of blood clots or lower blood pressure.

Although the use of garlic sounds like a fascinating and delicious way to lower blood cholesterol, there is no good scientific proof that indicates that garlic is useful for this purpose. Good science does not rely on only a few small studies to draw conclusions. Judgment about garlic's true therapeutic value for this problem, as well as others, awaits further testing. Many readers may still want to include more garlic in their diets and it is likely that bad breath will be the worst possible outcome. These individuals should remember, however, that the real harm that can come from using garlic as a treatment for high blood cholesterol is when it is used for more conventional and sounder approaches, such as diet modification.

Laxatives

The use of laxatives—specifically those containing psyllium—has recently been promoted as a way to lower blood cholesterol. Psyllium, the active ingredient in laxatives such as *Metamucil*, is a natural fiber product derived from the husks of psyllium seeds. It is one of a group of gel-forming, soluble fibers that have been shown to lower blood cholesterol values when added to the diet. What's more, even when the diet is already low in cholesterol, the addition of this type of fiber appears to decrease blood cholesterol levels further.

In the best study done on the cholesterol-lowering effects of this fiber, psyllium was added to the diet as sugar-free *Metamucil*. The subjects took 3.4 grams of *Metamucil* (one packet) before each meal three times daily. (*Metamucil* comes as a powder that is mixed with eight ounces of water and taken immediately.)

The patients in this study were 26 men with cholesterol values ranging from 188 to 314 mg/dl. The average blood cholesterol level for the treatment group was 247 and the average level for the placebo group was 249. The average LDL level was 162 for the treatment group and 159 for the placebo group. These cholesterol levels are less than those seen in the major cholesterol-lowering trials that have been reported in the last four years. So on average, these men had a milder form of high cholesterol.

After eight weeks of treatment, the psyllium reduced the treatment group's average blood cholesterol level to 211 and average LDL level to 130. These are excellent results. Since the study lasted only eight weeks, however, it is difficult to draw conclusions about the long-term benefits of this therapy. The therapeutic effects of powders have been known to wane over time. Also, it is difficult to tell how this treatment would work for men with lipid problems that are characterized by high triglycerides, low HDL-cholesterol, or higher levels of total cholesterol.

In terms of safety, psyllium has been prescribed by physicians for decades to prevent constipation or to regulate bowel habits in patients with irritable bowel syndrome, diverticular disease, or hemorrhoids. Allergic reactions and gastrointestinal blockage appear to be rare.

The use of psyllium as a treatment for elevated blood cholesterol does appear to hold promise, but final word is still out. It would be one of the least expensive therapies considering the cost of some drugs for lowering cholesterol (drug therapy may range from several dollars to more than a hundred dollars for a month's worth of treatment, while a month's worth of Metamucil would cost only a few dollars). Laxatives like Metamucil, however, come in a powder form that must be mixed with liquid before each dose, so it might be somewhat less convenient than taking a pill. If you are considering the use of psyllium for lowering blood cholesterol, be sure to discuss this with your physician first.

Lecithin

Lecithin is a powder that is produced commercially from soybeans. One of the major uses for commercial lecithin is in the processing of foods. As one of the more common food additives, lecithin can be found in margarine, chocolate, baked goods, and breakfast cereals. A natural source of dietary lecithin is egg yolk. The human liver also produces lecithin and the brain and nerves are rich in this substance. Lecithin is important for conducting nerve impulses through the body. As part of the structure of lipoproteins, lecithin also functions in the transport of triglycerides and cholesterol through the blood.

Lecithin is also sold as a popular dietary supplement. Its popularity has been attributed to claims that it can improve memory as well as help with a variety of ailments including arthritis, gallstones, and skin disorders. None of these claims has ever been substantiated.

Lecithin supplements have also been strongly promoted as a method for lowering blood cholesterol. Any effect these supplements might have on blood cholesterol, however, cannot be from the lecithin itself, since this compound is first digested before it is absorbed into the body. Lecithin in the blood comes from the liver, not the diet.

One of the products of lecithin digestion, however, is the polyunsaturated fatty acid, linoleic acid. Because polyunsaturated fat is well known for its ability to lower blood cholesterol, it is the linoleic acid that is probably responsible for the cholesterol-lowering effect attributed to lecithin. Linoleic acid is also important for healthy skin and normal nervous system functioning, which may explain some of the other claims attributed to lecithin. Vegetable oils, however, are a more economical source of linoleic acid than lecithin supplements because the oils provide more linoleic acid for the money.

Oats and Other Sources of Dietary Fiber

Dietary fiber has long been considered important for preventing constipation. Today, however, we are beginning to appreciate fiber for more than its role in maintaining regularity. Recent research seems to indicate that increasing the amount of fiber in the diet may lower blood cholesterol. This benefit of dietary fiber could explain why heart disease occurs less frequently in populations that consume diets that are high in fiber. Dietary fiber may also help in regulating blood sugar and may have a favorable effect on blood pressure as well. In addition, cancers of the colon and rectum are less common in people who consume twice the fiber typically found in the American diet.

Dietary fiber is found exclusively in plant foods. It serves as the structural framework in plants and is one of the most abundant compounds in nature. Fiber is the part of the plant that cannot be broken down in the intestines by human digestive enzymes. Because it is not digested, fiber is not absorbed in the body. Instead it stays in the intestines to do its job, and then it is excreted from the body in the feces.

Several different types of fiber are found in the diet. Fruits, vegetables, whole grain breads and cereals, nuts, and legumes such as dried beans are all sources of fiber in the diet. The properties and benefits afforded by a particular source of fiber depend on whether the fiber it contains is soluble or insoluble in water.

Insoluble fiber speeds up the movement of food through the intestines and promotes regularity. Cellulose, hemicellulose, and lignins are insoluble fibers. They can be found in asparagus, peas, kidney and pinto beans, and the wheat bran found in whole wheat breads and cereals.

Soluble fibers do just the opposite; they slow down the movement of food through the intestines. They also appear to be more effective than insoluble fibers at lowering blood cholesterol. Pectins, gums, and mucilages are examples of soluble fibers in the diet. Oat bran is a source of soluble fiber, as are rolled oats, broccoli, brussels sprouts, grapefruit, apples, and pinto and navy beans.

Much of the attention directed toward the connection between fiber and blood cholesterol has centered around oat bran. Oat bran and oatmeal are rich in a water-soluble form of fiber, a gum called **beta-glucan**. This gum is thought to be one of the most effective forms of dietary fiber for lowering blood cholesterol. Studies have shown that two ounces of oats incorporated into a low-fat diet each day can produce decreases of about five to ten percent in blood cholesterol levels. This decrease is slightly more than the decrease produced by the low-fat diet alone. What's more, the oat fiber had this effect even in people who did not have high blood cholesterol levels. Research has shown that the soluble fiber in legumes and fruits also lowers blood cholesterol when these foods are consumed in amounts that are twice what is usually found in the American diet. Although excellent for preventing constipation, the *insoluble* fibers found in most vegetables, soybean hulls, and wheat bran appear to have little or no impact on cholesterol levels in the blood.

One of the ways fiber may lower blood cholesterol is through its ability to bind bile in the intestines. When fiber binds bile in the intestines, the bile is excreted in the feces. To make up for this loss of bile, the liver makes more bile salts. The body uses cholesterol to make bile salts. So in order to obtain the cholesterol necessary to make more bile salts, the liver increases its production of LDL receptors. These receptors, you will remember, are responsible for pulling cholesterol out of LDL molecules in the bloodstream. Therefore, the more bile salts the liver makes, the more LDL-cholesterol is pulled from the blood. There's still more that needs to be learned about the relationship between fiber and cholesterol, however. There's probably an additional mechanism at work that would explain why soluble fibers have a greater effect on blood cholesterol levels than insoluble fibers since both types have the ability to bind with bile. It is possible that soluble fiber may inhibit the amount of cholesterol produced by the liver.

The typical American diet is notoriously low in dietary fiber. It is estimated that most Americans are getting about 10 to 20 grams of dietary fiber, about half the current recommendation of 20 to 40 grams. Diets rich in fat are typically low in fiber because the most common sources of dietary fat—foods of animal origin or commercially prepared baked goods—contribute little or no fiber to the diet.

The best way to increase fiber in the diet is to eat more fruits, grains, vegetables, whole grain breads and cereals, and legumes. (Nuts also contribute fiber to the diet, but they are higher in calories and contain more fat than these other sources.) Incorporating high-fiber foods into recipes—like using oat bran in muffins—also helps to increase the amount of fiber in the diet. Sources of water-soluble fibers, such as oats, apples, citrus fruits, dried beans, broccoli, and brussels sprouts, can also be included in meals more often in order to lower blood cholesterol. Of course, this does not mean that other sources of dietary fiber should be ignored; health benefits, such as protection against colon and rectal cancers, can be gained by increasing the *total* amount of fiber in the diet regardless of its source. Fiber supplements can also be purchased, but they should not be necessary if plenty of fiber-rich foods are included in the diet.

Switching from a low-fiber to a high-fiber diet should be done gradually to avoid diarrhea, gas, and other types of stomach and intestinal discomfort. Care should also be taken not to go overboard with fiber. Very high intakes of fiber may reduce the body's ability to absorb dietary minerals like calcium, magnesium, zinc, copper, and iron. This may cause problems if the diet is not providing adequate amounts of these nutrients to begin with. It also explains why recommendations for dietary fiber emphasize food sources of fiber over fiber supplements; fruits, vegetables, whole grains, and legumes contribute minerals, as well as fiber, to the diet.

Olive Oil

Olive oil has always been popular for both cooking and seasoning in the Mediterranean countries of Italy and Greece. These days, however, it's being rediscovered in America. The low frequency of heart disease in the Mediterranean countries, despite their Western industrialized lifestyles, has caught our attention and made us look more closely at their diets. By American standards, the Mediterranean diet is slightly lower in fat and cholesterol; but it is not as low as you might expect given the lower blood cholesterol levels found in people living in that area. The most distinct feature of the Mediterranean diet is not its general fat content, however, but the amount of monounsaturated fat it contains.

The heavy use of olive oil by people living in that part of the world is the source of the high level of monounsaturated fat in their diets. Olive oil is rich in **oleic acid**, the most common dietary monounsaturated fatty acid. Previously, this type of fat was not considered useful in lowering blood cholesterol. Recently, however, that idea has been challenged. Numerous studies now indicate that monounsaturated fat is about as effective as polyunsaturated fat in lowering total blood cholesterol and LDL-cholesterol. But unlike polyunsaturated fat, monounsaturated fat does not appear to lower beneficial HDL-cholesterol. In studies, monounsaturated fat either raised HDLs or had no effect on them at all. Either way, the ratio of LDL-cholesterol to HDL-cholesterol was improved by monounsaturated fat.

One way of increasing monounsaturated fat in the diet is to substitute olive oil for some of the vegetable oil you usually use. "Substitute" is the key word here because you do not want to raise your total intake of fat when you add more olive oil to your diet. Even though polyunsaturated fat is preferrable to saturated fat in the diet, there are still concerns about too much of it in the diet. Whether it is desirable to lower total blood cholesterol at the expense of HDL-cholesterol, as polyunsaturated fat does, remains unresolved. Also at issue is whether large amounts of polyunsaturated fat contribute to the development of colon and rectal cancers.

Because olive oil burns easily even at low temperatures, its use in cooking is limited. It is best suited for salad dressings, marinades, and low-temperature cooking methods. For general cooking, canola or rapeseed oil, which is also rich in monounsaturated fat, is a better alternative because it is able to withstand higher temperatures.

Vitamin and Mineral Supplements

In a world where miracle cures are supposed to come in tablets and capsules, we want to reach into our medicine cabinets for solutions to our health problems. This mentality is what makes vitamin and mineral supplements so attractive. A survey by the Gallup Organization reported in 1982 that 45 percent of Americans who took vitamin supplements did so "to stay healthy."

The use of vitamin and mineral supplements to help lower blood cholesterol is a habit that actually has some basis in scientific knowledge. In fact, vitamin B_3 (niacin) is commonly used in cholesterol-lowering therapy. We'll be discussing niacin in the chapter on drugs, however, because the large doses prescribed for cholesterol lowering make this vitamin act more like a drug than a dietary supplement.

Some vitamins and minerals are promoted for cholesterol lowering because they appear to play important roles in the handling of cholesterol and fat in the body. Vitamin C (ascorbic acid), vitamin E, copper, and chromium are the ones most commonly advocated. There is no question that these vitamins and minerals are important for health. Research in this area, however, is wholly inadequate to even suggest that vitamin and mineral supplements (other than niacin) be used for treating high blood cholesterol.

Taking a vitamin and mineral supplement seems like an easy way to correct poor nutritional habits. The problem with relying on these supplements is that they may provide a false sense of assurance. You may be tempted to think that if you're taking supplements, you don't have to make wise food choices. Those same wise food choices, however, can provide your body with the vitamins and minerals you need for health *and* decrease your dietary fat and cholesterol intake at the same time.

Yogurt

The current trendiness of yogurt belies the centuries-old tradition of this food. It was even mentioned in the Bible. Yet yogurt was not really dubbed a health food until the twentieth century, when Francois I of France used it to treat a persistent intestinal disorder. Since that time, the health claims made for yogurt have included boosting immunity, prolonging life, and arresting the growth of tumors. The validity of these claims is currently being evaluated in scientific tests.

Yogurt is a fermented milk product. In other words, it is produced from pasteurized homogenized milk through the process of **fermentation**, in which bacteria convert the milk sugar lactose into lactic acid. Modern science has attributed any possible health benefits from yogurt to the live bacterial cultures it contains.

The long-lived inhabitants of the Caucasus region in the Soviet Union are often pointed to as examples of the health benefits of yogurt. It has been suggested that their regular consumption of yogurt has prolonged their lives by helping to keep them free of the usual causes of death (heart disease and cancer) plaguing industrialized countries.

Interest in the use of yogurt specifically to lower blood cholesterol was piqued by a recent study of African warriors. The warriors showed a drop of 28 mg/dl in their blood cholesterol when the four to five quarts of milk they drank each day was replaced by an equivalent amount of fermented milk. Subsequent studies, however, have been unable to confirm a direct cholesterol-lowering effect for yogurt. On the other hand, as a low-fat replacement for fat-rich foods like ice cream, and as a substitute for cream or mayonnaise in recipes, low-fat yogurt has a definite place in a dietary plan for lowering blood cholesterol.

If yogurt appeals to you, you need to be aware of the different kinds that are available, since not every one is equally acceptable in a low-fat diet. As a milk product, the fat contents of yogurt are the same as those in milk. There are whole-milk yogurts, low-fat yogurts, and non-fat yogurts. Whole-milk yogurts present the same problems for a low-fat diet that whole milk does—they are rich in saturated fat and cholesterol. The low-fat and non-fat yogurts provide the same amount of fat and cholesterol as skim milk. To be sure the yogurt you purchase is low in saturated fat and cholesterol, check the label.

CHAPTER 7:

Weight Control

How Weight Affects Blood Cholesterol

These days, we're constantly reminded of the aesthetic benefits of being slim. Trim, fit figures parade across television screens, billboards, and magazine advertisements, encouraging us to hop on the fitness bandwagon. But the importance of weight control goes beyond appearance. If you are overweight, and especially if you are obese, chances are your total blood cholesterol level and your blood triglyceride level are also elevated. For some people, gaining weight also appears to lower HDL levels, although why this is so is not clear.

Dietary saturated fat may play a role in the high blood cholesterol levels in overweight people. Consuming too much saturated fat can raise your blood cholesterol level, even if you don't gain weight. A diet that is high in fat, however, makes weight gain very difficult to avoid (remember that a gram of fat contains more than twice the calories of a gram of carbohydrate or protein). Foods contributing large amounts of fat to the diet are very often the same foods that contribute unwanted calories. Those excess calories are stored in the body as fat. This process, if unchecked, leads to weight gain.

Of course, fat-rich foods are not the only ones that can add excess calories to the diet. Overeating protein- or carbohydrate-rich foods or overindulging in alcohol can add excess calories. You're simply more likely to pile up excess calories—and excess weight—when you eat a lot of foods that are high in calorie-laden fat.

Does Weight Loss Help?

There is more to weight loss than meets the eye. Perhaps no other single change you can make in yourself—except to quit smoking—will provide more health rewards than losing weight. For as long as they have been keeping records, insurance companies have known that overweight people tend to suffer more illnesses and die at an earlier age than people who maintain a desirable weight. So if you are overweight, losing weight may actually help to lengthen your life.

Heart disease is a common problem afflicting overweight people. Excess body weight may play several roles in the development of this disease. Overweight tends to raise the total blood cholesterol level and in some people lowers the HDL-cholesterol level. It also tends to increase blood pressure and increase the likelihood of developing diabetes. Elevated blood cholesterol, high blood pressure, and diabetes are all called **risk factors** for coronary heart disease because they increase the chance of developing this disease.

By targeting three of the major risk factors for coronary heart disease, weight control is a powerful weapon in the fight to protect your heart. Losing weight is one of the most effective strategies you can try for controlling blood cholesterol. Not only does it tend to lower blood cholesterol, it also lowers triglycerides, and for some people, it raises HDL-cholesterol. (While a high triglyceride level does not appear to be an independent risk factor for coronary heart disease in the general population, the Framingham study did indicate that it does appear to predict heart disease risk in older women.) Losing weight has also proven effective in lowering elevated blood pressure and in reducing the risk of diabetes.

If you have high blood cholesterol levels and are overweight, losing weight is an important first step in getting your cholesterol levels under control and decreasing your heart-disease risk. What's more, *you do not necessarily have to lose large amounts of weight to be successful.* Studies have shown that even modest changes in weight can lower blood cholesterol levels. Whether the weight loss itself is responsible or whether it is due to the type of change in diet that is required for a successful weight loss is not yet known. More than likely, the combination of weight loss and a decrease in saturated fat and dietary cholesterol provides the greatest benefit to blood cholesterol levels.

What's the Best Way to Lose Weight?

The weight-loss method you choose is important in determining how successful you will be at both losing weight and keeping it off. As difficult as it is, losing the weight is really the easy part. The true challenge is being able to keep the weight off over the long haul. About 95 percent of dieters gain their weight back within two years of losing it. This cycle of weight loss and weight gain is more than just frustrating. Research is beginning to show that it may be as harmful to health as staying overweight.

The reason most diets fail to remove weight permanently is that they do not get to the root of the problem. A successful long-term diet program has to replace poor eating habits with a healthy, balanced diet plan that is flexible enough to be followed for life. The diet also has to target the excess body *fat* that caused the weight gain.

Many diet programs promise weight reductions of more than two or three pounds a week, but they are not being completely honest. Yes, the amount of weight that can be lost with some diets is considerable—ten to 20 pounds in a couple of weeks or even days! But these weight reductions come mostly from the loss of water and the breakdown of muscle protein—not the loss of fat. When you eventually replace these vital substances—as you will when you resume normal eating habits—you gain back the weight. Diets that promote these transient weight losses are the ones that really do

the most psychological harm. Nothing can be more discouraging than watching a 20-pound weight loss evaporate into a two-pound one.

A diet plan to remove excess body *fat* has to be low in energy (calories). A low-calorie diet creates an energy deficit in the body by supplying less energy than the body needs for daily functions. To meet its energy needs, the body then has to draw upon the energy stored in body fat. This is why exercise—which increases the body's demand for energy—is such a useful adjunct to diet therapy. By exercising *and* switching to a low-calorie diet, you increase your body's energy needs and force your body to pull energy from body fat.

Many people are unsuccessful at losing weight because they get discouraged with the results. If you don't have realistic expectations, it is easy to become frustrated. Becoming overweight is not an overnight phenomenon; it takes months, even years, to accumulate that added weight. Reversing the process takes an equal amount of time. You have to be willing to invest the time and effort if the weight you want to lose is body fat.

A good weight-loss program will cause an *average* weight loss of two to three pounds a week. This is all the body fat it is possible to lose, on average, in that amount of time. "Average" is a key word here, because the pattern of weight loss is not a steady one. In the beginning, weight losses can be quite large as the body adjusts to a new diet. Eventually, this will taper off to an average of about one to three pounds a week.

Many dieters will experience "plateaus" during their attempts to lose weight. These are the people who swear they are following the diet, yet appear to stop losing weight. These plateaus can often last for weeks, but they are temporary. If you are one of these people, don't be discouraged! Staying with the diet during these critical periods is essential if you want to continue to lose weight in the long run. Increasing exercise will help. Sooner or later most people make it through this period and continue to lose weight.

In addition to reducing body fat, a successful diet program has to provide your body with the essential nutrients it needs and show you how to make wise food choices to meet those needs. If a diet doesn't provide your body with enough of the protein, carbohydrates, fat, vitamins, and minerals that it needs for health, the diet will end up doing more harm than good. And if a diet doesn't teach you how to change your eating habits, you're likely to fall back on the poor food choices that caused the weight gain in the first place. And before you know it, those lost pounds of body fat will be back to haunt you.

How to Lose Weight and Control Blood Cholesterol

The key to a successful weight loss is to reduce body fat. Reducing body fat is also necessary before blood cholesterol will fall. Body fat can be measured by the thickness of the folds of skin at normally lean parts of the body, such as the upper arm or back. It is actually the loss of body fat, and not the weight loss itself, that causes changes in LDL- and HDL-cholesterol levels in the blood. When weight is lost from losing water or muscle protein, there is no real benefit to blood cholesterol levels.

The best weight-reduction program for lowering blood cholesterol is a low-calorie diet combined with exercise. This is the approach that mobilizes body fat best. Not only does exercise help with the weight loss, but it also raises HDL-cholesterol by its own merits (see Chapter 8 for more on exercise).

The composition of the diet is also important. If the low-calorie foods recommended by a diet plan are not also low in fat, saturated fat, and cholesterol, then efforts to lower blood cholesterol by weight loss and exercise will be diminished. Studies have shown that people who lose weight on a low-fat diet have a larger fall in blood cholesterol than people losing the same amount of weight on other types of weight-reduction diets. Lowering dietary fat intake while losing weight has a bigger impact on blood cholesterol than does weight loss alone.

Sorting through the Options

Deciding to lose weight is the first step toward improving your health. Choosing the diet that works best for you is the next step. Hundreds of different diets have been promoted for weight loss, but there are actually just a few general types of weight-loss diets. Most of the popular diets fit into one of these general types. Only a few of these diets are really appropriate for controlling blood cholesterol. To help you sort through the many diets currently available, the main features of the most common types of weight-reduction diets are described here. Once you become familiar with them, you will be able to recognize the latest diet trends for what they are. Before you choose one to help you lower blood cholesterol, examine the diet carefully and ask yourself these questions:

- *Does it promise too much too soon?* Remember that weight is gained slowly and has to be lost slowly. Speedier losses will not greatly decrease body fat, the key to a long-term weight loss.
- *Is it low in calories?* You cannot lose body fat without this feature.
- *Is it low in fat, saturated fat, and cholesterol?* If it's not low in fat, chances are it's not low in calories, so it won't help you lose body fat. If it's not low in saturated fat and cholesterol, your efforts may not pay off in lower blood cholesterol.
- *Does it teach you new eating behavior that you can continue after you lose the weight?* Without this, you may gain the weight back once you resume your old eating habits.
- *Is it nutritionally sound?* A diet has to be balanced, with enough foods from each of the major food groups, or it may not provide adequate vitamins and minerals. The diet should include lean meats, fish, poultry, or legumes; low-fat dairy products; fruits; vegetables; and breads and cereals.
- *Is it safe?* It simply does not make good sense to trade the health problems caused by being overweight for a whole new set of problems caused by a shoddy weight-loss diet.

Low-Calorie Diets

A low-calorie diet is a low-energy diet. The goal is to create an energy deficit by providing fewer calories than your body needs. In order for you to lose one pound of body fat, a low-calorie diet has to provide 3,500 fewer calories than you need. (Most adults need only about 1,500 to 3,000 calories of energy each day to meet their needs.) Since low-calorie diets provide 500 to 1,000 fewer calories than you need each day, one to two pounds of body fat will be used over the course of a week to make up the energy shortfall.

A low-calorie diet can be recognized by the types of foods it recommends. Fresh fruits and vegetables, skim milk, and lean meats, chicken, or fish make up the bulk of the menu. Small servings are stressed. Fried foods, sugary snacks, rich sauces, pies, cakes, and other sugary, fat-rich desserts are restricted. Alcoholic beverages are sometimes included, but not on a regular basis. Foods are prepared using low-calorie cooking methods. Meats, poultry, and fish are roasted, baked, or broiled. Steaming or boiling keeps vegetables low in calories. Margarine and oils are used sparingly.

Although the number of calories you usually eat has to be reduced before you can expect to lose weight, it is possible to lower your calorie intake too far. A real irony of dieting is that you lose more weight if you eat some food than if you eat nothing at all. If too few calories are eaten, the body protects itself from the energy shortage by using the available energy more economically. The body does this by slowing its **metabolic rate**, the rate at which it uses energy. This shift in the rate of metabolism when food is scarce has its roots early in human development. As hunter-gatherers, our ancestors could not always count on regular meals. They ate whenever they found food. As protection against the possible ill effects of an unreliable food supply, early humans developed this metabolic adjustment in order to conserve energy when food was not available.

As the body becomes more efficient at using the energy on hand, it actually *needs* less. A smaller energy deficit results and less body fat is lost. To avoid this response, modern humans need to feed their bodies at least 1000 calories every day. Diets recommending less than this number of calories should not be followed without the supervision of a physician. They can do more than frustrate efforts to lose weight. If followed for an extended period of time, these extremely low-calorie diets can also lead to nutritional deficiencies. Another repercussion of following a very-low-calorie diet for a long time is that eventually the body will begin to break down muscle protein to provide energy. While a vitamin-mineral supplement added to a very-low-calorie diet may protect against nutritional deficiencies, it cannot ward off the loss of muscle protein.

Low-Fat Diets

A low-calorie diet is usually low in fat. The high energy value of fat, which makes it so perfect for storing energy, also makes its presence in food synonymous with a high calorie content. Fat has more than twice the energy potential (caloric content) of either protein or carbohydrate and slightly more than alcohol. So as a general rule, foods high in fat will also be high in calories. Low-calorie diets take advantage of this fact and make lowering fat intake a priority. This conveniently allows a low-calorie diet to also be low in fat, making it appropriate for both losing weight and lowering blood cholesterol.

The types of foods prescribed by a low-fat diet are almost identical to those recommended in a low-calorie diet, making it almost impossible to distinguish between the two. But while a low-calorie diet is usually also a low-fat one, a low-fat diet does not always need to be low in calories. Once the desired amount of weight is lost, the low-fat nature of this diet can still be preserved while raising the number of calories. This is achieved by adding more low-fat foods and by increasing the size of the serving.

Whether or not calories are restricted, a low-fat diet is made up primarily of foods that are rich in carbohydrate. Carbohydrate-rich foods are natural replacements for fat-rich foods because they are almost always low in fat. Fruits, vegetables, breads, cereals, rice, pasta, and dried beans and peas are the carbohydrate-rich staples of a low-fat diet. By increasing carbohydrate-rich grains and vegetables at the expense of animal foods that are rich in saturated fat, the amount of polyunsaturated and monounsaturated fat in the diet will be raised and the amount of saturated fat will be lowered. The protein in this diet is provided by such low-fat sources as lean meats, chicken, fish, legumes, and low-fat dairy products.

A low-fat diet contains fewer foods from animal sources and more from plant sources. Plant sources provide almost all of the carbohydrate-rich foods in the diet. The only animal source of carbohydrate in a low-fat diet is low-fat milk. Foods of plant origin do not contain cholesterol and are also usually lower in total fat and saturated fat than foods of animal origin. So when foods of animal origin are restricted in the diet, your intake of dietary cholesterol and saturated fat, as well as total fat, are lowered.

A low-fat diet also limits commercially prepared snacks and baked goods. These foods are not only high in saturated fat and cholesterol, they are also high in calories and cannot be included regularly in a weight-loss diet.

Weight control is only one of several uses for a low-fat diet. Blood cholesterol is successfully lowered by a low-fat diet (regardless of whether weight is lost or not), making this type of diet important for preventing and treating heart disease. People who suffer from diseases of the gallbladder also need a low-fat diet because they usually find fat-rich foods difficult to tolerate.

There is also some limited but suggestive evidence that a low-fat diet may offer some protection against some common forms of cancer, such as those of the breast and colon. In places around the world where these cancers rarely occur, the people consume diets low in fat. Although fat is not a cause of cancer, it is possible that eating large quantities may promote its development.

Despite all the benefits a low-fat diet can bring, some dietary fat is essential both from a practical and a nutritional standpoint. Dietary fat is responsible for the feeling of **satiety** or fullness experienced after a meal. Because fat is digested more slowly than carbohydrate or protein, it stays in the stomach longer, so you do not feel hungry soon after a meal. Since nothing will sabotage a diet faster than hunger, it is especially important to include some fat in a low-calorie diet where the total amount of food eaten is small.

Dietary fat also promotes the absorption of the fat-soluble vitamins, A, D, E, and K. We get most of the vitamin A we need from low-fat plant sources, such as carrots, squash, spinach, broccoli, and tomatoes, which contain a substance that the body converts into vitamin A. Without some fat present, we would probably not be getting enough vitamin A. One of the essential nutrients, **linoleic acid**, is also provided by dietary fat. Linoleic acid is a poly-unsaturated fatty acid needed for growth and healthy skin. It is also vital for the production of a group of hormones called **prostaglandins**. Prostaglandins are responsible for regulating functions of the heart, blood vessels, kidneys, lungs, nerves, and reproductive organs.

Large amounts of dietary fat are not necessary to provide sufficient linoleic acid or to insure adequate absorption of fat-soluble vitamins. Vegetable oils are the primary source of linoleic acid. Since there is no requirement for either saturated fat or cholesterol in the diet, just two tablespoons of vegetable oil or six pats of vegetable-oil-based margarine can supply all the linoleic acid and fat needed each day.

Low-Carbohydrate, High-Fat Diets

Popular forms of this type of diet include the Atkins Diet, the Mayo Diet, the Air Force Diet, the Drinking Man's Diet, the Calories Don't Count Diet, the Grapefruit Diet, the Ski Team Diet, and the Stillman and Scarsdale diets. The appeal of these diets is and always has been the quick weight losses they promise. These diets also allow dieters the freedom to eat most foods that are normally restricted in weight-loss programs. Weight losses of as many as ten to 20 pounds can occur within a few days or weeks after starting on these diets. While this amount of weight can actually be lost, the drawback to it is that only a small part of the weight lost is body fat.

Any weight-reduction diet should be suspect if it allows you to consume all the calories you want as long as those calories do not come from carbohydrate. In doing this, the diet violates the basic rule of long-term weight loss. It does not achieve the energy deficit required for body fat to be removed. Before ten pounds of body fat can be lost, a calorie deficit of 35,000 calories has to be created. For this to occur over a week, a daily deficit of 5,000 calories is needed. It would be impossible for most people to manage a deficit this large even if they ate nothing and performed heavy labor.

In actuality, these low-carbohydrate diets may lower calories—because they simply do not taste very good. Lowering the amount of carbohydrate in the diet removes all the colorful and many of the flavorful foods. Fruits, vegetables, grains, and cereals are restricted. Meat, fish, poultry, eggs, cheese, milk, ice cream, and peanut butter are emphasized instead. Hard liquor, but not beer or wine, is also allowed.

Low-carbohydrate diets work by depriving the body of carbohydrate, the primary fuel source of the brain, nerves, and lungs. To compensate for this, the body produces acids called **ketones** that can be used for energy in place of carbohydrate. Ketones are made from body fat. Besides being used for energy, ketones are also excreted in the urine. Proponents of low-carbohydrate diets claim that by excreting calories, weight loss will be faster than if the calories are used only to provide energy. This may sound good in theory. In reality, however, ketones can only be excreted in small quantities. Only 100 calories a day can be excreted in ketones. At that rate, it would take 35 days to equal the 3,500 calories needed to lose a pound of fat.

Large weight losses do occur rapidly on a low-carbohydrate diet, but not because ketones are excreted. High levels of ketones in the blood interfere with appetite, so less food is eaten. The carbohydrate deficiency promoted by a low-carbohydrate diet also causes large amounts of salt and water to be lost from the body. Muscle protein is also broken down to make carbohydrate for use by the brain, nerves, and lungs. The loss of water and muscle responsible for most of the weight lost on a low-carbohydrate diet is only a temporary loss. As soon as normal eating patterns are resumed, the body will replace the water and muscle and the weight will be regained.

Low-carbohydrate diets are not recommended for lowering blood cholesterol because they do not promote the loss of body fat, which is key to long-term weight loss and lowering blood cholesterol. They also encourage the consumption of foods that are high in fat, saturated fat, and cholesterol. By restricting carbohydrate-rich foods, they limit the only sources of dietary fiber, which plays a role in lowering blood cholesterol (see Chapter 6 for more information about fiber). Indeed, blood cholesterol levels are actually elevated in people who follow these diets.

The high level of blood ketones caused by a low-carbohydrate diet can also be dangerous. For pregnant women, damage to the unborn child is an especially serious consequence. Blood sugar can also fall to very low levels in those following low-carbohydrate diets. **Hypoglycemia**, or low blood sugar, causes dizziness, fatigue, weakness, irritability, and fainting spells. The most serious threat of this diet is a condition called **ketoacidosis**. Followers of this type of diet are usually instructed to monitor their urine for ketones to prevent this condition from developing. Nevertheless, ketoacidosis can develop if ketone production is allowed to continue for a long time. Ketoacidosis can lead to coma and death.

High-Protein Diets

One type of high-protein diet is the low-carbohydrate diet just described. Foods contain only three nutrients that contribute calories—protein, carbohydrate, and fat. When, by your choice of foods, you change the amount of any one of these, you automatically change the proportions of the other two. So lowering carbohydrate will automatically raise the proportion of fat or protein or both.

A high-protein diet is usually one that is also high in fat, saturated fat, and cholesterol, because the foods that are richest in protein are those from animal sources. Grains, nuts, and dried beans contain plant protein but only in small amounts relative to the quantities of protein found in meat, eggs, cheese, and milk. It would be very difficult to make a diet high in protein if it included nothing but plant foods. A high-protein diet has to be rich in foods from animal sources. Therefore, it would not be appropriate for lowering blood cholesterol.

Since it is difficult to create a low-calorie, high-protein diet using foods, the high-protein diets that are promoted for weight loss are usually liquid or powdered formula diets. Formula diets allow nutrients to be manipulated in proportions that would not be possible with food. The protein in these formula diets, however, is not the same structurally as the proteins found in foods. Instead, it has usually been predigested into mixtures of the individual units, called **amino acids**, that make up a protein.

To be considered a high-protein diet, a formula preparation has to contain enough protein to provide at least 50 percent of total calories. Typically, about 16 percent of the total calories we eat come from protein, while 35 to 40 percent come from fat and 45 to 50 percent come from carbohydrate. When protein makes up 50 percent of all the calories consumed, then the amount of both fat and carbohydrate is much lower than usual. Unlike a diet high in protein-rich *foods*, which would also be high in fat, a high-protein formula diet is manipulated to be low in both fat and carbohydrate.

The composition of high-protein formula preparations is also manipulated to be low in calories. The majority of these diets provide about 800 calories a day, but some preparations may contain as few as 300 to 600 calories. This level of calories is supposed to create the energy deficit necessary to mobilize body fat. This highly restricted calorie intake, however, dips below the necessary minimum to prevent the body from slowing down its rate of metabolism. Therefore, less body fat will be lost on this type of diet than on a more moderately restrictive diet.

High-protein formula diets promote rapid and considerable *weight* losses because they are low in carbohydrate as well as calories. The carbohydrate deficiency accentuates the amount of weight lost by increasing loss of salt and water. The very low calorie intake should promote the breakdown of muscle protein to provide energy, but the large amount of protein supplied by the formula is supposed to prevent this from happening. By providing protein for the body to burn for energy, these diets should enable muscle protein to be preserved. For this reason, high protein diets offering less than 800 calories a day are often referred to as **protein-sparing modified fasts**.

The experience with these high-protein formula diets indicates that they may be a risky undertaking. Although the more modern ones have been improved over the earlier ones, the Food and Drug Administration now requires that warning labels appear on all of these preparations. First introduced in 1977 as The Last Chance Diet, the high-protein diet was promoted in a formula preparation called *Pro-linn*. One year after its introduction, 46 deaths had been linked to its use. Although the reasons for these deaths are still debated, the people who died were all consuming the 300- to 600-calorie preparations with amino acid mixtures derived exclusively from collagen or gelatin proteins. Deficiencies in a number of minerals including potassium, magnesium, copper, and selenium were thought to have played a role.

High-protein formula diets are not appropriate for long-term weight loss, nor are they good candidates for lowering blood cholesterol. (In certain situations when a very large amount of weight—50 pounds or more—needs to be lost and the more conventional weight-loss therapies have failed, a liquid protein diet may be temporarily incorporated into an overall program of weight loss; this is done only under a doctor's supervision.) Temporary elevations in blood cholesterol are so common in people who follow these diets that potential users are warned of the possibility. But temporary or not, without the needed long-term weight loss, blood cholesterol will still not benefit from these diets. Overweight is not a short-term problem, but a lifelong one. A safe and long-term solution is the only reasonable approach. Any short-term toxic effects brought on by a weight-reduction program are simply not acceptable. They just do not make good sense if the whole point of losing weight is to improve your health.

Fasts

A fast is defined as partial or complete abstinence from food. Fasting implies a severe restriction of calories. Completely abstaining from food is impossible over the long run, so most fasts are really very-low-calorie diets.

Although calorie intake is greatly reduced in these diets, the loss of body fat is slowed because metabolic rate decreases. Indeed, fasting has been shown to lower the rate of metabolism by as much as 20 percent within a few days. This lack of body-fat loss is hidden by the accelerated loss of salt and water and the breakdown of muscle protein brought about by a carbohydrate deficiency.

Like the other diets that base their weight losses on limiting carbohydrate, fasting produces quick and impressive results. These weight losses, however, are accompanied by the possibility of developing hypoglycemia and ketoacidosis. Also, as with other carbohydrate-deficient diets, weight lost from fasting is only transitory. Water and muscle protein are replaced once the fasting stops. Consequently, the amount of body fat lost will not be much different from what would be lost on a conventional low-calorie diet, but the price paid in discomfort will certainly be much greater.

Elevations in blood cholesterol levels often occur during fasting. As with high-protein diets, these elevations are transient. But because long-term weight loss is difficult to attain from fasting, blood cholesterol will not be improved in the long run.

CHAPTER 8:
Exercise

The Benefits of Exercise

In increasing numbers, Americans are pursuing exercise in their leisure time. Their reasons are nearly as numerous as the exercisers themselves. Like the rewards of losing weight, however, the benefits of regular exercise go beyond what it can do for your physique. Regular exercise that gives your muscles and your heart a workout even appears to benefit blood cholesterol and help protect against coronary heart disease.

The benefits from exercise depend, in part, on what type of exercise you do and how regularly you do it. **Aerobic exercise**, which forces the heart and lungs to work harder to meet the muscles' demand for oxygen, appears to provide the greatest health benefits. Examples of aerobic exercise include jogging, brisk walking, swimming, cycling, and cross-country skiing. These activities involve regular, repeated activity that is performed at a pace intense enough to quicken your breathing and get your heart pumping faster than usual. To do the most good, aerobic exercise needs to be performed for at least 20 minutes a day, at least three times a week, at a heart rate (pulse) that is between 60 and 90 percent of your maximum (in general, your maximum heart rate per minute is approximately equal to 220 minus your age).

The rewards of aerobic exercise are numerous. First, regular aerobic exercise increases cardiovascular fitness by decreasing resting heart rate, decreasing blood pressure, and increasing the capacity of the heart and body tissues to exercise for longer periods using less energy. In other words, the heart and muscles become more efficient at using oxygen and can work harder and longer using less energy. It's like being able to go farther on a gallon of gas.

In addition, many studies show that regular aerobic exercise can improve blood lipid levels. Most of the studies show that this type of exercise can decrease blood triglyceride levels and increase HDL levels. LDL levels, however, do not appear to be directly affected by exercise.

Exercise can also play a vital role in weight control. Regular aerobic exercise may increase the body's metabolism. When combined with a sound, balanced diet, aerobic exercise can help prevent the loss of lean muscle tissue that may occur with diet alone. Studies have also indicated that people who participate in regular, aerobic exercise tend to adopt healthier lifestyle habits, including quitting smoking, maintaining desirable weight, and choosing healthier foods.

Many people also report that regular exercise helps to alleviate stress and improve mental outlook. Improvements in self-esteem and self-image may also occur as a result of successfully maintaining a regular exercise program and improving physical appearance.

Finally, there appears to be substantial but inconclusive evidence suggesting that people who are more physically active have fewer heart attacks and less angina. They also appear to live longer than their sedentary counterparts.

Exercise and Risk of Heart Attack

Two studies from Massachusetts have provided important insights into how regular aerobic exercise can affect your risk of having a heart attack. The Framingham study found that those subjects who were more than 20 percent overweight, were short-of-breath (decreased vital capacity), and had a rapid resting pulse (heart rate at rest of more than 85 beats per second) had five times the risk of dying of coronary heart disease compared to those subjects who had none of these sedentary traits. They also had more than twice the coronary heart disease risk of those subjects who had only one of these sedentary traits.

In addition to the Framingham study, a study of Harvard alumni showed lower death rates among those alumni who were physically active as opposed to those who were sedentary. The results of this study showed that, by the age of 80, those alumni who had exercised regularly could look forward to living one to two years longer than their sedentary counterparts.

A Finnish study, on the other hand, did not show an increase in longevity among subjects who were physically active. The study did show, however, that there were fewer deaths from coronary heart disease among the most active participants as compared to those subjects who were less active.

In addition to its apparent role in protecting against coronary heart disease, exercise seems to be beneficial for those who already have coronary heart disease. In one study, when exercise was added to a cholesterol-lowering diet, the patients appeared to experience less angina (chest pain). After one year, they also showed improvement on a special treadmill test that measures impaired blood flow to the heart.

It's important to note that in this study of patients with heart disease, the diet and exercise therapy also caused weight loss, which appears to play a beneficial role in the prevention and treatment of coronary heart disease. Another carefully done study of the effect of exercise training in monkeys with high blood cholesterol, however, showed improvement even without weight loss. The researchers showed that exercise training greatly lowered triglycerides and LDL-cholesterol and raised HDL-cholesterol significantly, even though there was no significant change in weight. Narrowing of the coro-

nary arteries and sudden death were seen only in those monkeys who had not undergone the conditioning. Indeed, exercise appeared to produce a reduction in atherosclerosis in the conditioned monkeys.

Exercise and Blood Cholesterol

There is a growing body of data highlighting the effects of various kinds of aerobic exercise on blood cholesterol and blood triglyceride levels. One study, for instance, showed that after an endurance race, triglycerides and blood cholesterol fell (after an initial delay). This effect lasted up to 66 hours after the participants completed the race. In another study of men with elevated triglycerides, 40 minutes of more moderate exercise caused a decrease in triglycerides with no decrease in cholesterol.

It is possible, of course, that people who choose to exercise may be more conscious of their health and may make healthier food and lifestyle choices that would also benefit blood cholesterol. To avoid this possible bias, the most informative studies randomly divide participants into exercise and non-exercise (sedentary) groups. In one such study, Finnish investigators showed that along with increased measures of aerobic fitness, the exercise group had increased HDL levels and decreased triglyceride values, which were not dependent on weight reduction. A similar study in California showed basically the same results, although in this study, LDL-cholesterol values were also lowered.

These beneficial changes in HDL- and LDL-cholesterol, however, were not found in the National Exercise and Heart Disease Project, which looked at 223 middle-aged, male heart attack survivors who participated in moderate exercise. Other smaller studies, on the other hand, have shown increases in HDL-cholesterol in patients who participated in moderate exercise after a heart attack. Interestingly, in one study, HDL-cholesterol increased in heart attack survivors who exercised, but did not increase in heart attack survivors who exercised and continued to smoke cigarettes. This is not surprising, however, since cigarette smoking substantially lowers HDL-cholesterol levels.

One very recent study further highlighted the role that aerobic exercise can play in a comprehensive approach to controlling blood cholesterol. This small but well-executed study showed that losing weight through exercise is as helpful in improving blood cholesterol levels as is losing weight through dieting.

In the study, 46 men were randomly assigned to the aerobic exercise group, 42 were assigned to the dieting group, and 42 were assigned to a control group. Both the aerobic exercise and the diet were designed to decrease body fat by one-third over the course of a year.

After one year, the exercise group and the dieting group showed comparable increases in HDL-cholesterol levels and decreases in blood triglycerides (the control group did not show similar improvements). Although the dieters lost an average of 16 pounds of body weight and the exercisers lost an average of nine pounds, both lost about the same amount of body *fat*. What's more, while the dieters lost lean muscle tissue as well as fat, the exercisers lost fat without losing muscle. Thus, exercise appeared to lower body fat and consequently improve lipid levels even without dieting. These results further suggest that a combination of diet and exercise may bring the greatest rewards by decreasing body fat and consequently increasing HDL levels while preserving lean tissue.

Many other studies have also shown that regular aerobic exercise, such as swimming, tennis, cross-country skiing, skating, cycling, rowing, and running, is associated with increased HDL levels and lower triglyceride levels. With all this seemingly good news about exercise, however, there is a point you should keep in mind to avoid being disappointed. In the California study discussed previously, there appeared to be a minimum amount of exercise needed to obtain these desirable effects on lipid values. The lower limit in the California study was about ten miles of running per week for at least nine months.

This is an important qualifier because the most desirable cholesterol and triglyceride values are seen in lean, elite distance runners. That's not to say, however, that beginning exercisers will not benefit from less strenuous aerobic exercise. Moderate aerobic exercise performed regularly can improve blood lipid levels in these individuals, but it won't be enough to bring lipid levels into the range found among lean, well-conditioned athletes. A couple of studies do suggest that two groups in whom moderate exercise may not have a significant impact on HDL include women who take oral contraceptives and young, sedentary, non-smoking men with low levels of both HDL and LDL; the reasons for this are not completely clear.

CHAPTER 9:

Stress Management

What is Stress?

Stress. We may not be able to define it precisely, but we all know what it feels like. It's that pressure you feel when the boss tells you to hand in that report two weeks early. It's the frustration that comes from having too many demands made on your time. It's the craziness preceding that big wedding day. It's the anxiety you feel when a loved one is very ill. The examples go on and on. Indeed, stress appears to be an ongoing feature of modern life.

Stress can arise from a variety of factors around us that disturb or interfere with our everyday functioning. When faced with a stressful situation, the body automatically prepares us for action. It produces hormones that quicken the pulse, tense the muscles, raise blood pressure, and sharpen the senses. This automatic "fight or flight" mechanism was a lifesaver in earlier times when humans needed to cope with physical danger every day. Even today it comes in handy when your environment demands a quick, physical response from you, like when you race to keep a small child from falling down the stairs.

Unfortunately, most of the potentially stressful situations we face in modern life don't require a physical response. So the physiological commotion builds up—putting us on edge and keeping us there. We feel tense, frustrated, and anxious. Of course, not all stress is negative. Sometimes stress can help us to perform better by challenging us and keeping us on our toes. But when demands are too great or when we can't find a way to cope with stressful changes and use them to our advantage, stress can have a detrimental effect on our emotional and even physical health.

Often when we think of stress and its effects on health, the infamous "Type A" behavior pattern comes to mind. We picture the competitive, harried executive swigging down antacids in between high-powered meetings. The concept of this Type A behavior pattern was first defined and then refined through years of research by two cardiologists, Meyer Friedman, M.D., and Ray Rosenman, M.D. The Type A behavior pattern that they described is marked by ambition, drive, competitiveness, aggressiveness, hostility, and a sense of time urgency. "Type B" behavior, on the other hand, is the opposite of Type A and shows none of these traits. It is the stressful Type A behavior pattern that has been considered to be a predictor of coronary heart disease.

Stress and Coronary Heart Disease

Although the concept of stress is very old, evidence linking a stressful behavior pattern to coronary heart disease is quite recent. It's only been within the past 25 years that major studies of this possible connection have been performed.

Stress can affect cardiovascular health in a variety of ways. Sometimes, this relationship is blatant. For example, certain stress responses, such as denial or fear, often prevent patients with symptoms of a heart attack from seeking immediate medical treatment.

A stressful behavior pattern may also prevent an individual from making the type of lifestyle changes that can help to prevent coronary heart disease, such as consuming a low-fat, low-salt diet, exercising regularly, and quitting smoking. Driven, aggressive individuals who always seem to be racing against the clock may simply find these changes too time-consuming, despite the fact that such changes would be beneficial.

The effects of stress on cardiovascular health, however, are often less obvious. For example, anger has been shown to reduce coronary flow (blood flow to the heart) in dogs that have experimentally narrowed arteries. Indeed, the powerful effect of anger in precipitating angina or even heart attack in people who have coronary heart disease was hauntingly forecast by John Hunter, a famous eighteenth-century English surgeon. Hunter, who had angina pectoris (chest pain caused by reduced blood flow to the heart), was apparently quoted as saying, "My life is in the hands of any rascal who chooses to annoy or tease me!" Hunter later died during an argument. In more scientific terms, anger has been linked to cardiac death because of its tendency to provoke the recurrence of **ventricular arrhythmias** (rapid, irregular heartbeats) that can lead to death.

Lack of social support, which is considered to be stressful, also appears to affect heart health. In fact, the lack of social support that occurs when persons migrate to new environments is seen as a risk factor for coronary heart disease. In a random sample of California adults followed for nearly ten years, those adults who lacked social ties were more likely to die of coronary heart disease than were those adults who had such ties.

The Ni-Hon-San study discussed in Chapter 2 also appears to support this link. In this study, Japanese who migrated to Hawaii and San Francisco experienced a higher rate of coronary heart disease than did their counterparts who remained in Japan. While the study results suggested that this increased risk was due, in part, to the adoption of a more Western diet that was higher in saturated fat and cholesterol, they also suggested that the loss of the high level of social support in traditional Japanese culture was also a risk factor for coronary heart disease among these immigrants.

A pivotal study in assessing the relationship between behavior pattern and heart attack rate was the Western Collaborative Group Study. The results of this study showed that men considered to be Type A developed coronary heart disease at twice the rate of those men considered to be Type B. In this study, Type A behavior was found to be an independent risk factor for coronary heart disease.

In addition, in 1981, after reviewing all of the existing evidence, a blue ribbon panel of biochemists and behavioral scientists concluded that the available data supported a link between Type A behavior and risk of coronary heart disease. What's more, the risk of coronary heart disease from Type A behavior appeared to be on the same order of magnitude as the risk from hypertension, cigarette smoking, and high blood cholesterol. As you'll see in the section entitled "Does 'Type A' Predict Heart Risk?", however, recent studies have cast some doubts on the link between the Type A behavior pattern and heart disease risk.

Stress and Blood Cholesterol

The available research appears to indicate that stress can have a detrimental effect on blood cholesterol levels. Many studies have shown that various groups of individuals have higher levels of blood cholesterol during periods of marked job stress, frustration, and fear than they do at less stressful times. Accountants, for example, have been shown to have significantly higher cholesterol levels during the first two weeks of April—the two weeks before the deadline for filing income tax—than during February or March. Similar types of blood cholesterol elevations have been shown to occur in medical students taking examinations.

A possible link between stress and increases in blood cholesterol may be **cortisol**, a hormone produced in the adrenal glands and released into the bloodstream when we are experiencing stress. Elevated levels of cortisol appear to coincide with elevated levels of blood cholesterol in people who have coronary heart disease and exhibit Type A behavior.

Adrenaline, another hormone released from the adrenal glands when we experience stress, may also be a factor. Research has shown that in situations in which competition is coupled with harassment, there is a marked increase in blood adrenaline levels in Type A individuals as compared to Type B individuals. This possible connection was also highlighted by the same researcher who first observed that excess dietary cholesterol was essential for producing atherosclerosis in animals. The researcher noted that injecting adrenaline into these experimental animals could intensify the buildup of cholesterol in the walls of the coronary arteries.

A recent study of female monkeys also suggests that changes in hormone levels caused by stress may play a role in disturbing blood cholesterol levels. This study of female monkeys living in a social unit showed that the subordinate females had more extensive coronary heart disease than the dominant females. In addition, the subordinate females showed lower levels of HDL-cholesterol that were felt to be related to impaired ovarian function. In other words, the stress these subordinate monkeys experienced due to their social status appeared to affect the functioning of their ovaries, which in turn may have affected their levels of estrogen (one of the female hormones produced by the ovaries). This decrease in estrogen levels may have caused a lowering of HDL-cholesterol levels in their blood. This research is suggestive since, in women, total blood cholesterol levels and risk of coronary heart disease tend to increase in the later years, when estrogen levels fall.

Does "Type A" Predict Heart Disease Risk?

Despite the impressive array of evidence that appears to support a connection between behavior pattern and coronary heart disease, the relationship is not as strong or clear-cut as it was once presumed to be. For example, Type A behavior (as determined by questionnaire) has not been found consistently in patients with coronary heart disease.

Two recent studies cast further doubts on the ability of the Type A behavior pattern to actually predict first, as well as second, heart attacks. In the Multiple Risk Factor Intervention Trial (MRFIT), for example, researchers could not confirm the results of the Western Collaborative Group Study, which showed Type A behavior to be an independent risk factor for coronary heart disease.

Moreover, a recent follow-up of the male patients in the Western Collaborative Group Study who were felt to be Type A and who developed coronary heart disease provided surprising results. The follow-up showed that after 12.7 years, the death rate among those with Type A who had heart attacks was actually lower than the death rate among those who were classified as Type B. These results suggest that not all patients defined as Type A are at increased risk of having a second heart attack.

They also suggest that further study needs to be done on the relationship between stress and coronary heart disease.

One of the problems in assessing this relationship has been that the definition of Type A varies depending on whether an interview or a questionnaire is used to determine behavior pattern. It has been pointed out that the questionnaires describe Type A behavior from a job-involvement point of view, with attention paid to both impatience and overcompetitiveness. These questionnaires neglect to consider the presence of hostility. A growing body of evidence suggests, however, that hostility is the key feature of Type A behavior that correlates with coronary heart disease. Therefore, before any conclusions can be drawn, new methods for assessing behavior that take hostility into account will have to be defined, tested, and put into practice.

Does Changing Behavior Help?

A standard form of therapy for altering Type A behavior has not been developed. Various attempts at toning down Type A behavior and increasing strategies for coping with stress do appear to be of benefit, however.

The Recurrent Coronary Prevention Project, for example, looked at middle-aged heart attack survivors who were randomly selected to receive either the usual cardiac (post-heart attack) counseling alone or a combination of cardiac counseling and special behavior counseling aimed at altering Type A behavior. After 4.5 years, the researchers felt that 35 percent of those who received the special behavior counseling had markedly reduced their Type A behavior, as opposed to less than ten percent of those who had only received cardiac counseling. Furthermore, the total rate of recurrent heart attacks and cardiac deaths was significantly reduced in the group that received special behavior counseling in addition to cardiac counseling.

Despite the less-than-conclusive data supporting the link between the specific Type A behavior pattern and cardiovascular disease, it's likely that changing stressful behavior patterns can benefit both physical and emotional health. There is hope that continuing research will not only clarify this relationship, but will provide physicians and their patients with improved methods for coping with stress constructively and altering the harmful aspects of stressful behavior.

CHAPTER 10:
Drugs & Surgery

When Diet isn't Enough

Although diet therapy is the treatment of choice for lowering blood cholesterol levels, sometimes it is not enough to lower stubbornly high blood cholesterol to a desirable level. In such cases, the physician may decide to add drug therapy to a cholesterol-controlling diet. The key word here is "add," since even when drug therapy is prescribed, a low-fat, low-cholesterol diet must be continued during drug therapy.

In general, diet therapy alone will be tried before drug therapy is considered. According to the guidelines established by the Adult Treatment Panel of the National Cholesterol Education Program (NCEP), LDL-cholesterol level should be reevaluated after a minimum of six months of diet therapy. If the LDL-cholesterol level is 190 mg/dl or greater, or if it is in the 160 to 189 mg/dl range and the patient has definite coronary heart disease or two or more risk factors for coronary heart disease, then the addition of drug therapy to diet should be considered.

In rare instances, shorter periods of diet therapy may be tried before drug therapy is added. Such exceptions to the rule include patients who have LDL-cholesterol levels above 225 mg/dl indicating an underlying genetic disorder and patients who have active coronary heart disease. The decision to initiate drug therapy prior to the minimum six months of diet therapy, however, will be made by the physician. And, once again, diet therapy must be continued during drug therapy.

How Cholesterol-Lowering Drugs Work

The aim of cholesterol-controlling therapy is to lower LDL-cholesterol levels, either by limiting the production of LDL in the body or by increasing its processing or removal. As discussed in Part I, large lipoprotein molecules carry various proportions of dietary cholesterol and triglyceride through the bloodstream to the liver. The liver produces triglyceride-rich VLDL molecules that also carry cholesterol. These VLDL molecules are converted in the blood (when they drop off their triglycerides) into cholesterol-rich LDL molecules. LDL levels are regulated in the body by special receptors that are concentrated mainly on the cells of the liver. Along this complicated system for handling fat, there are several points at which drug therapy can influence the usual balance between production and removal of cholesterol, thereby lowering levels of total cholesterol and LDL-cholesterol.

Drugs designed to limit the production of cholesterol can do so either by interfering with the absorption of cholesterol or by interfering with one of the stages of cholesterol synthesis. One drug, *beta sitosterol*, was designed to retard the absorption of cholesterol in the intestines. This drug, however, proved to be only mildly effective. Drugs that interfere with the later stages of cholesterol synthesis are no longer marketed because of the tragic experience with a drug called *Mer 29*. This drug was briefly marketed in the late 1950s but was removed from the market because it caused cataracts.

Lovastatin, on the other hand, is an example of a new class of drugs called **HMG-CoA-reductase inhibitors**, which affect an earlier stage of cholesterol synthesis. This type of drug works by inhibiting the key enzyme in cholesterol synthesis called HMG-CoA reductase. By reducing the production of cholesterol in the liver, this drug causes new LDL receptors to be produced and thus restores the liver's ability to control cholesterol levels in the blood.

Niacin, when prescribed in adequate doses, affects the production of cholesterol in another manner. Niacin alters the flow of fatty acids from fat tissue to the liver. With fewer fatty acids coming in from fatty tissue, the liver produces fewer triglycerides and thus fewer VLDL molecules. Since much of the LDL-cholesterol in the blood comes from VLDL molecules, the level of LDLs in the blood drops.

Drugs that improve the body's ability to process or remove cholesterol are also valuable in lowering blood cholesterol levels. **Resins**, for example, bind bile acids and prevent them from being reabsorbed and sent to the liver, where they are usually recycled. This results in the loss of bile, which is needed to digest fatty foods. The liver compensates for this loss by breaking down cholesterol into bile acids. This lower level of cholesterol in the liver causes the production of more LDL receptors, which pull LDL-cholesterol out of the bloodstream. Unfortunately, the liver does try to compensate for its lowered level of cholesterol by increasing cholesterol synthesis, so the total reductions in blood cholesterol seen with these drugs is not always as great as expected. Drugs like **psyllium derivatives** (*Metamucil*) and **neomycin** are less effective than resins but appear to work in a similar manner.

The drug **gemfibrozil** appears to affect both the synthesis of cholesterol and the removal of fats. By stimulating an enzyme system called lipoprotein lipase, gemfibrozil lowers triglyceride and LDL-cholesterol levels and raises HDL-cholesterol levels.

The drug **probucol**, on the other hand, may have a unique anti-atherosclerosis effect. It may interfere with the actual process by which LDL-cholesterol is deposited in the arteries. It may therefore be very useful in patients with the highest levels of LDL-cholesterol who are at the greatest risk of having cholesterol deposited in their artery walls.

Comparing the Drugs

In this section, we'll compare the various lipid-lowering drugs commonly prescribed. As a basis of comparison, each drug will be reviewed in terms of its ability to lower lipid levels; its proven ability to reduce the risk of coronary heart disease in clinical trials; its long-term safety; and how convenient it is to use. Convenience of use, which relates to factors such as how the drug is administered, how palatable it is, whether it has side effects, and how expensive it is, is considered because all of these can affect long-term adherence to a drug.

The **bile-acid binding resins** are important drugs of first choice in cholesterol-lowering therapy. They are known as **cholestyramine** (*Questran*) and **colestipol** (*Colestid*). The dosage form is a powder, which as *Questran* contains four grams of active medication and as *Colestid* contains five grams. Lipid experts consider them to be comparable in their effects on blood cholesterol. As mentioned earlier, they produce a moderate decrease in LDL-cholesterol levels and a slight increase in HDL-cholesterol levels. Both have been associated with lower rates of new cases of coronary heart disease in several trials of men with and without coronary heart disease. They have an enviable safety record due to the fact that they are not actually absorbed by the body.

With such an outstanding record of efficacy and long-term safety, it may come as a surprise that resins are not always popular with patients. This appears to be due to the gritty texture of the powder, the inconvenience of carrying and consuming a packet of powder away from home, and troublesome gastrointestinal side effects such as bloating, constipation, and aggravation of hemorrhoids. It therefore takes a considerable amount of patient education for this type of drug therapy to be adhered to successfully by patients, especially when moderate to high dosages are prescribed. What's more, since resins cause elevated triglyceride levels to rise further, they are not recommended for patients who have high triglyceride as well as high cholesterol levels.

Yet patients who desire the safest possible drug therapy for lowering blood cholesterol can successfully tolerate this medication. The key to therapy is to "start low and go slow." A gradual increase in dosage often succeeds. One practical tip is to add a psyllium derivative like *Metamucil* to the resin (you should discuss this with your physician first, however). This may prevent some of the bowel problems that can occur when the resins are used alone.

A useful tip for consumers on resin therapy is that you pay extra for convenience forms of packaging, such as individual packets. The best buys among resins are the cans of powder. To minimize the problems of carrying this medication with you, a useful habit is to take the medication in the morning before leaving home and then again in the evening upon returning home.

One important problem with resins is their ability to interfere (bind) with other medications, particularly commonly prescribed drugs such as thyroid, digoxin, and antibiotics. Patients should therefore remember to take these and any other medications at least one hour before, or four or more hours after, taking the resin. Although drug adherence can be a problem, the remarkable safety record of resins makes them an excellent choice for patients who are young, motivated, and concerned about the safety of medications and who have no gastrointestinal problems.

The other drug of first choice in cholesterol-lowering therapy is **niacin** or **nicotinic acid**. Niacin comes in tablet form and in a sustained-release form. The usual initial dose is either 100 mg of niacin in the tablet form or 250 mg in the sustained-release form. The dosage must be built up slowly; lipids and other blood chemistry must be monitored as the dosage is raised. While some patients with mild to moderate high blood cholesterol respond to lower dosages of niacin (500 to 1000 mg daily), those with moderate to severe high blood cholesterol (240 mg/dl or more) may require one to three grams or more of niacin daily.

Consumers must be aware of the difference between niacin and niacinamide. Niacinamide has many of the vitamin properties of niacin but regrettably little of the lipid-lowering power. Niacinamide is not the generic form of niacin as some might believe. *Niacinamide is another form of the drug and is not effective in lowering blood lipid levels.*

Niacin lowers total blood cholesterol, LDL-cholesterol, and triglyceride levels while it raises HDL-cholesterol levels. When given to heart attack survivors, niacin has been shown to reduce the chance of a second heart attack. Long-term follow-up has also shown increased longevity among these patients. In addition, coronary bypass patients who were given a combination of niacin and a resin showed less progression of their coronary atherosclerosis.

Since niacin has been used in patients for decades, it appears to be safe in long-term therapy. Side effects are more likely when higher doses are used, and at least one study suggests that the sustained-release forms may cause side effects in the liver more easily than the unmodified form. Nonetheless, side effects do appear to cause an adherence problem. Since niacin is a potent vasodilator (it causes blood vessels to widen), niacin causes flushing and itching. The intensity of these reactions can be reduced by taking an aspirin before taking the niacin and by taking the niacin with food. Niacin therapy can aggravate peptic ulcer disease and can interfere with liver function. In certain individuals it can also elevate blood sugar and uric acid (the substance that produces gout) levels. These levels must be monitored as the dosage of niacin is increased. Therefore, like other drug therapy for reducing lipid levels, niacin therapy must be prescribed and supervised by a physician.

In those individuals who have both elevated cholesterol and elevated triglycerides, niacin is the preferred drug therapy. Unmodified niacin is also extremely inexpensive and is therefore the drug of choice in patients for whom cost is an issue. Because of its record in such patients, niacin is also an attractive choice for patients with coronary heart disease who have had either a heart attack or coronary bypass surgery.

A new class of drugs now commonly prescribed for lipid lowering are the **HMG-CoA-reductase inhibitors**. The only one currently available to consumers is known as **lovastatin** (*Mevacor*). Other HMG-CoA-reductase inhibitors will probably be introduced on the market within the next five years. Lovastatin is produced in 20 mg tablets that should be taken with food for maximum efficacy. The exact daily dosage of the drug depends on the patient's LDL-cholesterol level at the start of drug therapy.

This type of drug is very effective in lowering LDL-cholesterol levels. It also lowers triglyceride levels and raises HDL-cholesterol levels. In general, this drug is well tolerated and appears to have fewer side effects than do the resins. Since lovastatin has only recently been introduced into the marketplace, however, no final judgment as to its long-term safety has been made. Possible side effects from lovastatin include abnormal liver function, which occurs in about two percent of patients and can be reversed by discontinuing the drug, and muscle injury that appears serious only when lovastatin is used in conjunction with cyclosporine (a drug used in transplant patients), gemfibrozil (another lipid-lowering drug) or, less often, niacin. Because lovastatin is such a powerful lipid-lowerer, it was suspected that the drug might cause an increased incidence of cataracts (similar to the way that *Mer 29* did); after investigation, however, no such increased incidence was found. Nonetheless, patients are currently required to have their eyes examined for cataracts prior to beginning lovastatin therapy and then annually thereafter.

Because lovastatin is such a new drug, there are no studies available yet on its ability to affect the incidence of coronary heart disease. Nonetheless, because lovastatin favorably affects lipid levels, it is likely that this drug's ability to reduce the incidence of coronary heart disease is considerable. Lovastatin's ability to lower LDL-cholesterol levels considerably, with a minimal amount of medication and tolerable side effects, makes it a good choice in patients who have multiple illnesses (in addition to high blood cholesterol) or take several medications and in patients with severely elevated blood cholesterol.

Another group of drugs prescribed for lipid lowering are the **fibric acid derivatives**. Gemfibrozil and clofibrate are examples of this type of drug. **Gemfibrozil** (*Lopid*) is produced as 300 mg tablets and is usually taken twice daily. Gemfibrozil lowers LDL-cholesterol and is particularly effective at lowering triglyceride levels and raising HDL-cholesterol levels. The results of the Helsinki Heart Study showed gemfibrozil to be safe and effective for significantly lowering the risk of coronary heart disease in middle-aged Finnish men with average cholesterol levels of 280 mg/dl. This beneficial effect appeared to be due to both a decrease in LDL-cholesterol levels and an increase in HDL-cholesterol levels. The results also appeared to support gemfibrozil's long-term safety. There were fewer deaths due to coronary heart disease although there were slightly more deaths due to violence, accidents, and hemorrhage in the gemfibrozil group as compared to the placebo group. This was an interesting, although as yet unexplained finding, since another trial also appeared to show a slight increase in deaths due to accidents and violence in patients taking gemfibrozil. Compared to the placebo group, there was also a slight increase in gastrointestinal symptoms in the gemfibrozil group; otherwise, the drug is well tolerated.

Clofibrate (*Atromid-S*) is a fibric acid derivative that comes in 500 mg capsules. The usual dosage is 1500 to 2000 mg daily. Clofibrate was a very popular drug in the late 1960s and 1970s. It's popularity waned, however, after the publication of the results of the World Health Organization (WHO) Clofibrate Trial. This large study looked at the total mortality and heart disease rates in 15,745 middle-aged men. The study showed that a nine percent reduction in blood cholesterol was associated with a 20 percent decrease in new cases of coronary heart disease in those men with high blood cholesterol who received clofibrate. The most distressing finding in this study, however, was an increase in the number of deaths in the clofibrate group as compared to the placebo group, despite the reduction in heart attacks. The men who took clofibrate also had an increased incidence of gallstones. This study gave the consumer an important warning: The true measures of a cholesterol-lowering drug's worth are its long-term safety as well as its ability to reduce coronary heart disease.

The final drug to be considered is **probucol**. Probucol comes in 250 mg and 500 mg tablets and is taken twice daily. The usual maintenance dose (the dose prescribed once cholesterol levels have stabilized) is 500 mg taken twice daily. Probucol lowers LDL-cholesterol levels slightly and has no effect on triglyceride levels. It also lowers HDL-cholesterol to a variable degree. It is not clear whether this lowering of HDL-cholesterol is an adverse effect since there is no clinical trial data to determine probucol's long-term safety or its ability to decrease the incidence of coronary heart disease. It's ability to retard atherosclerosis in rabbits with inherited high blood cholesterol (in terms of research, they resemble adult humans with inherited high blood cholesterol) holds out the promise that further studies will define probucol's role in the treatment of elevated lipid levels and coronary heart disease. It appears to be a safe drug, but again, lack of controlled, long-term clinical trials means that its safety has not been proven. It also appears to be well tolerated.

Special Situations

There are some special situations in drug therapy that need to be mentioned. One such situation is the use of low dosages of a safe medication in patients whose LDL-cholesterol levels are above the goals set for dietary therapy but are not high enough to warrant intensive drug therapy. In such patients who are judged to be at increased risk for coronary heart disease, many physicians use small doses of resins to successfully lower LDL-cholesterol levels. Because of the small doses used, there are few side effects with this type of therapy.

In addition, combination therapy is often beneficial in patients with very high levels of LDL-cholesterol, those with combined elevations of cholesterol and triglycerides, and those in whom side effects at higher doses prohibit the maximum dosage of just one drug. Combinations that are beneficial for those with very high levels of LDL-cholesterol (patients with inherited high blood cholesterol) include resins plus niacin and resins plus lovastatin. These combinations have produced reductions in LDLs as great as 35 to 50 percent. Since gemfibrozil and niacin both raise blood sugar levels in patients with borderline diabetes, the use of lovastatin may be preferred in diabetics who have elevated cholesterol and elevated triglycerides.

For patients with combined elevations of cholesterol and triglycerides, resins can't be used as the initial therapy because they would aggravate the existing elevated triglyceride levels. Successful therapy for these individuals begins with niacin or, if the niacin is not well tolerated, gemfibrozil. Resin therapy may be added for extra cholesterol lowering once triglyceride levels have been controlled.

For those patients in whom smaller doses of medication are required in order to minimize side effects, resin plus probucol may be well tolerated.

Surgery in Patients with High Blood Cholesterol

In patients who have severe or progressive symptoms of coronary heart disease that indicate a marked impairment of blood flow to the heart, it may be impossible to wait the one to two years that may be necessary for cholesterol-lowering therapy to work its magic. In such cases, a coronary angiogram (an X ray of the coronary arteries obtained after a cardiologist injects a dye into the coronary arteries) is often performed to determine the location and severity of the blockages and to determine the state of the heart's main pumping chamber, called the left ventricle (LV). Studies have shown that maintaining good LV function is important; with declining LV function, the patient's prognosis worsens. Therefore, the object of therapy is to improve blood flow and to preserve the function of the LV muscle. Often, this can be done through medication. If the symptoms can't be controlled or if there's a critical blockage surgery is suggested.

Coronary Artery Bypass Surgery

Coronary bypass surgery is performed on one or more of the coronary arteries, which lie on the outer surface of the heart and supply the heart muscle with the oxygen and nutrients it needs. The purpose of the operation is to bypass the obstructed area and permit blood to flow freely to the heart muscle. To bypass the blocked area, the surgeon uses a segment of vein taken from the patient's leg or a segment of artery taken from the patient's chest. A small hole is made in the aorta (the main artery), and one end of the bypass blood vessel is sewn to it. The other end is then attached to the blocked blood vessel beyond the point of the obstruction. Thereafter, blood will flow freely around the obstructed part of the artery to nourish the heart muscle.

Studies have shown that coronary artery bypass grafting prolongs the life of patients with blockages in the left main coronary artery and in those with significant blockages in three blood vessels who also have impaired function of the LV. A European study further showed that there was a significant advantage to surgery in certain patients with two blocked coronary arteries.

Although bypass surgery in these circumstances does appear to prolong life and relieve symptoms of coronary heart disease, bypass operations do not always improve the patient's quality of life. For example, a study of patients enrolled in the Coronary Artery Surgery Study, all of whom were men with mild angina (chest pain), failed to show an improvement either in work status or activity level during leisure-time activity.

It is important to note that bypass surgery is not truly a curative procedure. During the decade following bypass surgery, atherosclerosis is seen with increasing frequency in the arteries that were originally bypassed as well as in the blood vessels used to bypass the obstructions. Although this appears less likely when the bypass vessel comes from the chest rather than from the leg, blood vessels from the chest cannot always be used. What's more, in patients with multiple bypasses, blood vessels from both the leg and chest must be used.

Bypass surgery also does not make controlling cholesterol easier. In the study of patients enrolled in the Coronary Artery Surgery Study, for instance, the number of patients with blood cholesterol levels above 250 mg/dl prior to surgery did not change five years after surgery. So while bypass surgery may be necessary in critical situations, long-term cholesterol-controlling therapy is essential to decrease lipid levels and help decrease the risk that the arteries will become critically blocked again.

Balloon Angioplasty

Percutaneous Transluminal Coronary Angioplasty (PTCA), also known as balloon angioplasty, is performed by guiding a catheter, with a balloon attached, into the coronary arteries. When the catheter reaches the site of the obstruction, the balloon is blown up and the plaque is pressed against the artery walls, thus easing the flow of blood through the artery.

This procedure can eliminate the symptoms of angina (chest pain caused by a decrease in the flow of blood to the heart) when such symptoms are not severe enough to warrant bypass surgery. It may also allow improved blood flow in patients for whom bypass surgery is not possible. It has the appeal of allowing some patients to avoid major open-heart surgery. This makes it more likely that the patient can return to his or her previous level of activity reasonably soon after a successful procedure.

In 1987 it was estimated that there were more than 150,000 PTCA procedures performed. Results from the National Heart, Lung, and Blood Institute registry showed that the success rate was over 90 percent for dilating one or more blockages. The mortality rate with such procedures was one percent and the incidence of emergency bypass surgery was 3.4 percent. In 30 percent of cases, there is a failure of the dilation to keep the blood vessel open, requiring a second PTCA. This usually occurs in the first six months after the initial successful PTCA. If the artery does not close up within that time, chances are the artery will not close up at a later time. Thus, angioplasty is a reasonably safe and effective therapy for significant narrowing of coronary arteries that causes impaired blood flow to the LV. Once again, however, angioplasty will not prevent blockages from occurring in other segments of the coronary arteries. Therefore, angioplasty, like bypass surgery, is not a replacement for a lifetime plan for controlling blood cholesterol.

Surgery to Lower Blood Cholesterol

You may be asking yourself, "What if there were an operation that could lower blood cholesterol permanently?" Then you wouldn't have to worry about your blood cholesterol and you wouldn't have to rely on your own willpower to keep your cholesterol levels under control. Well, such an operation is available. It is called the **partial ileal bypass**. This operation, however, is only for the one-in-a-million patient who has virtually no functioning LDL receptors.

In this operation, the surgeon bypasses the last part of the small intestines. This prevents vitamin B_{12} and bile acid from being absorbed and permanently lowers blood cholesterol. It should be noted that this operation is not a form of weight-loss therapy; it should not be confused with the more extensive jejunoileal bypass procedure used to treat massive obesity.

The side effects of a partial ileal bypass include mild diarrhea that eventually subsides and the life-long need for monthly injections of B_{12}. The real disadvantages are the risks associated with an operation that requires general anesthesia and the possibility of long-term gastrointestinal complications. The incidence of these complications, however, appears to be low.

Careful studies have shown the partial ileal bypass to be successful in lowering total blood cholesterol, triglycerides, and LDL-cholesterol. In addition, the results of this procedure appear superior to those obtained from therapy with resins, such as cholestyramine, in which long-term adherence to medication can be a real problem. For patients with inherited high blood cholesterol who lack LDL-receptor function, the results are less striking. In these patients, the addition of lovastatin has proven beneficial in bringing LDL-cholesterol values into the normal range.

For those patients with the most severe cholesterol problems, in which the absence of LDL-receptor function causes blood cholesterol to reach the 600 to 1000 mg/dl range, an innovative approach to a surgical cure has been developed. The procedure was first performed on a six-year-old girl with severe heart disease who required a heart transplant. The surgeons implanted a normal liver, as well as a new heart, in the hope of surgically correcting the girl's LDL-receptor problem. The little girl's new liver, with abundant LDL receptors, was able to correctly dispose of the excess cholesterol in her body. This caused her blood cholesterol level to fall from over 1000 mg/dl to the mid-200 mg/dl range. The transplant had literally corrected the genetic defect that produced an absence of LDL receptors. Of course, because of the great risks involved in these types of surgical procedures, surgery to lower blood cholesterol levels is considered a last resort for patients who have critically elevated cholesterol levels that do not respond to intensive diet and drug therapy and that would otherwise cause fatal coronary heart disease before the end of the second or third decade of life.

CHAPTER 11:

The Big Picture

Don't Stop at Cholesterol

Once you have decided to take the necessary steps to control your blood cholesterol levels, you are on your way to improving the health of your heart. That is not to say, however, that improving your cholesterol profile is the only thing you need to do to protect your heart. A variety of factors, such as tobacco use, blood pressure, diet, weight, exercise, and stress, can affect your risk of heart disease. Neglecting any of these aspects of your lifestyle may increase your risk. So while you make those beneficial changes to keep blood cholesterol in line, you need to pay attention to your lifestyle in general to be sure you are moving forward on that heart-healthy path.

As discussed in Part I, some of the factors that increase your risk of heart disease are beyond your control. These include your age, your sex, and your family history. While you can't change these factors, you may be able to make other changes that might minimize their effects. For example, if you are at increased risk due to a family history of coronary heart disease, you may be able to minimize that risk somewhat by working with your doctor to get your cholesterol levels into a desirable range. There are also a variety of risk factors like high blood cholesterol that are within your control.

Smoking

Perhaps the most important of the controllable risk factors for heart disease is cigarette smoking.

We've already mentioned that smokers tend to have lower levels of the protective HDL-cholesterol. Smoking's effect on the health of your heart and blood vessels goes beyond its effect on cholesterol levels, however. Smoking appears to damage the arteries, making it easier for cholesterol and other debris to accumulate and clog the arteries that supply your heart with blood. Smoking is also considered to be the major risk factor for sudden cardiac death. Indeed, smokers have two to four times the risk of sudden cardiac death of nonsmokers. A smoker who has a heart attack is also more likely to die from that heart attack.

To rid yourself of this risk factor, you need to quit smoking (of course, if you don't smoke now, don't start). By quitting smoking now, you can greatly decrease your risk of heart disease. Research indicates that ten years after a pack-a-day smoker quits, his or her risk of heart disease is almost the same as the risk for people who have never smoked. Luckily, a variety of methods are now available to help smokers break the habit. These include special clinics and classes, hypnosis, and nicotine chewing gum.

High Blood Pressure

In addition to high blood cholesterol and cigarette smoking, high blood pressure (hypertension) is considered a major controllable risk factor for heart disease. According to 1985 estimates, nearly 60 million Americans have high blood pressure. While the actual death rate from high blood pressure appears relatively low (about 30,000 deaths in 1985), many more people die from heart attacks that are a direct result of high blood pressure. Unfortunately, high blood pressure is considered a *silent killer* because most often there are no apparent signs or symptoms of the disease.

Blood pressure is the amount of force exerted on artery walls as blood is pumped through the body. The pressure is exerted by the heart. Thus, a high blood pressure means the heart is working extra hard to move blood through your body. When the heart has to keep up this extra work for long periods, it can become significantly enlarged. The larger the heart gets, the harder it is for the heart to meet the demands placed on it. High blood pressure can also damage the arteries and this damage may speed up the plaque formation that causes coronary heart disease.

Blood pressure is measured in terms of millimeters of mercury (mm Hg). A blood pressure reading takes into account both the maximum pressure when the heart beats (systolic pressure) and the minimum pressure between beats (diastolic pressure). Blood pressure is considered high when the systolic pressure is 140 mm Hg or higher and/or when the diastolic pressure is 90 mm Hg or higher.

Scientists don't know the exact cause of most cases of high blood pressure. Some of the factors that appear to increase a person's risk are age (the older you are the more likely you are to have high blood pressure) and heredity (you are more likely to have high blood pressure if you are black or if your parents have high blood pressure). But other controllable factors, such as overweight and a high salt intake, appear to play a role as well. There are a variety of medications that can be used to lower blood pressure and keep it under control. For mildly elevated levels, however, losing weight and limiting the amount of salt in the diet can often help bring blood pressure into a more desirable range.

Lifestyle

This brings us back to lifestyle. Many other aspects of your lifestyle, including diet, exercise habits, weight control, and stress, influence not only your blood cholesterol and blood pressure, but your total risk of heart disease. To adopt a healthier lifestyle, therefore, you need to pay attention to all of these factors.

Dietary change, for instance, is only as effective as the number of risk factors it addresses. Making one beneficial change in your diet at the expense of others defeats your purpose. For example, by using more salt to add flavor to low-fat foods, you may simply be trading one risk factor (high blood cholesterol) for another (high blood pressure).

Sometimes dietary habits can be more subtle in the way they sabotage your efforts to make healthier lifestyle choices. Coffee drinking may be a good example. Coffee itself has not been conclusively linked to an increased risk of heart disease. But if you add cream and sugar and if you're in the habit of smoking when you drink coffee, the combination of saturated fat (from the cream), empty calories (from the sugar), and cigarettes can make indulging in several cups a day a risky habit. Popcorn is another example. Air-popped popcorn is a good low-fat, low-sodium snack that adds fiber to the diet. You are probably better off without popcorn, however, if you pop it in oil and pour on salt and butter.

As discussed in Chapter 7, overweight, especially when it leads to obesity, can affect your blood cholesterol levels, your risk of heart disease, and your overall health. The more excess body fat you accumulate, the worse it gets. Obesity is generally defined as 20 percent or more over ideal body weight (some guidelines use 30 percent as the cutoff). In addition to affecting blood cholesterol, obesity also puts a strain on your heart. Your heart simply has to work harder when you carry around that much extra weight. Being overweight also appears to increase your risk of high blood pressure as well as diabetes, a disease that also tends to increase the risk of heart disease.

On the other hand, bringing body weight down to an ideal level and then maintaining that weight can have a beneficial effect on your blood cholesterol, your blood pressure, and your heart. Decreasing your consumption of fat-rich foods and cutting your calorie intake can help you lose excess weight. If most of the fatty foods that you exclude from your diet are rich in saturated fat and cholesterol, you'll also help lower your blood cholesterol level.

A sedentary or inactive lifestyle may also increase your risk of cardiovascular disease. When combined with a high-fat, high-calorie diet, inactivity can lead to overweight and obesity. Aerobic exercise (see Chapter 8), on the other hand, is a good all-around approach to improving cardiovascular health. In addition to increasing the strength and efficiency of your heart, aerobic exercise can help you control your weight, your blood cholesterol, and your blood pressure. Making aerobic exercise a habit may also make it less likely that you will begin or continue to smoke.

Another aspect of lifestyle that can have an impact on the health of your heart is stress. While we discussed the scientific research linking stress to blood cholesterol and cardiovascular disease in Chapter 9, there are less obvious ways in which stress and your responses to it can affect your heart. Think for a minute about what you do when you are under a great deal of stress. Do you spend the time and effort necessary to prepare healthy meals or do you opt for fast food? Do you skip meals completely and then satisfy those hunger pains with a candy bar and a soda? Do you reach for a cigarette at the first sign of a stressful situation? Does exercise end up getting left off your list of "things to do"? For many people, the answer to one or more of these questions is "yes." When stress is a daily occurrence, these unhealthy stress responses can translate into an unhealthy lifestyle.

Ideally, it might be best for our hearts and our health if we could avoid stress completely. Unfortu-nately, avoiding all stress is impossible to do. Besides, some stress can be good. It can prompt us to do our best and it can add challenge to life. So what we need to do in order to avoid as many of the unhealthy side effects of stress as possible is to learn to avoid some stress and learn how to respond constructively to the stress we do feel. There are a variety of methods advocated for reducing the adverse effects of stress, including meditation and exercise. You may find one of these approaches helpful or you may need to develop your own strategy for dealing with stress. In terms of heart health, however, the most important thing to realize is that how we respond to stress affects how we treat our hearts.

So while controlling blood cholesterol is of major importance in warding off heart disease, it needs to be part of an overall plan to protect the health of your heart. Taking care of your heart for life requires adopting a heart-healthy lifestyle that you can stick with for good.

PART III:

Help Yourself to a Heart-Healthy Diet

CHAPTER 12:

How to Change Your Diet

Look at What You Eat

Now that you know how diet affects blood cholesterol levels and how blood cholesterol levels affect your heart, it's time to take a look at your diet. By figuring out how your eating habits and food choices compare with the experts' recommendations, you'll have a better idea of how you can make changes that will benefit your heart.

As mentioned in previous chapters, the American Heart Association (AHA) and the National Cholesterol Education Program (NCEP) have developed dietary guidelines (for adults) designed to lower high blood cholesterol levels and keep them in a desirable range. According to these guidelines, less than 30 percent of your total calorie intake should come from fat. Less than ten percent of your total calories (or less than one-third of your total fat calories) should come from saturated fat and no more than ten percent of your total calories should come from polyunsaturated fat; the remaining fat calories (ten to 15 percent of your total calorie intake) should come from monounsaturated fat. You should consume 50 to 60 percent of your total calories as carbohydrate. You should also consume less than 300 mg of dietary cholesterol each day.

In the *typical* American diet, however, 35 to 40 percent of calories come from fat, about 47 percent come from carbohydrates, and about 16 percent come from protein. The average adult diet also provides anywhere from 400 to 500 mg of cholesterol each day. In other words, the average American adult gets too many calories from fat, not enough calories from carbohydrate, and too much cholesterol.

To give you a general idea of whether or not your diet is high in saturated fat and cholesterol, read through the following list and make a check mark by each statement that applies to you.

DIET CHECK

____ You frequently eat hamburger, pork chops, luncheon meats, ham, hot dogs, sausages, bacon, or ribs.

____ You eat fast foods regularly.

____ You frequently eat hard cheeses, cheese foods, and cheese spreads.

____ You eat more than three egg yolks a week.

____ You drink whole milk and use half-and-half, sour cream, and dairy whipped cream.

____ When you eat chicken or fish, it is usually fried, or breaded and fried.

____ You prefer your vegetables to be deep-fried, breaded and fried, creamed, or served with cheese sauce.

____ You eat foods cooked in bacon grease or pan drippings from meats.

____ You use butter rather than margarine.

____ You frequently eat chocolate candy.

____ You frequently eat ice cream.

____ You frequently snack on chips, cookies, and crackers.

____ You frequently eat commercially prepared

baked goods like pastries, sweet rolls, doughnuts, pies, cakes, croissants, and cupcakes.

Each of these statements indicates a food choice or preference that is either high in saturated fat, high in cholesterol, or high in both saturated fat and cholesterol. So the fewer check marks you've made, the healthier your diet. Ideally, none of these statements should apply to you. On the other hand, the more statements that apply to you, the higher your diet is in saturated fat and cholesterol, and the more changes you'll need to make to improve the quality of your diet.

Your Plan of Action

To adopt a healthier diet that is low in total fat, saturated fat, and cholesterol, you need a plan of action. In other words, you need to set goals for yourself and then decide on changes that you can make to meet those goals. As just mentioned, the AHA and NCEP have developed guidelines or goals to help you create a heart-healthy diet. So before going any further, you need to take a look at what those goals mean in terms of your diet and your eating habits.

The guidelines recommend that you eat less than 30 percent of your total daily calorie intake as fat. What does that mean? Well, first of all, you need to know what your average daily calorie intake is (or should be). How many calories your body needs each day depends, to a great extent, on your gender, your age, and your level of activity. In general, men require more calories to maintain their weight than do women. In addition, as you grow older, your body needs fewer calories. Finally, the more active you are, the more energy—calories—your body needs to fuel that activity.

To help you determine your average calorie intake, we've set up two simple charts—one for adult men and another for adult women. The calorie information is taken from the Recommended Dietary Allowances (RDAs) of the Food and Nutrition Board of the National Science Council. These estimates are based on the calorie needs of men and women of average height and desirable weight. Each chart is broken down into age groups. In each age group, you'll find a range for total daily calorie intake. (We've also listed the total fat intake and saturated fat intake ranges, but we'll get to those in a moment.)

A range of calories is given for each group in order to account for differences in physical activity.

CALORIE, TOTAL FAT, AND SATURATED FAT RANGES* FOR ADULT MALES**

Age	19–22	23–50	51–75	76 and over
Daily Calorie Intake	2500–3300	2300–3100	2000–2800	1650–2450
Average Daily Total Fat Intake (in grams)	83–110	76–103	66–93	55–81
Average Daily Saturated Fat Intake (in grams)	27–36	25–34	22–31	18–27

CALORIE, TOTAL FAT, AND SATURATED FAT RANGES* FOR ADULT FEMALES**

Age	19–22	23–50	51–75	76 and over
Daily Calorie Intake	1700–2500	1600–2400	1400–2200	1200–2000
Average Daily Total Fat Intake (in grams)	56–83	53–80	46–73	40–66
Average Daily Saturated Fat Intake (in grams)	18–27	17–26	15–24	13–22

Where your calorie intake falls within the range for your age group depends on your level of physical activity. See text.

**Estimates of energy (calorie) needs from Food and Nutrition Board, National Research Council: Recommended Dietary Allowances. 9th ed. Washington, D.C., National Academy of Sciences, 1980. Ranges are for adult men and women of median height and desirable weight.*

In other words, those individuals who are most active would need a calorie intake closer to the upper limit of the calorie range while those who are least active would need a calorie intake that falls closer to the lower limit of the calorie range. For example, say that you're a 21-year-old male. In the chart for adult males under the 19 to 22 age group, the daily calorie intake range is 2500 to 3300. If you engage in intensive aerobic exercise for at least an hour several days a week and you lead a very active lifestyle, your daily calorie intake is likely to be closer to the 3300-calorie-a-day figure. On the other hand, if you have a sedentary job and spend almost all of your leisure time sitting in front of the television set, you're likely to require closer to 2500 calories a day. If your activity level falls in between, you can average the upper and lower values to estimate your daily calories intake. To do this, simply add the upper value and the lower value together and divide that total by two. For a 21-year-old male, the average is about 2900 calories.

Once you've estimated your daily calorie intake, you want to know how many of those calories should come from fat. According to the guidelines, less than 30 percent of your total calorie intake should come from fat. To find out the total number of calories that should come from fat, you multiply your total calorie intake by .30 (30 percent). Using the previous example of an active 21-year-old male, you would multiply 3300 by .3 and you would get 990. Therefore, no more than 990 of the calories you consume each day can come from fat. While this figure is helpful, you need to go one step further because most product labels and recipes list their fat content in terms of grams, not calories. Since one gram of fat (regardless of whether it is saturated or unsaturated) yields nine calories, dividing 990 by nine tells you how many grams of fat you are allowed. In this case, you should consume less than 110 grams (990 divided by nine) of fat each day. (You'll find the total fat intake range for each age group listed below the calorie range in the chart.)

The guidelines also specify how that daily fat intake should be divided between the three types of fat—saturated, polyunsaturated, and monounsaturated. They recommend that less than ten percent of your total daily calorie intake come from saturated fat. You can figure out the upper limit of saturated fat grams in the same way that you figured the total grams of fat. Instead of multiplying your daily calorie intake by .30 (30 percent), however, you

multiply your daily calorie intake by .10 (ten percent). For example, if you've estimated your total calorie intake to be 3300, then you should be consuming less than 330 (3300 multiplied by .10) of your total calories each day as saturated fat. Once again, since one gram of fat yields nine calories, you divide 330 by nine. Therefore, you should consume less than 36 grams (that's 330 divided by nine) of saturated fat each day. (You'll find the range of saturated fat grams for each age group listed in the chart as well.)

The guidelines also recommend that ten percent of your total daily calories come from polyunsaturated fat and the remaining fat calories come from monounsaturated fat. There's no need to do any extra figuring to determine these amounts, however. You've already figured out what ten percent of total calories means in terms of grams. In the example we've been using, 36 grams equal ten percent of total calories. So our young, active male should consume less than 36 grams of saturated fat and no more than 36 grams of polyunsaturated fat each day. The remaining 36 or so grams of fat should come from monounsaturated fat.

In order to reach these goals for fat intake, you need to *eat fewer high-fat foods, especially foods that are high in saturated fat*. Since high-fat food is usually also high in saturated fat, you will be decreasing your saturated fat intake by decreasing your total fat intake.

Much of the saturated fat in the typical American diet comes from animal products. Dairy products made from whole milk, for example, contain large amounts of saturated fat; butter, cheese, and ice cream add hefty doses of saturated fat to the diet. The marbling and visible fat in meat are also high in saturated fat. Poultry and fish generally contain lower amounts of saturated fat than meat. Most of the saturated fat in poultry is concentrated in the skin.

While vegetable fats are generally low in saturated fats, there are some exceptions. Coconut oil, palm oil, palm kernel oil, and cocoa butter are high in saturated fat. These are often referred to as hidden sources of saturated fat because they are not visible in foods. Unfortunately, they are used in a variety of prepared baked goods, snack foods, non-dairy creamers, cake mixes, and frozen dinners.

When you do choose foods that contain fat, you should choose those that contain mostly polyunsaturated and monounsaturated fats more often than those that contain mostly saturated fat. Good sources of polyunsaturated fats are cooking oils made from corn, sunflower, safflower, soybean, sesame, and cottonseed. (As explained in Chapter 1, however, the process of hydrogenation increases the saturated fat content of these oils. So you'll need to choose those oils that are not hydrogenated.) Fish oils also contain polyunsaturated fats known as omega-3 fatty acids (see the section on fish oils in Chapter 6). Oils rich in monounsaturated fatty acids include olive oil and rapeseed (canola) oil.

Since you will be decreasing the number of calories in your diet that come from fatty foods, you will need to increase the number of calories that come from other types of food in order to maintain your weight. According to the guidelines, *you should increase your intake of complex carbohydrates* (starch and fiber) to make up for the lost calories. Foods that are rich in complex carbohydrates include breads, pasta, rice, cereals, dried beans, vegetables, and fruits.

On the other hand, if you need to lose weight, you can decrease both your total calorie intake and your total fat intake by cutting out fatty foods and not replacing the lost calories. If you cut out 500 calories worth of fat from your diet each day and don't replace them with calories from other sources like carbohydrates, you can lose about a pound of fat a week on average. As discussed in Chapter 6, *if you are overweight, losing weight can actually help you to lower your blood cholesterol level* (especially if you lose that weight by removing saturated fat from your diet).

You also need to limit your dietary cholesterol intake. If you eat a typical American diet, chances are you're getting between 400 and 500 mg of cholesterol each day. The guidelines, however, recommend that you *decrease the amount of cholesterol in your diet* to less than 300 mg each day. Cholesterol is found exclusively in animal products, including dairy products, meat, eggs, poultry, fish, and shellfish. Foods from plant sources, on the other hand, do not contain cholesterol (unless, of course, they are served with animal products like creamy sauces or cheese). Since many of the foods that are high in saturated fat also contain cholesterol, your cholesterol intake should decrease as you decrease the amount of saturated fat in your diet. Also, since much of the cholesterol in the American diet comes from egg yolks (one egg yolk contains about 250 mg of cholesterol), you can make a concerted effort to decrease the number of eggs (including those in prepared or processed foods) you consume.

Check the Ingredients

To help you reach your heart-healthy diet goals, you need to pay attention to the ingredients in foods. More and more food producers have begun to list the fat and cholesterol content of their products. When you read labels, compare the amounts of saturated fat and cholesterol. The amounts of fat will be listed in grams. The amount of cholesterol will be listed in milligrams. By using the "Cholesterol & Fat Counter" in this book and by comparing the labels of similar products, you'll be able to choose those foods that are lowest in saturated fat and cholesterol.

Even when the food label does not list the amounts of fat, saturated fat, and cholesterol, you can get some valuable information about the product from the list of ingredients. All food labels list the ingredients in order of weight. The ingredient that is contained in the greatest amount is listed first, while the ingredient that is contained in the least amount is listed last. Therefore, if a product lists a fat (or oil) as the first ingredient, it contains more fat than it does any other ingredient. Also, if the product label lists several fats and oils, the product is likely to be high in fat.

You also want to pay special attention to the specific types of fats and oils the product contains. For example, some products simply list "vegetable oil" as an ingredient. While that sounds healthy, you need to keep in mind that two vegetable oils—coconut oil and palm oil—are highly saturated. So

---

COMMON SOURCES OF SATURATED FAT AND CHOLESTEROL

animal fat	egg	palm kernel oil
bacon fat	egg yolk solids	palm oil
beef fat or	ham fat	pork fat
tallow	hardened fat	turkey fat
butter	or oil	vegetable oil*
chicken fat	hydrogenated	vegetable
cocoa butter	vegetable oil	shortening
coconut	lamb fat	whole-milk
coconut oil	lard	solids
cream	meat fat	

* This could be coconut oil or palm oil—both of which are highly saturated—rather than one of the polyunsaturated vegetable oils.

look for those products that list a specific polyunsaturated vegetable oil like safflower, sunflower, corn, sesame, soybean, or cottonseed oil. The chart on page 73 lists common ingredients that are sources of saturated fat and cholesterol. To lower your intake of saturated fat and cholesterol, you'll want to avoid or at least cut back on foods that list these ingredients first or that list several of them.

Choosing and Preparing Foods

In this section, you'll find specific practical choices and changes that you can make to decrease the saturated fat and cholesterol content of your diet. It's important to keep in mind that both the foods you choose to eat and the way you choose to prepare them affect the amount of saturated fat and cholesterol they provide. For instance, chicken that is skinned, trimmed of fat, and baked is a good choice for a heart-healthy entree. If you leave the skin on, bread the chicken, and then fry it in butter or lard, however, you've created a saturated-fat monster. So we've included practical suggestions not only for choosing foods that are lower in saturated fat and cholesterol, but for preparing those foods without adding saturated fat and cholesterol. You'll find additional suggestions for preparing tasty, heart-smart meals in the recipe section.

Meats

—Meats provide protein and other important nutrients, but they also contribute saturated fat and cholesterol. To lower blood cholesterol, choose the leanest cuts of meat and cut down on the portion size. You should limit your daily meat intake to no more than six ounces and use low-fat foods like vegetables, pasta, and rice to fill in the meal.

—Well-marbled meat (meat with streaks of fat running through it) is higher in saturated fat than meat with less marbling. While marbling tends to make the meat tastier, meats from the "round" cuts, which have less marbling, can be quite tasty if prepared appropriately.

—The grade of meat indicates the fat content. "Prime" has the most fat, "choice" has less fat, and "good" has the least fat; choose "choice" and "good" more often than "prime."

—Certain cuts of meat are naturally lower in fat than others. See the chart at the end of the meat section to help you select the leanest cuts.

—Meats labeled "light," "lite," "leaner," or "lower fat" *may* be, but are not necessarily, low in fat. Check the nutrition label to find out how many grams of fat each serving contains.

—Avoid or decrease your consumption of luncheon meats and other high-fat processed meats, including hot dogs, bacon, bologna, and sausages; more than half of the calories they contain come from fat and much of that fat is saturated.

—Organ meats like liver, sweetbreads, and kidneys are high in cholesterol, so choose them less frequently.

—When preparing meats, trim visible fat.

—Instead of frying, try baking, broiling, or roasting. When roasting, place the meat on a rack so that fat can drip away. When basting, use wine, lemon juice, or tomato juice rather than fatty drippings from the meat itself.

Poultry

—Poultry is generally lower in saturated fat than meat, so replace some of the meat dishes in your weekly menu plan with poultry dishes.

—Processed products or luncheon "meats" that are made from poultry are often very high in saturated fat, so limit them in your diet. Instead, use leftovers from poultry meals prepared in a low-fat manner.

—Limit goose and duck, which are very high in saturated fat.

—To decrease the saturated-fat content of poultry, remove the skin and any visible fat before cooking.

—Instead of frying, try baking, broiling, or roasting. When basting, use wine, lemon juice, or tomato juice instead of fatty drippings. When roasting, place the poultry on a rack so that fat can drip away.

Fish

—Most fish is lower in saturated fat than poultry or meat, so choose fish more often than meat or poultry when planning your weekly menu.

—Shellfish has less saturated fat than meat, poultry, and most fish. Some shellfish, however, is relatively

FAT FIGHTER'S GUIDE TO MEAT

	CHOOSE			*AVOID*		
	Steaks and Chops	**Roasts**	**Potroasts, Stews, and Ragouts**	**Steaks and Chops**	**Roasts**	**Potroasts, Stews, and Ragouts**
Beef	flank steak; top round; fat-trimmed tenderloin and sirloin steaks	fat-trimmed tenderloin; top round; eye of round; rump; sirloin	rolled flank; fat-trimmed bottom round; chuck arm or shank	rib; club; porterhouse; T-bone steaks	rib roast	shoulder; chuck blade; short ribs; brisket; short plate
Veal	round steak; loin chops or cutlets	round; rump; sirloin	shoulder; arm; shank	rib chops	shoulder; rib; breast	breast
Lamb	centerbone leg steaks; fat-trimmed loin chops	fat-trimmed leg of lamb	shank	rib chops	rib; loin; shoulder	shoulder; breast
Pork and Ham	fresh or cured ham slice (pork leg steak); center-cut pork chops or loin cutlets; all fat-trimmed	fat-trimmed fresh or smoked ham; tenderloin; center-cut loin	fat-trimmed fresh or smoked bottom or rump; arm or picnic; cured ham	rib chops; spare-ribs; bacon	picnic; shoulder; rib-end roasts	shoulder; blade; ribs; hocks; jowl; feet

high in cholesterol. Check the shellfish listings in the "Cholesterol and Fat Counter" to help you choose shellfish that is lower in cholesterol.

—Instead of frying fish, try baking, broiling, or poaching.

—If you purchase tuna or fish packed in oil, rinse it in a strainer before preparing it—or buy it packed in water.

Dairy Products
—Dairy products can add calcium and other vitamins and minerals to the diet. Dairy products that contain fat, however, are also high in saturated fat and cholesterol. So you need to choose dairy products that come in low-fat varieties.

—Skim milk and 1% milk provide the same nutrients as whole milk and 2% milk but are much lower in saturated fat and cholesterol. To make the transition from whole milk to skim milk easier, switch first to 2% milk, then to 1% milk, and then to skim milk over the course of a few weeks.

—Cream, half-and-half, whipped cream, and most nondairy creamers and whip toppings (check the label) are high in saturated fat and should be avoided.

—Contrary to popular belief, substituting cheese for meat will not decrease the saturated fat and cholesterol content of your diet. Cheese has about the same amount of cholesterol, ounce for ounce, as meat or poultry. Most cheeses, however, contain much more saturated fat and provide fewer nutrients than does meat or poultry. So you need to decrease the amount of cheese that you eat.

—Most cheeses are high in saturated fat and cholesterol because they are made from whole milk. Natural and processed hard cheeses contain the most saturated fat. Imitation cheeses that are made with vegetable oil, cheeses made partly with skim milk, and cheeses labeled "low-fat" may contain less saturated fat, but they may still be higher in saturated fat than meat. Low-fat soft cheeses like cottage, farmer, and pot cheese are your best cheese choices.

—Cream cheese is high in saturated fat and should be avoided. "Light" cream cheese may be lower in saturated fat, but you should still go easy on it.

—Ice cream contains a good deal of saturated fat and cholesterol because it is made from whole milk and cream, so you'll need to cut back on it. Try substituting frozen ice milk, frozen yogurt, or sherbets, which are low in saturated fat.

—Low-fat or nonfat yogurt is a heart-healthy food that can also be used as a substitute for high-fat foods. For example, drained, plain, nonfat yogurt can be substituted for sour cream on baked potatoes. Plain, nonfat yogurt mixed with fresh fruits is a tasty substitute for high-fat desserts.

Eggs
—Egg yolks, which contain about 250 mg of cholesterol a piece, are too high in cholesterol to be regular items on your menu. Draw the line at three egg yolks a week, including those used in baked goods and processed foods.

—In recipes, substitute two egg whites, which contain no cholesterol, for one whole egg.

—To cut down on the number of eggs you eat, try one of the egg substitutes.

Fruits and Vegetables
—Because they come from plants, fruits and vegetables contain no cholesterol. With the exception of olives and avocados, fruits and vegetables are also low in fat. They make excellent side dishes and are nutritious substitutes for high-fat snacks and desserts.

—Avoid preparing vegetables with butter, cream, or cheese sauce.

Cereals, Breads, Pasta, Rice, and Dried Peas and Beans
—These types of foods are all high in complex carbohydrates (starch and fiber). They are also low in saturated fat and therefore should be included frequently in your meals.

—Pasta, rice, and dried peas and beans should be used as main dishes (in place of meat, poultry, and fish) frequently. They can also be combined with smaller amounts of meat, fish, and poultry, to create filling meals that are low in fat.

—Bread and cereal products are generally low in fat. Check labels to be sure that the commercially prepared bread and cereal products you choose were made with unsaturated fats—or make your own using polyunsaturated oils.

—Choose bread, English muffins, sandwich buns, and dinner rolls. Avoid or decrease your consumption of croissants, butter rolls, sweet rolls, danishes, and doughnuts.

—Choose low-fat crackers like saltines, rye krisp, and matzo, instead of snack crackers made with butter, cheese, or saturated oils.

Fats and Oils
—In cooking, use vegetable cooking spray, unsaturated vegetable oils, or margarine made from polyunsaturated vegetable oils instead of butter, lard, fatback, or solid shortening.

—Use margarine made from polyunsaturated vegetable oils, rather than butter, as a spread.

—Choose commercially prepared products made with unsaturated. unhydrogenated vegetable oils: avoid those made with palm oil, palm kernel oil, or coconut oil.

—Use peanut butter and peanut oil sparingly.

Sweets and Snacks
—Many commercially prepared baked goods and snacks, like cakes, cookies, pies, and some types of chips, are high in saturated fat and cholesterol. To

select those that are lowest in saturated fat and cholesterol, check the "Cholesterol and Fat Counter" or compare package labels.

—Substitute baked goods made at home (using margarine instead of butter, skim milk instead of whole milk, and egg whites instead of whole eggs) for commercially prepared baked goods, which are often high in saturated fat and cholesterol.

—Since even home-prepared baked goods can be high in fat, try cutting back on them. Instead, choose fruits, vegetables, popsicles, unbuttered popcorn, and breadsticks as snacks or desserts.

A Word about Sodium
—While you limit your cholesterol and saturated fat intakes, you also need to pay attention to dietary sodium. It has been estimated that the average adult needs between 1100 and 3300 mg daily. To keep your sodium intake in a healthy range, check food labels and try to choose foods that have the lowest sodium values. Also, limit the use of sodium in cooking and at the table.

Heart-Healthy Recipes

In this section, we provide you with a variety of tasty, heart-healthy recipes designed to help you decrease your intake of total fat, saturated fat, and cholesterol. Many of the recipes also include special "tips" that suggest alternative ingredients that can be used to lower the recipe's sodium or sugar content. You may also find that you can use many of these tips to modify your own favorite recipes. These substitutions may be especially helpful for readers who have been placed on special sodium-restricted diets or for those readers who are diabetic (if either of these conditions applies to you, however, you should have your physician or dietitian review the recipes and substitutions before you try them).

Every recipe is accompanied by a chart that lists the nutrition content of one serving. Included are figures for grams (g) of protein, carbohydrate, total fat, and saturated fat, along with figures for milligrams (mg) of cholesterol and sodium. The number of calories in each serving is also included.

All of these figures should be considered approximate, although we have tried to make them as exact as possible. The figures are based on findings of the U.S. Department of Agriculture, except for a few items for which information was obtained from manufacturers. Figures for the recipes from the American Dietetic Association and the American Diabetes Association were supplied by these associations.

The figures for a recipe include all the ingredients listed in the main body of the recipe, *except* for those indicated as "optional." If an ingredient is listed with one or more alternatives, such as "1 red or green bell pepper" or "1 cup fresh, frozen, or canned crab meat," the first item was used to calculate the nutrition figures for the recipe. Thus, for the two examples just cited, the recipe nutrient totals would include values for one *red* bell pepper and one cup *fresh* crab meat. Also, if a recipe calls for previously cooked vegetables, pasta, or rice, the total sodium figures are based on these foods having been cooked in water to which a moderate amount of salt was added.

A final reminder on the nutrition charts is that the figures include only those ingredients listed in the main body of the recipe (except optional items). They do not reflect any substitutions or deletions that are recommended in the "tips."

Soups & Salads

"Cream" of Turkey Soup

Makes 6 servings

1 small meaty turkey
    carcass
1 qt. water
1 onion, sliced
2 tbsp. sherry
Pinch nutmeg
1/2 lb. fresh mushrooms,
    finely chopped
2 tsp. safflower or corn oil
13-oz. can evaporated skim
    milk
1 tbsp. flour
Parsley flakes
Salt ● and pepper to taste
    (optional)

● *SODIUM TIP—Omit added salt.*

Combine turkey carcass, water, onion, sherry, and nutmeg in kettle. Simmer covered 2 hours. Strain broth; cool to room temperature. Refrigerate until fat hardens; remove and discard fat. Separate meat from bones; reserve meat. Discard bones and skin.
   Brown mushrooms in oil in large nonstick skillet. Add reserved turkey meat and broth. Heat to boiling. Mix together milk and flour; stir into skillet. Cool and stir over moderate heat until hot and bubbling. Sprinkle with parsley, salt, and pepper.

	Per Serving
Calories	128.4
Carbohydrate (g)	12.3
Protein (g)	12.9
Total Fat (g)	2.7
Saturated Fat (g)	0.5
Cholesterol (mg)	34.3
Sodium (mg)	105.2

Gringo Gazpacho

Makes 6 servings

4 ripe tomatoes, peeled,
    diced
1 large cucumber, pared,
    coarsely chopped
1 green pepper, coarsely
    chopped
1 medium onion, minced
1 clove garlic, minced
1 cup tomato juice or
    nonalcoholic Bloody
    Mary mix ●
1/4 cup low-calorie low-fat
    Italian salad
    dressing ●

● *SODIUM TIP—Use unsalted tomato juice or Bloody Mary mix and unsalted dressing.*

Mix together all ingredients. Chill several hours. Serve cold.

	Per Serving
Calories	54.2
Carbohydrate (g)	11.5
Protein (g)	2.4
Total Fat (g)	0.5
Saturated Fat (g)	0.1
Cholesterol (mg)	0.0
Sodium (mg)	109.4

Lamb-Barley Soup

Makes 10 servings

Meaty bone from roast leg
    of lamb
2 qt. water
1/4 cup chopped fresh
    parsley
Salt ● and pepper to taste
    (optional)
2 cups sliced carrots
2 cups sliced onions
2 cups sliced celery ●
16-oz. can tomatoes, well
    broken up,
    undrained ●
6 tbsp. medium pearl
    barley

● *SODIUM TIP—Omit added salt and celery. Use unsalted tomatoes.*

Combine lamb bone, water, parsley, salt, and pepper in kettle. Simmer covered 1 hour. Strain broth; cool to room temperature. Refrigerate until fat hardens; remove and discard fat. Separate meat from bones; discard bones. Wrap and refrigerate meat. Stir vegetables and barley into broth. Simmer covered 1 1/2 hours or until barley is tender. Stir in reserved meat and heat through.

	Per Serving
Calories	104.1
Carbohydrate (g)	12.9
Protein (g)	6.4
Total Fat (g)	3.3
Saturated Fat (g)	1.8
Cholesterol (mg)	16.6
Sodium (mg)	114.1

Jellied Tomato Consommé

Makes 4 servings

1 envelope unflavored
    gelatin
1³/₄ cups tomato juice ●
1 onion, chopped
2 tbsp. lemon juice
2 tsp. Worcestershire
    sauce ●
Salt ● and pepper to taste
    (optional)
Dash red pepper sauce
    (optional)

● *SODIUM TIP—Use unsalted
tomato juice. Omit Worce-
stershire and added salt*

Sprinkle gelatin over ¹/₄
cup of the tomato juice in
blender container. Simmer
remaining tomato juice and
the onion in saucepan 5
minutes. Add to blender;
cover. Blend on high speed.
Stir in lemon juice, Worcestershire, salt, pepper, and
pepper sauce. Pour into
individual molds or 2-cup
mold. Chill until set.

	Per Serving
Calories	38.8
Carbohydrate (g)	6.3
Protein (g)	2.9
Total Fat (g)	0.0
Saturated Fat (g)	0.0
Cholesterol (mg)	0.0
Sodium (mg)	245.1

Mushroom Clam Chowder

Makes 4 servings

4-oz. can mushroom stems
    and pieces ●
1 tsp. safflower or corn oil
1 can (7 or 8 oz.) minced
    clams, undrained ●
1 stalk celery, chopped ●
1 small onion, chopped
1¹/₃ cups nonfat dry milk
    powder
1¹/₂ cups cold water
1 tbsp. cornstarch or
    arrowroot
Salt ● and pepper to taste
    (optional)
Pinch cayenne pepper
2 tbsp. minced fresh
    parsley

● *SODIUM TIP—Use unsalted
mushrooms and clams. Omit
celery and added salt.*

Drain mushrooms; reserve
liquid. Sauté mushrooms in
oil in nonstick saucepan.
Stir in reserved mushroom
liquid, clams, celery, and
onion. Simmer covered 5
minutes. Mix together milk
powder, water, cornstarch,
salt, and peppers; stir into
saucepan. Cook and stir
over low heat just until
soup bubbles and thickens.
Sprinkle with parsley be-
fore serving.

	Per Serving
Calories	142.3
Carbohydrate (g)	17.8
Protein (g)	13.6
Total Fat (g)	1.7
Saturated Fat (g)	0.1
Cholesterol (mg)	20.7
Sodium (mg)	648.6

Asparagus Vichyssoise

Makes 6 servings

10¹/₂-oz. can cut asparagus
    spears, undrained ●
1 cup fat-skimmed chicken
    broth, canned or
    homemade ●
¹/₃ cup chopped onion
³/₄ cup instant potato
    flakes
1 cup evaporated skim milk
Salt ● and pepper to taste
    (optional)
Chopped chives

● *SODIUM TIP—Use unsalted
asparagus and broth. Omit
added salt.*

Puree asparagus in
blender; reserve. Combine
broth and onion in sauce-
pan. Heat to boiling. Re-
duce heat; simmer covered
5 minutes. Remove from
heat; stir in potato flakes.
Add pureed asparagus,
milk, salt, and pepper. Chill
thoroughly. Sprinkle with
chives before serving.

	Per Serving
Calories	70.1
Carbohydrate (g)	12.0
Protein (g)	5.0
Total Fat (g)	0.2
Saturated Fat (g)	0.0
Cholesterol (mg)	14.3
Sodium (mg)	290.1

Jellied Gazpacho

Makes 8 servings

1 envelope unflavored
   gelatin
1 1/2 cups fat-skimmed beef
   or chicken broth,
   canned or homemade ●
2 tbsp. vinegar
1 tsp paprika
1/2 tsp. basil
1/4 tsp. ground cloves
1/8 tsp. red pepper sauce
1 clove garlic, minced
   (optional)
1 1/2 cups finely chopped
   tomatoes
1/2 cup finely chopped
   cucumber
1/2 cup finely chopped
   green pepper
1/4 cup finely chopped
   celery
2 tbsp. finely chopped
   onion

● *SODIUM TIP—Use unsalted
broth.*

Sprinkle gelatin over 1/2
cup of the cold broth in
saucepan. Cook over low
heat, stirring constantly,
until gelatin dissolves. Remove from heat; stir in
remaining broth, vinegar,
and seasonings. Chill until
mixture is the consistency
of unbeaten egg white.
Fold in remaining ingredients. Place in serving bowl.
Chill until firm.

	Per Serving
Calories	22.2
Carbohydrate (g)	3.7
Protein (g)	2.3
Total Fat (g)	0.1
Saturated Fat (g)	0.0
Cholesterol (mg)	4.5
Sodium (mg)	155.3

"Cream" of Potato Soup

Makes 8 servings

3 potatoes, pared, sliced
1 onion, minced
2 cups fat-skimmed chicken
   broth, canned or
   homemade ●
1 1/2 cups water
13-oz. can evaporated skim
   milk
Salt ● and pepper to taste
   (optional)
3 tbsp. minced chives
   (optional)

● *SODIUM TIP—Use unsalted
broth. Omit added salt.*

Combine potatoes, onion,
broth, and water in saucepan. Simmer covered 35
minutes. Pour into blender.
Cover; blend until smooth.
Return to saucepan and
heat to boiling. Stir in milk.
Simmer covered 4 to 5
minutes. Sprinkle with salt
and pepper. Garnish with
chives, if desired.

	Per Serving
Calories	89.8
Carbohydrate (g)	16.1
Protein (g)	5.7
Total Fat (g)	0.0
Saturated Fat (g)	0.0
Cholesterol (mg)	18.1
Sodium (mg)	240.2

Fat-Skimmed Scotch Broth

Makes 4 servings

Meaty lamb bones
2 qt. water
2 onions, chopped
3 small carrots, sliced
3 stalks celery, sliced ●
3 tbsp. pearl barley
2 bay leaves
2 tsp. monosodium
   glutamate ● (optional)
Salt ● and pepper to taste
   (optional)

● *SODIUM TIP—Omit celery,
monosodium glutamate, and
added salt.*

Combine lamb bones with
water in kettle. Simmer
covered 1 1/2 to 2 hours.
Strain broth; cool to room
temperature. Refrigerate
broth until fat hardens;
remove and discard fat.
Separate meat from bones;
discard bones. Wrap and
refrigerate meat. Stir remaining ingredients into
broth. Simmer covered 50
to 60 minutes. Stir in reserved meat and heat. Re-
move bay leaves.

	Per Serving
Calories	65.1
Carbohydrate (g)	8.8
Protein (g)	3.8
Total Fat (g)	2.1
Saturated Fat (g)	1.1
Cholesterol (mg)	10.4
Sodium (mg)	38.1

Trim Turkey Soup

Makes 6 servings

1 small meaty turkey
  carcass
6 cups water
1 bay leaf
1/8 tsp. ground nutmeg
Salt ● and pepper to taste
  (optional)
3 small carrots, diced or
  sliced
4 stalks celery, diced or
  sliced ●
2 onions, sliced

● *SODIUM TIP—Omit added
salt and celery.*

Combine turkey carcass,
water, bay leaf, nutmeg,
salt, and pepper in kettle.
Heat to boiling; reduce
heat. Simmer covered
about 2 hours. Strain broth;
cool to room temperature.
Refrigerate broth until fat
hardens; remove and dis-
card fat. Separate meat
from bones; reserve meat.
Discard bones and skin.
Stir meat and vegetables
into broth. Simmer covered
25 to 30 minutes or until
vegetables are tender.

	Per Serving
Calories	58.3
Carbohydrate (g)	7.2
Protein (g)	6.5
Total Fat (g)	1.0
Saturated Fat (g)	0.3
Cholesterol (mg)	14.8
Sodium (mg)	70.7

Curried Chicken Gumbo Soup

Makes 4 servings

10³/₄-oz. can condensed
  chicken gumbo soup ●
1 soup can water
1/2 tsp. curry powder
1 unpared red apple, diced

● *SODIUM TIP—Use unsalted
soup.*

Combine all ingredients,
except diced apple, in
saucepan. Heat to boiling,
stirring occasionally. Stir in
diced apple before serving.

	Per Serving
Calories	51.8
Carbohydrate (g)	9.0
Protein (g)	1.9
Total Fat (g)	1.0
Saturated Fat (g)	0.6
Cholesterol (mg)	10.5
Sodium (mg)	590.5

"Cream" of Mushroom Soup

Makes 6 servings

1 lb. fresh mushrooms
4 cups fat-skimmed chicken
  broth, canned or
  homemade ●
13-oz. can evaporated skim
  milk
1/2 cup cold water
3 tbsp. instant-blend flour
Salt ● and pepper to taste
  (optional)
Chopped fresh parsley
  (optional)

● *SODIUM TIP—Use unsalted
broth. Omit added salt.*

Remove and chop mush-
room stems. Reserve caps.
Combine chopped stems
with broth in saucepan and
simmer covered over very
low heat 30 minutes. Strain
broth; discard the stems.
Return broth to saucepan;
heat to boiling. Reduce
heat; stir in the milk and
heat until simmering. Mix
water and flour into a
smooth paste; stir into the
simmering soup. Continue
to cook and stir over low
heat until soup is slightly
thickened. Slice the re-
served mushroom caps
very thin; stir into soup.
Simmer 6 to 8 minutes.
Sprinkle with salt and pepper. Garnish with parsley, if
desired.

	Per Serving
Calories	104.7
Carbohydrate (g)	15.3
Protein (g)	9.3
Total Fat (g)	0.3
Saturated Fat (g)	0.0
Cholesterol (mg)	28.8
Sodium (mg)	568.6

Eggless Salad

Makes 4 servings

1 cup liquid egg substitute
5 tbsp. low-calorie low-fat
    mayonnaise ●
2 tbsp. minced celery
2 tbsp minced green
    pepper (optional)
1 tbsp. minced onion
¹/₂ tsp. prepared mustard ●
    (optional)
Salt ● and pepper to
    taste (optional)
Dash red pepper sauce,
    or pinch red pepper
    (optional)

● *SODIUM TIP—Use unsalted mayonnaise. Substitute dry mustard to taste for prepared mustard. Omit added salt.*

Cook egg substitute covered in nonstick skillet over very low heat about 10 to 15 minutes, or until it thickens and is set. Remove from heat and cool slightly. Dice or shred cooked egg substitute; combine with remaining ingredients. Chill.

	Per Serving
Calories	66.6
Carbohydrate (g)	4.6
Protein (g)	7.1
Total Fat (g)	2.5
Saturated Fat (g)	0.0
Cholesterol (mg)	10.0
Sodium (mg)	158.7

Cottage-Style Tuna Salad

Makes 6 servings

¹/₂ cup low-fat cottage
    cheese ●
7-oz. can water-packed
    tuna, drained ●
¹/₂ small green pepper,
    diced
¹/₄ cup diced celery ●
1 tbsp. minced chives
1 tsp. lemon juice
Salt ● and pepper to
    taste (optional)

● *SODIUM TIP—Use unsalted cottage cheese and tuna. Omit celery and added salt; the quantity of green pepper can be doubled.*

Combine ingredients; toss lightly to mix.

	Per Serving
Calories	61.2
Carbohydrate (g)	1.4
Protein (g)	12.0
Total Fat (g)	0.5
Saturated Fat (g)	0.1
Cholesterol (mg)	22.6
Sodium (mg)	366.0

Pear Luncheon Salad

Makes 2 servings

1 cup low-fat cottage
    cheese ●
¹/₄ cup raisins
2 tbsp. low-calorie low-fat
    mayonnaise ●
8-oz. can juice-packed pear
    halves, drained
Lettuce
Cinnamon

● *SODIUM TIP—Use unsalted cottage cheese and mayonnaise.*

Combine cottage cheese, raisins, and mayonnaise. Slice each pear half into quarters. Arrange cottage cheese mixture and pear slices on lettuce. Sprinkle with cinnamon.

	Per Serving
Calories	198.9
Carbohydrate (g)	27.4
Protein (g)	15.7
Total Fat (g)	3.3
Saturated Fat (g)	0.6
Cholesterol (mg)	17.7
Sodium (mg)	439.9

Marinated Cucumbers

Makes 4 servings

¹/₂ cup plain low-fat yogurt
2 tbsp. lemon juice
1 tsp. sugar ▲ (optional)
Salt ● and pepper to
    taste (optional)
2 cucumbers, pared, thinly
    sliced

● *SODIUM TIP—Omit added salt.*
▲ *SUGAR TIP—Omit sugar or use sugar substitute.*

Combine yogurt, lemon juice, sugar, salt, and pepper. Toss with cucumber; chill.

	Per Serving
Calories	32.6
Carbohydrate (g)	5.7
Protein (g)	1.6
Total Fat (g)	0.5
Saturated Fat (g)	0.3
Cholesterol (mg)	2.5
Sodium (mg)	21.6

Strawberry-Orange Salad

Makes 1 serving

1/3 cup low-fat cottage cheese ●

5 or 6 fresh strawberries, hulled, sliced

1 tbsp. defrosted undiluted, unsweetened frozen orange juice concentrate

● *SODIUM TIP—Use unsalted cottage cheese.*

Place scoop of cottage cheese on salad plate; surround with strawberries. Top with juice concentrate.

	Per Serving
Calories	117.4
Carbohydrate (g)	15.8
Protein (g)	10.9
Total Fat (g)	1.2
Saturated Fat (g)	0.4
Cholesterol (mg)	6.5
Sodium (mg)	277.5

Banana Split Salad

Makes 1 serving

1 small ripe banana

1/3 cup low-fat cottage cheese ●

1 tbsp. defrosted undiluted, unsweetened frozen orange juice concentrate

● *SODIUM TIP—Use unsalted cottage cheese.*

Split banana; place halves in shallow dish. Add scoop of cottage cheese and top with juice concentrate.

	Per Serving
Calories	189.9
Carbohydrate (g)	35.3
Protein (g)	11.4
Total Fat (g)	0.7
Saturated Fat (g)	0.4
Cholesterol (mg)	6.5
Sodium (mg)	279.0

Mushroom Zucchini Salad

Makes 4 servings

1 cup sliced fresh mushrooms

2 cups thinly sliced zucchini

1 tomato, diced

6 green onions, sliced

1/2 cup low-calorie, low-fat Italian dressing ●

● *SODIUM TIP—Use unsalted dressing.*

Combine vegetables in large bowl. Add dressing and toss to mix.

	Per Serving
Calories	46.0
Carbohydrate (g)	7.4
Protein (g)	2.1
Total Fat (g)	1.5
Saturated Fat (g)	0.3
Cholesterol (mg)	0.0
Sodium (mg)	241.6

Blueberry-Pineapple Salad

Makes 1 serving

1/3 cup low-fat cottage cheese ●

1/4 cup fresh blueberries

1 tbsp. defrosted undiluted, unsweetened frozen pineapple juice concentrate

● *SODIUM TIP—Use unsalted cottage cheese.*

Place scoop of cottage cheese on salad plate; surround with blueberries. Top with juice concentrate.

	Per Serving
Calories	113.1
Carbohydrate (g)	15.3
Protein	10.6
Total Fat (g)	1.0
Saturated Fat (g)	0.4
Cholesterol (mg)	6.5
Sodium (mg)	277.5

Pineapple-Peach Salad

Makes 1 serving

1/3 cup low-fat cottage cheese ●

1 peeled fresh peach or unpeeled nectarine, pitted, sliced

1 tbsp. defrosted undiluted, unsweetened frozen pineapple juice concentrate

● *SODIUM TIP—Use unsalted cottage cheese.*

Place mound of cottage cheese on salad plate; surround with peach slices. Top with juice concentrate.

	Per Serving
Calories	126.9
Carbohydrate (g)	20.0
Protein (g)	11.3
Total Fat (g)	0.7
Saturated Fat (g)	0.4
Cholesterol (mg)	6.5
Sodium (mg)	278.2

Mock Sour Cream Dressing

Makes 1 1/2 cups

1 cup uncreamed
    small-curd cottage
    cheese ●
1/2 cup plain low-fat yogurt
2 tbsp. lemon juice
Salt ● and pepper to
    taste (optional)

● *SODIUM TIP—Use unsalted
cottage cheese. Omit added
salt.*

Combine all ingredients in
blender; cover; blend until
smooth. (Serve with baked
potato or as a base for
dips.)

	Per Tablespoon
Calories	8.0
Carbohydrate (g)	0.5
Protein (g)	1.2
Total Fat (g)	0.1
Saturated Fat (g)	0.1
Cholesterol (mg)	0.8
Sodium (mg)	20.2

Yogurt Dressing

Makes 1 1/4 cups

1 cup plain low-fat yogurt
3 tbsp. lemon juice
1/8 tsp. dry mustard
Salt ● and pepper to
    taste (optional)
Pinch garlic powder
    (optional)

● *SODIUM TIP—Omit added
salt.*

Combine all ingredients in
jar. Cover and shake well.
Store in refrigerator.

	Per Tablespoon
Calories	6.8
Carbohydrate (g)	0.9
Protein (g)	0.4
Total Fat (g)	0.2
Saturated Fat (g)	0.1
Cholesterol (mg)	1.0
Sodium (mg)	6.3

Celery Seed Dressing

Makes 1 1/4 cups

2/3 cup water
1/2 cup lemon juice
2 tbsp. safflower or corn
    oil
2 tsp. cornstarch or
    arrowroot
2 tsp. celery seed
1 tsp. prepared mustard ●
1 tsp. paprika
Salt ● and pepper to
    taste (optional)

● *SODIUM TIP—Substitute
dry mustard to taste for
prepared mustard. Omit
added salt.*

Combine all ingredients;
heat to boiling. Reduce
heat; simmer and stir until
thickened. Chill before
serving. Store covered in
refrigerator.

	Per Tablespoon
Calories	25.3
Carbohydrate (g)	1.3
Protein (g)	0.1
Total Fat (g)	2.4
Saturated Fat (g)	0.2
Cholesterol (mg)	0.0
Sodium (mg)	6.0

Curried Fruit Dressing

Makes 1 1/4 cups

1 cup plain low-fat yogurt
3 tbsp. golden raisins
2 tbsp. defrosted undiluted,
    unsweetened frozen
    pineapple juice
    concentrate
1/2 tsp. grated lemon rind
1/2 tsp. curry powder
1/4 tsp. cinnamon

Combine all ingredients;
mix well. Store in refrigerator.

	Per Tablespoon
Calories	13.5
Carbohydrate (g)	2.5
Protein (g)	0.4
Total Fat (g)	0.2
Saturated Fat (g)	0.1
Cholesterol (mg)	1.0
Sodium (mg)	6.7

Russian Dressing

Makes 2 cups

1 cup plain low-fat yogurt
1 cup low-calorie, low-fat
    Russian salad
    dressing ●
2 tbsp. catsup ● ▲

● *SODIUM TIP—Use unsalted
dressing and catsup.*
▲ *SUGAR TIP—Use sugarless
catsup.*

Combine all ingredients in
large jar. Cover and shake
well. Store in refrigerator.

	Per Tablespoon
Calories	19.8
Carbohydrate (g)	2.7
Protein (g)	0.3
Total Fat (g)	0.6
Saturated Fat (g)	0.1
Cholesterol (mg)	0.6
Sodium (mg)	111.2

Mock Mayonnaise

Makes 1 cup

1 cup low-fat cottage
  cheese ●
¼ cup liquid egg
  substitute
1 tbsp. vinegar or lemon
  juice
2 tsp. sugar ▲
½ tsp. salt ● (optional)
½ tsp. dry mustard
½ tsp. paprika
Pinch pepper

● *SODIUM TIP—Use unsalted
cottage cheese. Omit added
salt.*
▲ *SUGAR TIP—Use sugar
substitute, or omit.*

Combine all ingredients in
blender. Cover and blend
on medium speed until
smooth. Scrape down con-
tainer with rubber spatula.
Store in covered container
in refrigerator.

	Per Tablespoon
Calories	15.8
Carbohydrate (g)	1.1
Protein (g)	2.3
Total Fat (g)	0.1
Saturated Fat (g)	0.1
Cholesterol (mg)	1.2
Sodium (mg)	60.0

Parsley Dressing

Makes 1 cup

1 cup plain low-fat yogurt
3 tbsp. minced fresh
  parsley
1 tsp. dillweed
¼ tsp. garlic salt ●
  (optional)

● *SODIUM TIP—Substitute
garlic powder to taste for
garlic salt.*

Combine all ingredients;
mix well. Store in refrigerator.

	Per Tablespoon
Calories	8.0
Carbohydrate (g)	0.8
Protein (g)	0.5
Total Fat (g)	0.3
Saturated Fat (g)	0.1
Cholesterol (mg)	1.3
Sodium (mg)	8.2

Deviled Dressing

Makes about ¾ cup

6-oz. can cocktail vegetable
  juice ●
1 tbsp. safflower or corn
  oil
1 tbsp. vinegar
½ tsp. prepared
  mustard ●
½ tsp. Worcestershire
  sauce ●
Dash red pepper sauce
  (optional)

● *SODIUM TIP—Use unsalted
vegetable juice. Substitute dry
mustard to taste for prepared
mustard. Omit Worcestershire.*

Combine all ingredients in
jar. Cover and shake well;
chill. Store in refrigerator.

	Per Tablespoon
Calories	13.3
Carbohydrate (g)	0.7
Protein (g)	0.2
Total Fat (g)	1.2
Saturated Fat (g)	0.1
Cholesterol (mg)	0.0
Sodium (mg)	35.3

Savory Salad Dressing

Makes ⅔ cup

½ cup plain tomato sauce
  (check label for no
  added oil) ●
3 tbsp. lemon juice
2 tbsp. chopped onion
½ tsp. salt ● (optional)
½ tsp. sugar ▲ (optional)
½ tsp. steak sauce ●
¼ tsp. monosodium
  glutamate ● (optional)
¼ tsp. caraway seed

● *SODIUM TIP—Use unsalted
tomato sauce. Omit added
salt, steak sauce, and
monosodium glutamate.*
▲ *SUGAR TIP—Use sugar
substitute, or omit.*

Combine all ingredients in
jar. Cover and shake well;
chill. Store in refrigerator.

	Per Tablespoon
Calories	5.5
Carbohydrate (g)	1.4
Protein (g)	0.2
Total Fat (g)	0.0
Saturated Fat (g)	0.0
Cholesterol (mg)	0.0
Sodium (mg)	83.0

Meat

Italian Flank Steak

Makes 6 servings

1 1/2 lb. lean flank steak
1 cup sliced mushrooms
1 small onion, thinly sliced
1/2 cup lemon juice
1 tsp. dried oregano
1 tsp. grated lemon peel
1 small clove garlic, minced, or pinch garlic powder (optional)
Salt and pepper to taste (optional)

Score steak 1/8 inch deep on both sides in diamond design. Place steak in baking dish. Combine remaining ingredients and pour over steak. Refrigerate covered several hours, turning steak several times. Pour off marinade, including mushrooms and onion; reserve. Broil or grill steak 3 inches from heat 4 to 6 minutes on each side. Heat mushrooms and onion in marinade in tightly covered skillet 1 to 2 minutes. Slice steak very thin against the grain; top with onion and mushrooms.

	Per Serving
Calories	176.7
Carbohydrate (g)	3.5
Protein (g)	25.2
Total Fat (g)	6.6
Saturated Fat (g)	3.1
Cholesterol (mg)	73.8
Sodium (mg)	89.1

Venison Roast

Makes 8 servings

1 clove garlic, split
1/2 tsp. rosemary
2 lb. venison roast
5 strips bacon
2 baking potatoes (10 to 12 oz. each), unpeeled and cut into eighths
2 carrots, peeled and cut into 1/2-inch pieces
1 medium onion, cut into eighths
1/4 cup dry red wine
1/4 cup water

Rub garlic and rosemary over roast. Insert garlic in roast. Place in shallow roasting pan. Cover with bacon and tie with string. Add potatoes, carrots, and onion to pan. Pour in wine and water. Insert meat thermometer into roast and cook in preheated 350° oven until thermometer reaches 170°, about 1 1/2 hours. Baste often; if needed, add more water during cooking. Let stand, covered, about 10 minutes, before carving. Remove string and bacon before carving. Serve with vegetables.

	Per Serving
Calories	235.0
Carbohydrate (g)	20.0
Protein (g)	28.0
Total Fat (g)	4.0
Saturated Fat (g)	na
Cholesterol (mg)	18.0
Sodium (mg)	137.0

London Broil

Makes 8 servings

2 lb. lean flank steak
1 or 2 cloves garlic, minced, or 1/8 to 1/4 tsp. garlic powder
Meat tenderizer ● (optional)
Monosodium glutamate ● (optional)
Coarsely ground pepper

● *SODIUM TIP—Omit meat tenderizer and monosodium glutamate.*

With sharp knife, score steak 1/8 inch deep on both sides in diamond design. Sprinkle both sides of steak with remaining ingredients. Roll up. Wrap with plastic wrap or waxed paper; let stand 30 minutes at room temperature or several hours in refrigerator. (If refrigerated, allow to reach room temperature before broiling.) Broil or grill 4 inches from heat, turning once, until done as desired (best if served rare or medium-rare). To serve, slice very thin against the grain.

	Per Serving
Calories	163.8
Carbohydrate (g)	0.1
Protein (g)	24.5
Total Fat (g)	6.5
Saturated Fat (g)	3.1
Cholesterol (mg)	73.8
Sodium (mg)	85.9

Cantonese Pork

Makes 6 servings

1 lb. lean ground pork
1/4 tsp. salt
1/8 tsp. pepper
1/4 cup finely chopped onions
1/4 cup evaporated skim milk

Sweet and Sour Sauce

15 1/2-oz. can pineapple tidbits in unsweetened juice
1/4 cup vinegar
1 tbsp. sugar
1 tbsp. soy sauce
1/2 cup water
2 tbsp. cornstarch
1 tsp. margarine
1/4 cup slivered toasted almonds
1 cup sliced celery
1/2 cup sliced green onions
1/2 cup green pepper strips
2 medium tomatoes, cut in 6 wedges

Mix pork, salt, pepper, onions, and milk together thoroughly. Place on board and roll out in rectangle. Cut into 42 pieces. Roll each piece into a ball. Place in shallow pan and bake in 350° oven 30 to 40 minutes. Turn after 15 minutes. Drain juice from pineapple and combine with vinegar, sugar, soy sauce, water, and cornstarch in 2-qt. saucepan. Bring to a boil, stirring constantly, and cook until clear and thickened. Add margarine.

Ten minutes before serving, add almonds and vegetables to sauce. Heat until vegetables are just heated through. Serve meatballs over rice and cover with 2/3 cup sauce.

	Per Serving
Calories	235.0
Carbohydrate (g)	23.3
Protein (g)	19.5
Total Fat (g)	7.6
Saturated Fat (g)	na
Cholesterol (mg)	48.0
Sodium (mg)	355.1

Stew for Two

Makes 2 servings

1/2 lb. lean boneless bottom round chuck arm or steak, trimmed of fat, cut into cubes
1 tsp. safflower or corn oil
1/4 cup dry white wine or water
8-oz. can small white onions, drained, liquid reserved ●
8-oz. can sliced carrots, drained, liquid reserved ●
Salt ● and pepper to taste (optional)
Pinch garlic powder (optional)
2-oz. can mushroom stems, drained, liquid reserved ●

SODIUM TIP—Omit carrots and added salt. Use unsalted onions and mushrooms.

Brown meat in oil in non-stick skillet over high heat, stirring constantly. Pour off oil. Stir in wine, vegetable liquids, salt, pepper, and garlic powder. Simmer covered 1 hour or until tender. Cool to room temperature. Cover and refrigerate meat and vegetables separately overnight.

Remove and discard hardened fat. Cover skillet and heat to boiling; stir in vegetables. Simmer uncovered over low heat, stirring often, until most of liquid has evaporated.

	Per Serving
Calories	331.0
Carbohydrate (g)	19.9
Protein (g)	26.5
Total Fat (g)	14.1
Saturated Fat (g)	5.6
Cholesterol (mg)	73.7
Sodium (mg)	743.0

Apple Basting Sauce

Makes 1 cup

1/2 cup unsweetened applesauce
1/2 cup dry white wine

Combine thoroughly. (Use as a baste for meat during roasting.)

	Per Tablespoon
Calories	9.4
Carbohydrate (g)	1.1
Protein (g)	0.1
Total Fat (g)	0.1
Saturated Fat (g)	0.0
Cholesterol (mg)	0.0
Sodium (mg)	0.4

Grilled Venison Steak

Makes 4 servings

4 venison steaks (4 oz. each), trimmed
2 cloves garlic, split
1/4 tsp. onion powder
1/4 tsp. salt
1/4 tsp. black pepper
4 strips bacon
2 tsp. dry white wine (optional)

Rub garlic on both sides of each steak. Combine onion powder, salt, and pepper; rub on both sides of steaks. Place 1 strip of bacon on each steak. Roll up and secure with a bamboo skewer. Grill for 3 to 5 minutes per side over moderately hot fire or preheated broiler. Steaks should be well done. Transfer to a warm platter, remove skewers, and sprinkle with wine.

	Per Serving
Calories	187.0
Carbohydrate (g)	1.0
Protein (g)	31.0
Total Fat (g)	5.0
Saturated Fat (g)	na
Cholesterol (mg)	23.0
Sodium (mg)	305.0

Beef Burgundy

Makes 8 servings

2 lb. top round steak
3-oz. can mushrooms, sliced
1 tbsp. flour
1 envelope dry onion soup mix
1 3/4 cups water
1/2 cup dry red wine

Cut steak into 1-inch cubes. Brown meat slowly in skillet sprayed with vegetable cooking spray. Transfer to 1 1/2-qt. casserole. Add remaining ingredients. Stir well. Cover tightly and bake in preheated 350° oven for 1 1/2 hours. Remove cover and bake 15 minutes or until tender.

	Per Serving
Calories	138.0
Carbohydrate (g)	3.9
Protein (g)	19.5
Total Fat (g)	4.5
Saturated Fat (g)	na
Cholesterol (mg)	48.0
Sodium (mg)	539.6

Pineapple-Tenderized Steak

Makes 8 servings

2 lb. lean flank steak or top round steak, trimmed of fat
3 oz. undiluted defrosted frozen unsweetened pineapple juice concentrate

If using flank steak, score 1/8 inch deep on both sides in diamond design with sharp knife. Spread both sides with pineapple concentrate. If using round steak, place in shallow bowl and spread both sides with pineapple concentrate; puncture repeatedly with fork. Refrigerate covered several hours. Allow to reach room temperature before broiling. Broil or grill 4 inches from heat, turning once, until done as desired.

	Per Serving
Calories	187.1
Carbohydrate (g)	5.9
Protein (g)	24.7
Total Fat (g)	6.5
Saturated Fat (g)	3.1
Cholesterol (mg)	73.8
Sodium (mg)	86.1

Swiss Steak

Makes 6 servings

1/4 cup flour
1 tsp. salt
1/4 tsp. pepper
1 lb. beef round steak (about 3/4 inch thick)
1 tbsp. vegetable oil
1 large onion, sliced
16-oz. can tomatoes
1/2 cup beef broth
2 cups sliced, peeled carrots

Combine flour, salt, and pepper. Coat steak with seasoned flour. With wooden mallet pound meat between wax paper until it's 1/2 inch thick. Cut into 6 serving pieces. Heat oil in large skillet. Brown steak well on both sides. Move to one side of skillet to sauté onion until tender. Add tomatoes and broth. Cover and simmer 1 1/2 hours. Add carrots, cover, simmer 1/2 hour or until meat and carrots are tender.

	Per Serving
Calories	173.0
Carbohydrate (g)	14.3
Protein (g)	15.8
Total Fat (g)	6.0
Saturated Fat (g)	na
Cholesterol (mg)	35.0
Sodium (mg)	392.2

Poultry

"Southern Fried" Chicken

Makes 8 servings

2 frying chickens (about 2 lb. each), cut up, trimmed of fat
Water
1/2 cup plain bread crumbs ●
1/2 tsp. paprika
1/4 tsp. salt ●
1/4 tsp. celery salt ●
1/4 tsp. celery seed ●
Pinch pepper

● *SODIUM TIP—Use low-sodium bread crumbs. Substitute marjoram, thyme, and poultry seasoning for salt and celery seasonings.*

Brush chicken pieces with water to moisten. Combine remaining ingredients in heavy paper bag. Place chicken pieces, a few at a time, in paper bag; shake to coat chicken. Arrange, skin-side up, in nonstick pan or baking sheet. Bake uncovered in a preheated 375° oven about 50 minutes or until crisp.

	Per Serving
Calories	240.2
Carbohydrate (g)	4.6
Protein (g)	33.4
Total Fat (g)	8.9
Saturated Fat (g)	3.5
Cholesterol (mg)	139.0
Sodium (mg)	275.2

Turkey Spaghetti Sauce

Makes 8 servings

3 frozen turkey legs (about 3 lb. total)
4 cups canned tomatoes, undrained, well broken up ●
3 cups water
2 cans (6 oz. each) tomato paste
1 cup dry red wine
1 onion, minced
2 tsp. dried oregano or mixed Italian seasoning
1 tsp. garlic salt ● (optional)

● *SODIUM TIP—Use unsalted tomatoes. Substitute garlic powder to taste for garlic salt.*

Combine all ingredients in large stockpot. Heat to boiling. Simmer covered over very low heat 1 1/2 to 2 hours or until turkey is tender. Cool. Remove and discard turkey skin, bones, and tendons. Cut meat into small pieces; return meat to sauce. Refrigerate covered several hours.

Remove and discard hardened fat from surface of sauce. Heat sauce to boiling. Reduce heat; simmer uncovered until sauce is the consistency of thick gravy.

	Per Serving
Calories	276.6
Carbohydrate (g)	15.6
Protein (g)	30.1
Total Fat (g)	8.1
Saturated Fat (g)	2.2
Cholesterol (mg)	92.8
Sodium (mg)	266.1

Turkey Steaks with Mushrooms

Makes 4 servings

1 lb. turkey breast steaks
1 tbsp. diet margarine ● ■
2 cups sliced fresh mushrooms
1/2 cup sherry
Salt ● and pepper to taste (optional)

● *SODIUM TIP—Use unsalted margarine. Omit added salt.*

■ *CHOLESTEROL TIP—Use polyunsaturated margarine.*

Sauté steaks in margarine in nonstick skillet until done. Remove to serving platter. Sauté mushrooms; stir in sherry, salt, and pepper. Cook 2 to 3 minutes. Top steaks with mushroom mixture.

	Per Serving
Calories	242.2
Carbohydrate (g)	2.7
Protein (g)	38.3
Total Fat (g)	6.0
Saturated Fat (g)	1.5
Cholesterol (mg)	101.7
Sodium (mg)	126.5

Coq au Vin Rouge

Makes 4 servings

1 frying chicken (about 2 lb.), cut up, trimmed of fat
1 cup fresh, frozen, or drained canned small onions ●
3/4 cup dry red wine
1/4 cup tomato juice ●
1 small bay leaf
1/8 tsp. thyme
1/8 tsp. sage
Salt ● and pepper to taste (optional)

● *SODIUM TIP—Use fresh, frozen, or unsalted canned onions. Use unsalted tomato juice. Omit added salt.*

Broil chicken pieces skin-side up 10 to 15 minutes or until skin is crisp. Pour off fat. Blot chicken; combine with remaining ingredients in heavy Dutch oven. Simmer covered over moderate heat or bake in a preheated 350° oven 45 to 50 minutes or until chicken is tender. Uncover and continue to cook until liquid is reduced to a thick sauce.

	Per Serving
Calories	267.3
Carbohydrate (g)	4.9
Protein (g)	33.1
Total Fat (g)	8.6
Saturated Fat (g)	3.4
Cholesterol (mg)	138.9
Sodium (mg)	134.3

Chicken Stroganoff

Makes 6 servings

2 lb. chicken thighs, trimmed of fat
3/4 cup tomato juice ●
1 onion, chopped
4-oz. can sliced mushrooms, undrained ●
1/4 tsp. dry mustard
1/2 cup skim milk
1/2 cup plain low-fat yogurt
2 tbsp. flour
Salt ● and pepper to taste (optional)
4 cups tender-cooked wide noodles ● ■

● *SODIUM TIP—Use unsalted tomato juice and mushrooms. Omit added salt. Cook noodles without salt.*

■ *CHOLESTEROL TIP—Use noodles made without egg yolks.*

Broil chicken skin-side up 10 to 15 minutes or until skin is crisp. Pour off fat. Blot chicken. Combine tomato juice, onion, mushrooms, and mustard in large saucepan; add chicken. Simmer covered over very low heat about 50 minutes or until chicken is tender, adding water if needed. Skim off fat.
　Mix milk, yogurt, and flour. Stir into saucepan. Cook and stir until sauce thickens. Sprinkle with salt and pepper. Serve over hot noodles.

	Per Serving
Calories	180.3
Carbohydrate (g)	7.7
Protein (g)	27.8
Total Fat (g)	3.6
Saturated Fat (g)	1.7
Cholesterol (mg)	85.0
Sodium (mg)	70.0

Hungarian Turkey Skillet

Makes 4 servings

1 1/4 lb. package frozen turkey thigh, defrosted, skinned, boned, cut into 1/4-inch cubes
2 cups onions, cut into strips
2 green peppers, cut into strips
1 red bell pepper, cut into strips
2 tomatoes, peeled, seeded, diced
1 cup water
Salt ● and pepper to taste (optional)
Pinch cayenne pepper (or to taste)

● *SODIUM TIP—Omit added salt.*

Combine all ingredients in heavy skillet. Simmer covered 35 minutes or until meat is tender. Uncover and continue to simmer until sauce is thick.

	Per Serving
Calories	211.1
Carbohydrate (g)	12.5
Protein (g)	25.5
Total Fat (g)	6.5
Saturated Fat (g)	1.9
Cholesterol (mg)	77.3
Sodium (mg)	89.7

Moo Goo Gai Pan

Makes 4 servings

1 tsp. safflower or corn oil
4 chicken fillets (about 1
  lb.) (2 whole breasts,
  split, skinned, and
  boned), cut into 1-inch
  cubes
1 lb. Chinese or savoy
  cabbage
9-oz. package frozen snow
  peas, defrosted
8-oz. can sliced
  mushrooms, drained ●
1 cup drained canned
  Chinese vegetables ●
3/4 cup fat-skimmed
  chicken broth, canned
  or homemade ●
1/4 tsp. ground ginger
1 tsp. cornstarch or
  arrowroot

● *SODIUM TIP—Use unsalted
mushrooms, Chinese vege-
tables, and broth.*

Heat oil over high heat in
large nonstick skillet. Add
chicken to skillet; stir-fry
until chicken turns white.
Stir in cabbage, snow peas,
mushrooms, Chinese vege-
tables, 1/2 cup of the
chicken broth, and the
ginger. Cook covered 2
minutes. Reduce heat. Mix
together cornstarch and
remaining 1/4 cup broth;
stir into skillet. Cook and
stir 1 to 2 minutes, until
mixture thickens.

	Per Serving
Calories	201.3
Carbohydrate (g)	11.5
Protein (g)	30.3
Total Fat (g)	4.6
Saturated Fat (g)	1.6
Cholesterol (mg)	81.7
Sodium (mg)	775.3

Cornish Hens with Cherries

Makes 8 servings

4 Rock Cornish hens (about
  4 lb. total), cut into
  halves lengthwise
16-oz. can juice-packed
  dark cherries, drained,
  juice reserved
1/4 tsp. poultry seasoning
Salt ● and pepper to taste
  (optional)
1/2 cup undiluted bottled
  unsweetened red grape
  juice
Water
2 tsp. cornstarch or
  arrowroot

● *SODIUM TIP—Omit added
salt.*

Broil hen halves skin-side
up 10 to 15 minutes or
until skin is crisp. Pour off
fat. Blot hen halves; place
skin-side up in shallow baking dish. Pour 1/2 cup of
the reserved juice from the
cherries over the hen
halves. Sprinkle with poultry seasoning, salt, and
pepper. Bake uncovered in
a preheated 350° oven,
basting frequently, about 1
hour or until hen halves
are tender. Meanwhile,
pour remaining cherry
juice into a 2-cup measure;
add grape juice and
enough water to measure
1 3/4 cups liquid; combine
liquid and cornstarch in
saucepan. Cook and stir
over low heat until mixture
thickens and clears. Stir in
cherries and heat through.
Pour sauce over hens and
serve.

	Per Serving
Calories	245.5
Carbohydrate (g)	12.5
Protein (g)	30.0
Total Fat (g)	7.9
Saturated Fat (g)	3.1
Cholesterol (mg)	125.6
Sodium (mg)	90.9

Temple Chicken Breasts

Makes 4 servings

2 whole chicken breasts
  (about 1 1/4 lb.), split,
  trimmed of fat
1/4 tsp. pepper
1/8 tsp. garlic powder
  (optional)
1/4 cup unsweetened
  orange juice
2 tbsp. dry white wine
1 large Temple orange,
  peeled, segmented

Sprinkle chicken with pepper and garlic; broil skin-
side up 10 to 15 minutes or
until skin is crisp. Pour off
fat. Blot chicken; place
skin-side up in shallow baking dish. Mix orange juice
with soy sauce and wine;
pour over chicken. Bake
uncovered in a preheated
350° oven, basting fre-
quently, 45 to 50 minutes.
Add orange sections and
bake 5 minutes or until just
heated through. Serve
chicken with sauce.

	Per Serving
Calories	164.1
Carbohydrate (g)	6.9
Protein (g)	25.3
Total Fat (g)	3.2
Saturated Fat (g)	1.6
Cholesterol (mg)	79.3
Sodium (mg)	60.1

Chicken Teriyaki

Makes 6 servings

3 whole chicken breasts
(about 2 lb.), split,
trimmed of fat
1/2 cup dry white wine
1/4 cup water
3 tbsp. soy sauce
1/4 tsp. ground ginger
1/8 tsp. garlic powder

Place chicken in glass or
ceramic bowl. Mix together
remaining ingredients; pour
over chicken. Marinate
covered several hours or
overnight in refrigerator.
Drain and reserve mari-
nade. Grill or broil chicken,
turning once, about 10
inches from heat, about 30
minutes or until tender.
Baste frequently with re-
served marinade.

	Per Serving
Calories	161.7
Carbohydrate (g)	1.3
Protein (g)	27.2
Total Fat (g)	3.3
Saturated Fat (g)	1.7
Cholesterol (mg)	85.0
Sodium (mg)	613.5

White Wine Sauce

Makes about 2 cups

1 cup fat-skimmed chicken
or turkey broth, canned
or homemade ●
3 tbsp. dry white wine
3 tbsp. instant-blend flour
2/3 cup skim milk
Onion salt ● and pepper to
taste (optional)
Pinch nutmeg (optional)
1 tbsp. minced fresh
parsley

● *SODIUM TIP—Use unsalted
broth. Substitute onion
powder to taste for onion salt.*

Combine broth and wine in
nonstick saucepan. Heat to
boiling; reduce heat. Mix
together flour and milk;
stir into simmering broth.
Cook and stir until mixture
is thick and bubbling.
Sprinkle with onion salt,
pepper, and nutmeg. (Thin
with a little water, if necessary.) Sprinkle with parsley.

	Per 1/4 Cup
Calories	26.2
Carbohydrate (g)	3.8
Protein (g)	1.4
Total Fat (g)	0.0
Saturated Fat (g)	0.0
Cholesterol (mg)	2.2
Sodium (mg)	101.4

High-Fiber Fruit Stuffing

Makes 4 servings

4 slices stale high-fiber
bread, crumbled ●
1 1/2 cups finely diced
unpared apple
1 medium onion, chopped
5 tbsp. raisins
3/4 tsp. salt ● (optional)
1/2 tsp. pepper
1/4 tsp. dried sage
1/4 tsp. dried rosemary

● *SODIUM TIP—Use low-
sodium bread. Omit added
salt.*

Toss all ingredients to-
gether. Use to stuff chicken
or Cornish hens.

	Per Serving
Calories	117.3
Carbohydrate (g)	27.2
Protein (g)	3.1
Total Fat (g)	0.7
Saturated Fat (g)	0.0
Cholesterol (mg)	0.0
Sodium (mg)	163.9

Summer Chutney

Makes 24 servings

2 lb. fresh or frozen
blueberries (if frozen,
defrost and drain)
1 1/2 tbsp. fresh ginger,
peeled, chopped
1 medium onion, chopped
3/4 cup cider vinegar
1/4 cup golden raisins
24 packets sugar substitute
1 1/2 tsp. cinnamon
1/2 tsp. dry mustard
1/2 tsp. ground cloves
1/4 tsp. cayenne pepper
1/4 tsp. cardamom
2 cups water

Combine all ingredients in
large noncorrosive sauce-
pan. Bring to boil over
medium heat. Lower heat
and boil gently, uncovered,
for about 2 hours or until
thick. Store in sterilized
jars and process in boiling
water bath according to
manufacturer's instructions,
or freeze in separate air-
tight containers for up to 6
months. (Chutney is served
like a relish with poultry.)

	Per Serving
Calories	28.0
Carbohydrate (g)	7.0
Protein (g)	0.0
Total Fat (g)	0.0
Saturated Fat (g)	0.0
Cholesterol (mg)	0.0
Sodium (mg)	3.0

Fish & Seafood

Quick Seafood Newburg

Makes 4 servings

1 cup skim milk
2 tbsp. instant-blend flour
1/4 cup sherry
Salt ● and black pepper to taste (optional)
Pinch nutmeg
Pinch cayenne pepper
2 cups cold cooked shelled lobster or shrimp, or 2 cans (7 oz. each) water-packed tuna ● ■
4 slices toasted high-fiber bread, cut into halves diagonally ●
2 tbsp. minced parsley
Paprika
Lemon wedges (optional)

● *SODIUM TIP—Use unsalted tuna (do not use lobster or shrimp) and low-sodium bread. Omit added salt.*

■ *CHOLESTEROL TIP—Use lobster or tuna (do not use shrimp).*

Stir milk and flour together in saucepan; cook and stir over low heat until sauce simmers and thickens. Stir in sherry, salt, black pepper, nutmeg, and cayenne pepper. Stir in seafood until heated through. Spoon over toast triangles and sprinkle with parsley and paprika. Garnish with lemon wedges, if desired.

	Per Serving
Calories	177.7
Carbohydrate (g)	17.1
Protein (g)	18.8
Total Fat (g)	1.6
Saturated Fat (g)	0.0
Cholesterol (mg)	61.3
Sodium (mg)	343.3

Hearty Halibut

Makes 8 servings

2 lb. halibut steaks or other fish steaks, fresh or frozen, defrosted ●
2/3 cup thinly sliced onion
1 1/2 cups chopped fresh mushrooms
1/3 cup chopped tomato
1/4 cup chopped green pepper
1/4 cup chopped parsley
3 tbsp. chopped pimiento
1/2 cup dry white wine
2 tbsp. lemon juice
1/4 tsp. dillweed
1/8 tsp. pepper

Cut steaks into serving-size pieces. Spray baking dish with cooking spray. Arrange onion over bottom of dish. Place fish in a single layer over onion. Combine mushrooms, tomato, green pepper, parsley, and pimiento and spread over top of fish. Combine wine, lemon juice, and seasonings; pour over vegetables. Bake in a preheated 350° oven for 25 to 30 minutes or until fish flakes easily with a fork.

Saucy Seafood

Makes 8 servings

2 lb. fish fillets, fresh or frozen, defrosted ●
1/4 cup tomato juice ●
1/4 cup steak sauce ●
2 tbsp. low-calorie Italian salad dressing ●
Pinch curry powder
Dash red pepper sauce (optional)

● *SODIUM TIP—Use fresh fish, unsalted tomato juice, and unsalted salad dressing. Omit steak sauce.*

Cut fillets into serving-size pieces; place in nonstick broiler pan sprayed with cooking spray. Combine remaining ingredients; spread half of mixture on fish. Broil 4 to 5 minutes. Turn fillets carefully; spread with remaining sauce. Broil 4 to 5 minutes more until fish flakes easily.

	Per Serving
Calories	140.2
Carbohydrate (g)	3.6
Protein (g)	24.5
Total Fat (g)	1.5
Saturated Fat (g)	0.5
Cholesterol (mg)	56.8
Sodium (mg)	67.8

	Per Serving
Calories	98.9
Carbohydrate (g)	2.4
Protein (g)	19.0
Total Fat (g)	1.2
Saturated Fat (g)	0.3
Cholesterol (mg)	56.8
Sodium (mg)	272.7

Italian Fish Stew

Makes 4 servings

1 tsp. safflower or corn oil
1 tbsp. water
1 cup chopped onion
1 clove garlic, minced (optional)
16-oz. can tomatoes, undrained, well broken up ●
1 green pepper, diced
2 stalks celery, diced ●
3 tbsp. chopped Italian parsley
3 tbsp. dry white wine
1 small bay leaf
Salt ● and pepper to taste (optional)
1 tsp. dried oregano
1 tsp. fennel seeds
1 lb. frozen cod fillets, slightly defrosted ●

● *SODIUM TIP—Use fresh fish fillets; freeze until firm. Use unsalted tomatoes. Omit celery and added salt.*

Spray a large nonstick skillet with cooking spray. Add oil, water, onions, and garlic. Cook, stirring frequently, until water evaporates and onions are lightly browned. Add remaining ingredients except fish. Cover and simmer 25 to 30 minutes. With a sharp knife, cut fillets into 1¹/₂-inch chunks. Add to the skillet. Cover and simmer 12 to 15 minutes, only until fish flakes easily with a fork. Remove bay leaf before serving.

	Per Serving
Calories	157.3
Carbohydrate (g)	10.9
Protein (g)	22.2
Total Fat (g)	1.8
Saturated Fat (g)	0.2
Cholesterol (mg)	56.8
Sodium (mg)	260.6

Flounder Fillets

Makes 4 servings

1 lb. flounder or sole fillets, fresh or frozen, defrosted ●
¹/₂ cup dry white wine
¹/₂ cup water
¹/₂ tsp. dried dillweed
Salt ● and pepper to taste (optional)
1 cup plain low-fat yogurt
2 tbsp. chopped parsley

● *SODIUM TIP—Use fresh fish. Omit added salt.*

Cut fillets into serving-size pieces; place in a shallow baking dish. Add wine and water. Sprinkle with dillweed, salt, and pepper. Bake in preheated 350° oven 20 to 25 minutes or until fish flakes easily with a fork. Baste several times with liquid while baking. Drain liquid from dish into a saucepan. Cook liquid over high heat until reduced to about ¹/₃ cup. Reduce heat, stir in yogurt; heat (do not boil) just until sauce is heated through. Place fish on platter. Cover with sauce and parsley.

	Per Serving
Calories	146.8
Carbohydrate (g)	4.6
Protein (g)	21.0
Total Fat (g)	1.9
Saturated Fat (g)	0.8
Cholesterol (mg)	61.8
Sodium (mg)	121.8

Baked Orange Roughy with Tomatoes and Herbs

Makes 2 servings

¹/₄ cup onion, chopped
1 clove garlic, minced
¹/₂ tsp. margarine
¹/₂ large tomato, seeded, chopped
¹/₄ tsp. salt
¹/₈ tsp. oregano
¹/₈ tsp. thyme
Pinch black pepper
¹/₂ lb. orange roughy fish fillets (defrosted if frozen)
¹/₄ cup dry white wine
1¹/₂ tsp. tomato paste

In oven-proof skillet over medium heat, sauté onion and garlic in margarine until soft, about 5 minutes. Stir in tomato and seasonings. Cover and simmer for 5 minutes. Place fish in skillet; cover with sauce. Pour wine over fish. Cover and bake in preheated 350° oven for 15 to 20 minutes or until fish just flakes with fork. Remove fish to heated platter. Reduce sauce on top of range to ¹/₃ cup. Stir in tomato paste and pour over fish. Serve with lemon wedges, if desired.

	Per Serving
Calories	144.0
Carbohydrate (g)	5.0
Protein (g)	26.0
Total Fat (g)	2.0
Saturated Fat (g)	na
Cholesterol (mg)	37.0
Sodium (mg)	510.0

Succulent Sea Bass

Makes 8 servings

2 lb. sea bass fillets or other fish fillets, fresh or frozen, defrosted ●
1/2 cup unsweetened pineapple juice
1/4 cup steak sauce ●
Salt ● and pepper to taste (optional)

● *SODIUM TIP—Use fresh fish. Omit steak sauce and added salt.*

Cut fillets into serving-size pieces. Place fish in single layer in shallow baking dish. Combine remaining ingredients and pour over fish. Refrigerate covered for 30 minutes, turning once. Remove fish, reserving marinade for basting. Place fish on a broiler pan sprayed with cooking spray. Broil about 4 inches from heat source for 4 to 6 minutes. Turn carefully and brush with marinade. Broil 4 to 6 minutes longer or until fish flakes easily with a fork.

	Per Serving
Calories	119.9
Carbohydrate (g)	3.5
Protein (g)	21.8
Total Fat (g)	1.4
Saturated Fat (g)	0.5
Cholesterol (mg)	62.3
Sodium (mg)	214.5

Barbecued Sea Steaks

Makes 4 servings

1 lb. fresh or frozen, defrosted, cod or halibut steaks ●
6-oz. can tomato juice ●
2 tbsp. lemon juice
1 tsp. Worcestershire sauce ●
1 tsp. instant minced onion
Salt ● and pepper to taste (optional)
1/4 tsp. grated lemon rind
1/8 tsp. dried oregano
Few drops liquid smoke seasoning (optional)
Few drops red pepper sauce (optional)

● *SODIUM TIP—Use fresh fish. Use unsalted tomato juice. Omit added salt and Worcestershire.*

Cut cod into 4 serving pieces. Combine remaining ingredients in small saucepan; heat to boiling. Reduce heat; simmer, uncovered, for 5 minutes. Place fish 4 inches above medium coals; grill about 7 minutes. Turn; brush with sauce. Grill 7 minutes longer or until fish flakes easily with fork, brushing occasionally with more sauce.

	Per Serving
Calories	100.2
Carbohydrate (g)	3.0
Protein (g)	20.4
Total Fat (g)	0.4
Saturated Fat (g)	0.1
Cholesterol (mg)	56.8
Sodium (mg)	185.0

Red Snapper Provençale

Makes 4 servings

1 medium onion, finely chopped
2 cloves garlic, minced
1 tbsp. olive oil
1 zucchini, julienned
2 medium tomatoes, seeded, diced
2 tbsp. parsley, chopped
2 tbsp. tomato paste
1/2 tsp. basil
1/2 tsp. oregano
1/4 tsp. salt
1/8 tsp. black pepper
1/8 tsp. thyme
1 lb. red snapper fillets

Sauté onion and garlic in oil for 5 minutes or until soft. Stir in zucchini, tomatoes, parsley, tomato paste, and seasonings; simmer for 10 to 15 minutes. Rinse and pat dry fillets. Pour half of sauce on bottom of 8-inch square baking dish. Top with fillets and remaining sauce. Cover with foil and bake in preheated 350° oven for 20 to 25 minutes or until fish flakes with fork.

	Per Serving
Calories	173.0
Carbohydrate (g)	8.0
Protein (g)	24.0
Total Fat (g)	5.0
Saturated Fat (g)	na
Cholesterol (mg)	52.0
Sodium (mg)	284.0

Fish Kebabs

Makes 8 servings

2 lb. fresh or frozen,
  defrosted cod steaks ●
1 cup dry white wine
3 tbsp. Worcestershire
  sauce ●
2 tsp. garlic salt ●
1/2 tsp. pepper
2 tsp. dried oregano
1 tbsp. safflower or corn
  oil

● *SODIUM TIP—Substitute
1/4 tsp. garlic powder for
garlic salt. Omit Worces-
tershire. Use fresh fish.*

Cut cod into 2-inch cubes;
arrange cubes in shallow
dish. Combine remaining
ingredients except oil; pour
mixture over fish. Cover
and refrigerate 2 to 4
hours. Drain fish and re-
serve marinade. Thread
cubes on skewers. Brush
with oil. Grill over hot
coals or in oven broiler,
turning frequently, for 12
to 15 minutes or until fish
becomes opaque and flakes
with a fork. While grilling,
baste occasionally with
marinade.

	Per Serving
Calories	131.7
Carbohydrate (g)	2.5
Protein (g)	20.1
Total Fat (g)	2.1
Saturated Fat (g)	0.3
Cholesterol (mg)	56.8
Sodium (mg)	650.2

Slim Seafood Sauce

Makes 1 1/4 cups

1 cup canned condensed
  tomato soup ●
2 tbsp. lemon juice
2 tbsp. minced onion (or 2
  tsp. dried)
2 tsp. prepared horseradish

● *SODIUM TIP—Use unsalted
soup.*

Combine all ingredients
thoroughly and chill. (Use
for dipping chilled sea-
food.)

	Per Tablespoon
Calories	10.0
Carbohydrate (g)	1.8
Protein (g)	0.2
Total Fat (g)	0.3
Saturated Fat (g)	0.0
Cholesterol (mg)	0.0
Sodium (mg)	99.6

Seafood Dressing

Makes 2 3/4 cups

1 cup plain low-fat yogurt
1 cup low-calorie low-fat
  mayonnaise ●
1/2 cup hot chili sauce ●
2 tbsp. lemon juice
1 tbsp. minced onion
1 tbsp. prepared
  horseradish
Pinch tarragon
Salt ● and pepper to taste
  (optional)

● *SODIUM TIP—Use unsalted
mayonnaise. Substitute tomato
paste with chili powder to
taste for chili sauce. Omit
added salt.*

Combine all ingredients;
mix well. Store in refrigerator.

	Per Tablespoon
Calories	13.6
Carbohydrate (g)	1.5
Protein (g)	0.2
Total Fat (g)	0.8
Saturated Fat (g)	0.0
Cholesterol (mg)	3.4
Sodium (mg)	46.7

Dill Sauce

Makes 3/4 cup

1/4 cup plain low-fat yogurt
2 tbsp. fresh dillweed,
  minced
1/2 cup low-calorie low-fat
  mayonnaise ●

● *SODIUM TIP—Use unsalted
mayonnaise.*

Combine all ingredients
thoroughly.

	Per Tablespoon
Calories	15.9
Carbohydrate (g)	0.9
Protein (g)	0.2
Total Fat (g)	1.4
Saturated Fat (g)	0.1
Cholesterol (mg)	5.8
Sodium (mg)	15.3

Yogurt Tartar Sauce

Makes 2 1/2 cups

1 cup plain low-fat yogurt
1 cup low-calorie low-fat
  mayonnaise
1/2 cup pickle relish
1 tbsp. prepared mustard

Combine all ingredients;
mix well.

	Per Tablespoon
Calories	15.7
Carbohydrate (g)	1.9
Protein (g)	0.2
Total Fat (g)	0.9
Saturated Fat (g)	0.1
Cholesterol (mg)	3.7
Sodium (mg)	36.8

Pasta & Rice

Macaroni Salad

Makes 12 servings

8 oz. protein-enriched elbow macaroni, tender-cooked ●
1 onion, chopped
2 stalks celery, diced ●
2 carrots, shredded ●
1 small red or green bell pepper, finely chopped
1/3 cup plain low-fat yogurt
1/3 cup low-calorie low-fat mayonnaise ●
1 tbsp. lemon juice
1 tsp. prepared mustard ●
12 medium stuffed green (Spanish) olives, sliced ●
Salt ● and freshly ground pepper to taste (optional)
Paprika

● *SODIUM TIP—Cook macaroni without salt. Substitute additional bell pepper for celery and carrots. Use unsalted mayonnaise. Substitute dry mustard to taste for prepared mustard. Omit olives and added salt.*

Rinse macaroni with cold water; drain. Combine all ingredients except paprika; cover and chill thoroughly.

	Per Serving
Calories	96.0
Carbohydrate (g)	17.6
Protein (g)	3.0
Total Fat (g)	1.8
Saturated Fat (g)	0.1
Cholesterol (mg)	4.1
Sodium (mg)	342.2

Alfie's Fettucine

Makes 8 servings

8 oz. uncooked wide egg noodles ● ■
1 cup low-fat cottage cheese, at room temperature ●
1/2 cup grated Parmesan cheese ● ■
1/4 cup minced fresh parsley
Salt ● and coarsely ground pepper to taste (optional)

● *SODIUM TIP—Cook noodles without salt. Use low-sodium cheese. Omit added salt.*

■ *CHOLESTEROL TIP—Use cholesterol-free noodles. Substitute a low-fat cheese.*

Boil noodles according to package directions. Drain and return to the same pot. Quickly toss together with remaining ingredients. Serve immediately.

	Per Serving
Calories	156.9
Carbohydrate (g)	21.8
Protein (g)	9.8
Total Fat (g)	3.0
Saturated Fat (g)	1.6
Cholesterol (mg)	34.5
Sodium (mg)	487.5

Italian Ground Beef and Macaroni

Makes 4 servings

3/4 lb. ground beef, extra lean
1/2 cup chopped onion
1/4 cup chopped green pepper
1/4 cup chopped celery
16-oz. can tomatoes ●
10³/4-oz. can tomato puree ●
1 tsp. oregano leaves
1 tsp. basil leaves
1/4 tsp. salt ●
1/8 tsp. pepper
3 cups cooked elbow macaroni, unsalted (about 1 cup uncooked)

● *SODIUM TIP—Use unsalted tomatoes. Omit added salt.*

Cook beef, onion, green pepper, and celery in large frypan until beef is lightly browned and onion is clear. Drain. Break up large pieces of tomatoes. Add tomatoes, tomato puree, and seasonings to beef mixture. Simmer 15 minutes to blend flavors. Stir in macaroni. Heat to serving temperature.

	Per Serving
Calories	330.0
Carbohydrate (g)	35.7
Protein (g)	22.3
Total Fat (g)	11.3
Saturated Fat (g)	na
Cholesterol (mg)	53.0
Sodium (mg)	679.5

Baked Macaroni and Cheese with Mushrooms

Makes 10 servings

3½ cups tender-cooked
   protein-enriched elbow
   macaroni ●
8-oz. can mushroom stems
   and pieces, drained ●
4-oz. can pimientos,
   drained, minced
1 cup skim milk
1 tsp. cornstarch or
   arrowroot
1 cup shredded low-fat diet
   sharp cheese (about 4
   oz.) ●
1 onion, chopped
2 tsp. prepared mustard ●
1 tsp. Worcestershire
   sauce ●
Salt ● and pepper to taste
   (optional)
1 tbsp. seasoned bread
   crumbs ●

● *SODIUM TIP—Cook
macaroni without salt. Use
unsalted mushrooms and
low-sodium cheese and bread
crumbs. Substitute dry
mustard to taste for prepared
mustard. Omit Worcestershire
and added salt.*

Combine macaroni, mushrooms, and pimientos in 1½-quart baking dish. Mix milk with cornstarch in nonstick saucepan. Cook and stir over low heat until simmering. Stir in cheese, onion, mustard, Worcestershire, salt, and pepper; cook and stir until cheese is completely melted. Stir sauce into macaroni mixture. Top with bread crumbs. Bake in a preheated 350° oven 25 minutes or until hot and bubbly.

	Per Serving
Calories	98.7
Carbohydrate (g)	16.0
Protein (g)	6.4
Total Fat (g)	1.4
Saturated Fat (g)	0.5
Cholesterol (mg)	4.5
Sodium (mg)	486.3

One-Step Skillet Spaghetti and Meat Sauce

Makes 4 servings

8 oz. lean beef round,
   trimmed of fat, ground
2 cups water
16-oz. can plain tomato
   sauce (check label for
   no added oil) ●
1 onion, chopped
1 tsp. dried oregano
Garlic salt ● and pepper to
   taste (optional)
4 oz. uncooked thin
   spaghetti, broken up

● *SODIUM TIP—Use unsalted
tomato sauce. Substitute garlic
powder to taste for garlic salt.*

Spray large nonstick skillet with cooking spray. Spread the meat in a thin layer in skillet. Cook over moderate heat until underside is browned. Break up into large chunks and turn over. When meat is brown, add 1 cup of water, then pour off the liquid into a cup. Set liquid aside and allow the fat to rise to the surface. Meanwhile, stir remaining ingredients except spaghetti into skillet. Heat to boiling. Add the broken spaghetti a little at a time, stirring after each addition. Skim fat from the reserved drained liquid. Stir the fat-skimmed liquid into skillet. Simmer uncovered, stirring frequently, until most of the liquid is absorbed and spaghetti is tender and coated with a thick sauce. Serve straight from the skillet.

	Per Serving
Calories	253.0
Carbohydrate (g)	32.2
Protein (g)	17.7
Total Fat (g)	6.2
Saturated Fat (g)	2.7
Cholesterol (mg)	36.9
Sodium (mg)	809.9

Macaroni-Apple Salad

Makes 4 servings

2 cups tender-cooked
   protein-enriched elbow
   macaroni, rinsed,
   drained, chilled ●
2 red apples, diced
1 cup diced celery ●
¼ cup low-calorie low-fat
   mayonnaise ●
¼ cup plain low-fat yogurt
¼ cup chopped walnuts
4 large lettuce leaves

● *SODIUM TIP—Cook
macaroni without salt.
Substitute cucumber for
celery. Use unsalted
mayonnaise.*

Combine macaroni, apples,
celery, mayonnaise, and
yogurt; cover and chill.
Serve on lettuce leaves;
garnish with nuts.

	Per Serving
Calories	194.7
Carbohydrate (g)	29.2
Protein (g)	4.9
Total Fat (g)	7.5
Saturated Fat (g)	0.4
Cholesterol (mg)	9.3
Sodium (mg)	310.8

Pineapple Rice

Makes 6 servings

1 cup unsweetened
   pineapple juice
1 cup instant rice
2 tbsp. soy sauce ●
   (optional)

● *SODIUM TIP—Omit soy
sauce.*

Combine all ingredients in
saucepan; heat to boiling.
Remove from heat; cover
tightly. Let stand 5 minutes.

	Per Serving
Calories	81.7
Carbohydrate (g)	18.7
Protein (g)	1.3
Total Fat (g)	0.1
Saturated Fat (g)	0.0
Cholesterol (mg)	0.0
Sodium (mg)	0.5

Orange-Raisin Rice

Makes 6 servings

1 cup unsweetened orange
   juice
1 cup instant rice
3 tbsp. golden raisins
Pinch pumpkin pie spice
1 tsp. chopped parsley
Salt ● and pepper to taste
   (optional)

● *SODIUM TIP—Omit added
salt.*

Combine orange juice, rice,
and raisins in saucepan.
Heat to boiling. Remove
from heat; cover tightly.
Let stand 5 minutes. Stir in
remaining ingredients.

	Per Serving
Calories	92.5
Carbohydrate (g)	21.4
Protein (g)	1.6
Total Fat (g)	0.1
Saturated Fat (g)	0.0
Cholesterol (mg)	0.0
Sodium (mg)	1.5

Quick Spanish Rice

Makes 8 servings

1 large onion, finely
   chopped
1 stalk celery, finely
   chopped ●
1 red or green bell pepper,
   diced
8-oz. can plain tomato
   sauce (check label for
   no added oil) ●
8-oz. can tomatoes, well
   broken up ●
1¼ cups fat-skimmed
   chicken, turkey, or beef
   broth ●, canned or
   homemade
1 tsp. prepared mustard ●
1 bay leaf
½ tsp. dried oregano
2 cups instant rice

● *SODIUM TIP—Omit celery.
Use unsalted tomato sauce,
tomatoes, and broth.
Substitute dry mustard to taste
for prepared mustard.*

Combine all ingredients
except rice in nonstick
saucepan. Simmer covered
10 minutes. Stir in rice.
Simmer covered over very
low heat, stirring occasionally, about 5 minutes.

	Per Serving
Calories	116.8
Carbohydrate (g)	25.4
Protein (g)	3.5
Total Fat (g)	0.3
Saturated Fat (g)	0.0
Cholesterol (mg)	2.2
Sodium (mg)	359.5

Green-Pea Curry with Rice

Makes 2 servings

1/2 cup green split peas
1 cup water
1/2 tsp. vegetable oil
1/3 cup chopped onion
1 tsp. curry powder
1/4 tsp. ground ginger
1 tbsp. raisins
Pinch salt (optional)
1/2 cup water
1 cup cooked rice

Wash peas, add water, bring to boil. Cover, remove from heat, and let stand 1 hour. Heat oil in saucepan. Add onions and sauté until limp. Add spices and raisins; stir to blend. Add green peas and water as needed to cover; stir. Bring to boil. Cover and simmer 1 hour. Serve over 1/2 cup cooked rice. Garnish with chutney, shredded fresh coconut, chopped olives, or chopped nuts.

	Per Serving
Calories	286.0
Carbohydrate (g)	55.8
Protein (g)	12.2
Total Fat (g)	1.9
Saturated Fat (g)	na
Cholesterol (mg)	0.0
Sodium (mg)	17.4

Apple-Curry Rice

Makes 6 servings

1/2 cup tomato juice ●
1/2 cup unsweetened apple juice
1 cup instant rice
1 tsp. curry powder
1 red apple, unpared, diced

● *SODIUM TIP—Use unsalted tomato juice.*

Combine all ingredients except apple in saucepan. Heat to boiling. Remove from heat; stir in apple. Cover tightly; let stand 5 minutes.

	Per Serving
Calories	86.1
Carbohydrate (g)	19.7
Protein (g)	1.3
Total Fat (g)	0.2
Saturated Fat (g)	0.0
Cholesterol (mg)	0.0
Sodium (mg)	41.3

Raisin-Curry Rice

Makes 6 servings

1/2 cup tomato juice ●
1/2 cup unsweetened pineapple juice
1 cup instant rice
3 tbsp. golden raisins
1 tsp. curry powder

● *SODIUM TIP—Use unsalted tomato juice.*

Combine all ingredients in saucepan; Heat to boiling. Remove from heat; cover tightly. Let stand 5 minutes.

	Per Serving
Calories	87.2
Carbohydrate (g)	20.2
Protein (g)	1.5
Total Fat (g)	0.1
Saturated Fat (g)	0.0
Cholesterol (mg)	0.0
Sodium (mg)	41.8

Rice with Currants

Makes 6 servings

1 cup instant rice
1 cup water
5 tbsp. dried currants
Pinch cinnamon
Salt ● and pepper to taste (optional)

● *SODIUM TIP—Omit added salt.*

Combine rice, water, currants, and cinnamon in saucepan; heat to boiling. Remove from heat; let stand 5 minutes. Season with salt and pepper to taste.

	Per Serving
Calories	63.8
Carbohydrate (g)	14.2
Protein (g)	1.3
Total Fat (g)	0.0
Saturated Fat (g)	0.0
Cholesterol (mg)	0.0
Sodium (mg)	0.4

Vegetables

Oriental Stir-Fried Vegetables

Makes 4 servings

1 lb. fresh broccoli, asparagus spears, green beans, or sliced zucchini
1/2 onion, thinly sliced
2-oz. can sliced mushrooms, undrained ●
2 tbsp. soy sauce, ● white wine, or water (optional)
2 tsp. safflower oil

● *SODIUM TIP—Use unsalted mushrooms. Substitute wine or water for soy sauce.*

Slice broccoli or asparagus spears into 1 1/2-inch lengths. Combine all ingredients in nonstick skillet. Cook and stir uncovered until liquid has evaporated and vegetables are crisp-tender.

	Per Serving
Calories	64.6
Carbohydrate (g)	8.3
Protein (g)	4.6
Total Fat (g)	2.5
Saturated Fat (g)	0.2
Cholesterol (mg)	0.0
Sodium (mg)	79.4

Swedish Potato Pancakes

Makes 7 servings

1 cup skim milk
1 cup all-purpose flour
2 cups red potatoes, peeled, shredded, and patted dry
1/4 cup onion, grated
1/2 tsp. salt
1/4 tsp. black pepper
Nonstick vegetable spray

Combine milk and flour to make a fairly stiff batter. Stir in potatoes, onion, salt, and pepper. Heat large skillet and spray well with nonstick spray. Drop 1 tbsp. batter per pancake into skillet; flatten with spoon. Fry until edges are brown, turn over, and continue to brown. Cook over medium heat for 15 to 20 minutes until brown and crisp. Drain on paper towels. May need to cook in batches; spray skillet each time. Serve with no-sugar-added apple sauce, low-fat sour cream, or plain yogurt. (One serving equals 2 pancakes.)

	Per Serving
Calories	114.0
Carbohydrate (g)	24.0
Protein (g)	4.0
Total Fat (g)	0.0
Saturated Fat (g)	na
Cholesterol (mg)	1.0
Sodium (mg)	173.0

Slow-Baked Italian Zucchini

Makes 12 servings

3 cups sliced zucchini
1 cup fat-skimmed chicken broth, canned or homemade ●
6-oz. can tomato paste
1 onion, chopped
1 tsp. dried oregano or mixed Italian seasoning
1 clove garlic, minced
2 tsp. Italian-seasoned bread crumbs ●
2 tbsp. grated extra-sharp Romano cheese ● (optional)

● *SODIUM TIP—Use unsalted broth and plain bread crumbs. Use low-sodium cheese, or omit.*

Combine zucchini, broth, tomato paste, onion, oregano, and garlic in casserole. Sprinkle with bread crumbs and cheese. Bake uncovered in a preheated 350° oven 2 hours.

	Per Serving
Calories	23.6
Carbohydrate (g)	5.1
Protein (g)	1.3
Total Fat (g)	0.0
Saturated Fat (g)	0.0
Cholesterol (mg)	2.2
Sodium (mg)	69.2

Baked Tomatoes

Makes 6 servings

3 large tomatoes, cut crosswise into halves
3 tbsp. Italian-seasoned bread crumbs ●
2 tsp. olive oil
1 tsp. onion powder

● *SODIUM TIP—Use low-sodium bread crumbs.*

Place tomatoes cut-sides up on baking sheet. Combine remaining ingredients; sprinkle over tomato halves. Bake in a preheated 375° oven about 12 minutes or until crumbs are golden.

Per Serving	
Calories	51.1
Carbohydrate (g)	8.1
Protein (g)	1.8
Total Fat (g)	1.7
Saturated Fat (g)	0.2
Cholesterol (mg)	0.1
Sodium (mg)	99.4

Crispy Scalloped Potatoes

Makes 2 cups

2 cups thinly sliced raw potatoes
1 tbsp. flour
1 tbsp. minced onion
1 tsp. salt
Dash pepper
1 cup skim milk
1 tbsp. margarine

Lightly coat 1-qt. casserole with vegetable cooking spray. Layer half of the potato in bottom of baking dish. Sprinkle with half of flour, onion, salt, and pepper. Repeat layers. Pour milk over the potatoes. Dot with margarine. Cover and bake in preheated 350° oven for 30 minutes. Uncover and bake an additional 35 to 40 minutes or until potatoes are tender.

Per 1/2-Cup Serving	
Calories	114.0
Carbohydrate (g)	18.1
Protein (g)	3.9
Total Fat (g)	3.0
Saturated Fat (g)	na
Cholesterol (mg)	1.0
Sodium (mg)	602.3

Saucy Green Beans

Makes 3 servings

10-oz. package frozen French-cut green beans
1/3 cup water
1 tbsp. instant cream of mushroom soup powder from single-serving packet

Combine green beans and water in saucepan; cook covered until tender. Stir soup powder into saucepan. Cook and stir until sauce thickens.

Per Serving	
Calories	51.3
Carbohydrate (g)	8.7
Protein (g)	1.9
Total Fat (g)	1.4
Saturated Fat (g)	0.9
Cholesterol (mg)	1.7
Sodium (mg)	340.0

Marinated Beans and Corn

Makes 12 salad-size servings

15-oz. can red kidney beans, drained
15-oz. can pink beans, drained; reserve 1/4 cup sauce
15-oz. can garbanzo beans, drained
10-oz. package frozen whole-kernel corn
1 cup sliced celery (about 2 large stalks)
1/3 cup wine vinegar
1 tbsp. vegetable oil
1 tbsp. chopped fresh parsley
2 tsp. minced garlic cloves
1/4 tsp. chili powder

Cook corn according to package directions; drain. Combine drained beans and corn in large mixing bowl. Combine all other ingredients and reserved bean sauce. Pour over bean-and-corn mixture. Toss lightly to mix. Cover and refrigerate overnight. Serve 1/2-cup portions on lettuce. Garnish with onion slice and tomato wedge.

Per 1/2-Cup Serving	
Calories	156.0
Carbohydrate (g)	27.9
Protein (g)	8.2
Total Fat (g)	2.3
Saturated Fat (g)	na
Cholesterol (mg)	0.0
Sodium (mg)	20.1

Confetti Cabbage

Makes 4 servings
1 onion, chopped
1 tbsp. diet margarine ● ■
3 cups shredded cabbage
1 cup shredded carrots ●
1/2 cup water
1/2 tsp. dried oregano
1/8 tsp. garlic powder
Salt ● and pepper to taste
(optional)

● *SODIUM TIP—Use unsalted margarine. Substitute additional cabbage for carrots. Omit added salt.*

■ *CHOLESTEROL TIP—Use polyunsaturated margarine.*

Sauté onion in margarine in large skillet until just transparent. Stir in remaining ingredients. Cook covered over moderate heat 5 minutes. Uncover and simmer until most of the liquid has evaporated.

	Per Serving
Calories	46.7
Carbohydrate (g)	8.0
Protein (g)	1.5
Total Fat (g)	1.6
Saturated Fat (g)	0.2
Cholesterol (mg)	0.0
Sodium (mg)	53.7

Baked Corn on the Cob

Makes 4 servings
4 ears fresh or frozen corn
4 tsp. diet margarine ●
Salt ● and coarsely ground
   pepper to taste
   (optional)

● *SODIUM TIP—Use unsalted margarine. Omit added salt.*

Husk corn and rinse well (or defrost at room temperature, if using frozen corn). Place each ear on a sheet of heavy-duty foil or use a double thickness of regular foil. Spread each ear with 1 tsp. margarine. Sprinkle with salt and pepper. Wrap each ear in foil and secure ends. Bake in a preheated 300° oven 15 to 20 minutes or place on a rack in a covered grill and turn frequently. Unwrap after 15 minutes to check for doneness.

	Per Serving
Calories	86.6
Carbohydrate (g)	16.0
Protein (g)	3.0
Total Fat (g)	3.0
Saturated Fat (g)	0.3
Cholesterol (mg)	0.0
Sodium (mg)	36.6

Dilled Brussels Sprouts

Makes 3 servings
10-oz. package frozen or 1
   pint fresh Brussels
   sprouts
1/2 cup fat-skimmed beef
   broth, canned or
   homemade ●
1 tsp. dill seed
1 tsp. instant minced onion
   (optional)
Salt ● and pepper to taste
   (optional)

● *SODIUM TIP—Use unsalted broth. Omit added salt.*

Combine all ingredients in saucepan; simmer covered 8 to 10 minutes or until sprouts are nearly tender. Uncover and continue to simmer until most of the liquid has evaporated.

	Per Serving
Calories	39.0
Carbohydrate (g)	7.4
Protein (g)	4.0
Total Fat (g)	0.2
Saturated Fat (g)	0.0
Cholesterol (mg)	4.0
Sodium (mg)	145.3

Zucchini Piquant

Makes 4 servings
2 medium zucchini or
   yellow summer squash,
   sliced
1/2 cup low-calorie low-fat
   Russian or Thousand
   Island salad dressing ●
1/4 cup water
2 tsp. instant minced onion

● *SODIUM TIP—Use unsalted dressing.*

Combine all ingredients in nonstick saucepan. Simmer uncovered, stirring occasionally, until most of the liquid has evaporated and zucchini slices are evenly coated. Serve hot.

	Per Serving
Calories	79.3
Carbohydrate (g)	12.1
Protein (g)	1.4
Total Fat (g)	2.1
Saturated Fat (g)	0.0
Cholesterol (mg)	0.0
Sodium (mg)	391.3

Broccoli-Potato Bake

Makes 4 servings

4 small potatoes, peeled, diced
2 tsp. margarine
1 tsp. salt
1/4 cup skim milk
10-oz. package frozen chopped broccoli
1/4 cup grated cheddar cheese (about 1 oz.)

Cook, drain, and mash potatoes with margarine, salt, and milk. Cook broccoli according to package directions. Drain well. Fold into mashed potatoes. Place mixture in casserole sprayed with vegetable cooking spray. Sprinkle with cheese. Bake in preheated 350° oven for 15 minutes or until cheese melts.

	Per Serving
Calories	152.0
Carbohydrate (g)	23.0
Protein (g)	6.7
Total Fat (g)	4.5
Saturated Fat (g)	na
Cholesterol (mg)	8.0
Sodium (mg)	629.8

Quickie Green Beans with Mushrooms

Makes 4 servings

1 tbsp. diet margarine ● ■
2-oz. can sliced mushrooms, drained ●
16-oz. can green beans, undrained ●

● *SODIUM TIP—Use unsalted margarine and vegetables.*

■ *CHOLESTEROL TIP—Use polyunsaturated margarine.*

Melt margarine in nonstick saucepan or small skillet. Add mushrooms; brown lightly, stirring occasionally with wooden spoon. Add the green beans (including liquid). Heat to boiling; cook uncovered until most of the liquid has evaporated.

	Per Serving
Calories	35.5
Carbohydrate (g)	5.1
Protein (g)	1.4
Total Fat (g)	1.6
Saturated Fat (g)	0.2
Cholesterol (mg)	0.0
Sodium (mg)	356.0

Simmered Black-Eye Peas

Makes 10 servings

1 lb. dried black-eye peas
2 qt. cold water
1 slice salt pork or bacon
1/2 tsp. salt
1 large onion, sliced

Wash peas and place in large pot. Add water, pork, and salt. Bring to boil, cover, and cook slowly for 2 hours. Water should cook down so peas are just covered. Add more water if needed. Serve peas with juice and slices of onion. Pepper sauce may be served with peas. Peas may be used in salads or to make dip.

	Per Serving
Calories	117.0
Carbohydrate (g)	17.8
Protein (g)	6.5
Total Fat (g)	2.7
Saturated Fat (g)	na
Cholesterol (mg)	2.0
Sodium (mg)	156.8

Quick Creamed Cauliflower

Makes 3 servings

10-oz. package frozen cauliflower
1/2 cup fat-skimmed chicken broth, canned or homemade ●
1/2 cup evaporated skim milk
2 tbsp. instant-blend flour
Salt ● and pepper to taste (optional)
Paprika (optional)

● *SODIUM TIP—Use unsalted broth. Omit added salt.*

Combine cauliflower and chicken broth in saucepan. Simmer covered 10 to 12 minutes or until cauliflower is tender. Combine milk and flour; mix well. Stir into saucepan; cook and stir until sauce simmers and bubbles. Sprinkle with salt, pepper, and paprika before serving.

	Per Serving
Calories	77.2
Carbohydrate (g)	13.2
Protein (g)	6.0
Total Fat (g)	0.3
Saturated Fat (g)	0.0
Cholesterol (mg)	4.0
Sodium (mg)	177.5

Creamy Stuffed Baked Potatoes

Makes 6 servings

3 large baking potatoes
3/4 cup plain low-fat yogurt
1/4 cup low-calorie low-fat blue cheese salad dressing ●
1 tbsp. grated onion

● *SODIUM TIP—Use unsalted dressing.*

Bake potatoes 1 hour in a preheated 400° oven. After removing potatoes, increase oven temperature setting to 450°. Slice potatoes in half lengthwise. Scoop out potato; reserve shells.

Combine potato, yogurt, salad dressing, and onion; beat until fluffy. Divide among reserved shells. Place filled potato shells on baking sheet and return to oven. Bake at 450° 12 to 15 minutes.

	Per Serving
Calories	95.8
Carbohydrate (g)	18.3
Protein (g)	3.3
Total Fat (g)	1.2
Saturated Fat (g)	0.6
Cholesterol (mg)	4.5
Sodium (mg)	134.5

Dried Beans in Seasoned Tomato Sauce

Makes 12 servings

1 lb. dried marrow or pinto beans
6 cups water
1 tbsp. olive oil
1 tbsp. vegetable oil
1 tbsp. minced fresh garlic (about 3 cloves)
1 1/2 lb. onions (about 4 medium), thickly sliced
1/4 tsp. marjoram or oregano
1/4 tsp. thyme
1 bay leaf, crumbled
2 tbsp. chopped fresh parsley
28-oz. can tomatoes or 4 large fresh tomatoes
2 tsp. salt ● (optional)

● *SODIUM TIP—Omit added salt.*

Wash beans and soak overnight. Bring to a boil, cover, and simmer 1 hour. Drain thoroughly and wash with cold water. Heat oils in a heavy iron pot. Add garlic, onions, and herbs. Sauté until onions are soft but not brown, about 5 minutes. Stir in tomatoes and simmer until well blended. Add drained beans, salt, and just enough water to cover. Bring to a boil, reduce heat, and simmer uncovered 1 hour.

	Per Serving
Calories	182.0
Carbohydrate (g)	30.3
Protein (g)	10.1
Total Fat (g)	3.1
Saturated Fat (g)	na
Cholesterol (mg)	0.0
Sodium (mg)	112.2

Rutabaga in Potato Nest

Makes 6 cups

5 small potatoes
2 tbsp. margarine, divided
1/3 cup skim milk
3 cups diced rutabaga
Salt ● (optional) and pepper to taste
1 tbsp. chopped fresh parsley

● *SODIUM TIP—Omit added salt.*

Peel, dice, and cook potatoes; mash with 1 tbsp. margarine and milk. Put potatoes in 2-qt. baking dish, forming a nest in center. Bake in preheated 400° oven for 20 minutes or until lightly browned. While potatoes are in oven, cook rutabaga until tender; drain. Season with salt, pepper, and remaining 1 tbsp. margarine. Spoon into potato nest. Sprinkle with chopped parsley. (One serving equals 1/2 cup potato plus 1/2 cup rutabaga.)

	Per Serving
Calories	126.0
Carbohydrate (g)	20.9
Protein (g)	2.5
Total Fat (g)	4.1
Saturated Fat (g)	na
Cholesterol (mg)	0.0
Sodium (mg)	66.2

Pineapple Glazed Yams

Makes 4 servings

8-oz. can pineapple chunks in own juice (drain and reserve juice)
2 tsp. cornstarch
1/4 tsp. salt
1/8 tsp. black pepper
1/8 tsp. cinnamon
1/2 lb. yams (2 small), cooked, peeled, sliced in 1/4-inch slices with each slice halved
1 tsp. margarine

In 1 1/2-qt. saucepan, combine reserved pineapple juice with cornstarch, salt, pepper, and cinnamon. Cook until thickened, stirring constantly. Combine yams and pineapple in 8-inch round casserole. Stir in sauce and coat well. Dot with margarine. Cover with foil and bake in preheated 350° oven for 10 minutes.

	Per Serving
Calories	105.0
Carbohydrate (g)	24.0
Protein (g)	1.0
Total Fat (g)	1.0
Saturated Fat (g)	na
Cholesterol (mg)	0.0
Sodium (mg)	149.0

Crisp Red Cabbage

Makes 3 cups

4 cups shredded red cabbage (about 3/4 lb.)
2 medium apples, cored, cut into wedges
1/4 cup red wine vinegar
2 tbsp. brown sugar
1/4 tsp. salt
1/4 tsp. ground nutmeg

Place cabbage, apples, vinegar, and brown sugar in saucepan over medium heat. Mix well. Cover and simmer about 10 minutes until cabbage is tender-crisp. Add salt and nutmeg. Mix well. Serve warm.

	Per 1/2-Cup Serving
Calories	62.0
Carbohydrate (g)	16.0
Protein (g)	0.8
Total Fat (g)	0.3
Saturated Fat (g)	na
Cholesterol (mg)	0.0
Sodium (mg)	5.5

Creole Corn

Makes 8 servings

16-oz. can stewed tomatoes, undrained, broken up ●
1 small green pepper, chopped
1 onion, chopped
1 stalk celery, chopped ●
2 cups fresh or defrosted frozen kernel corn
Salt ● and pepper to taste (optional)

● *SODIUM TIP—Use unsalted tomatoes. Omit celery and added salt.*

Simmer tomatoes, green pepper, onion, and celery in nonstick saucepan 20 minutes. Stir in corn, salt, and pepper. Cook 5 minutes.

	Per Serving
Calories	59.1
Carbohydrate (g)	13.5
Protein (g)	2.2
Total Fat (g)	0.5
Saturated Fat (g)	0.0
Cholesterol (mg)	0.0
Sodium (mg)	199.5

Red Beans and Brown Rice

Makes 2 servings

3 tbsp. brown rice
2/3 cup water
1/3 slice bacon, diced
1/3 cup chopped onions
3 tbsp. diced celery
2 tbsp. diced green pepper
1/3 15-oz. can red kidney beans (New Orleans Style), pinto beans, or black-eye peas
2 drops hot sauce
Dash pepper

Bring rice and water to boil. Cover tightly, reduce heat, and cook until water is absorbed, about 1 hour. In large skillet, cook diced bacon, onion, celery, and green peppers slowly over low heat, about 10 minutes. Add undrained canned beans or peas and seasonings. Bring to a boil, cover, and simmer 5 minutes. Add cooked rice and mix lightly. Add a little water if mixture is too dry.

	Per 2/3-Cup Serving
Calories	118.0
Carbohydrate (g)	18.7
Protein (g)	5.3
Total Fat (g)	2.6
Saturated Fat (g)	na
Cholesterol (mg)	3.0
Sodium (mg)	38.3

Desserts

Strawberry Apple Fizz

Makes 4 servings

3 oz. unsweetened frozen apple juice concentrate, defrosted, undiluted
1 envelope unflavored gelatin
1 cup boiling water
1¹/₂ cups frozen whole unsweetened strawberries, not defrosted

Put apple juice in blender container and sprinkle on gelatin. Wait 1 minute, then add boiling water. Cover and blend until gelatin granules are dissolved. Add frozen berries. Cover and blend until liquified. Pour into 4 glass dessert cups and chill until set. (Dessert separates into layers.) For variety use other fruits and juices, except pineapple.

	Per Serving
Calories	70.0
Carbohydrate (g)	16.2
Protein (g)	1.9
Total Fat (g)	0.1
Saturated Fat (g)	0.0
Cholesterol (mg)	0.0
Sodium (mg)	3.1

Lime or Lemon Sherbet

Makes 16 servings

1 envelope unflavored gelatin
1 cup sugar
1¹/₂ cups water
6 egg whites
1 tbsp. grated lemon or lime rind
³/₄ cup lemon or lime juice

Combine gelatin and ¹/₂ cup of the sugar in small saucepan. Stir in water. Heat to boiling, stirring until gelatin is completely dissolved; set aside. Beat egg whites at high speed until soft peaks form. Gradually add remaining sugar; beat until stiff. Continue to beat while adding the warm gelatin mixture in a thin steady stream. Beat in rind and juice. Pour into shallow metal trays. Freeze until slushy, stirring occasionally. Transfer to large chilled mixer bowl. With chilled beaters, quickly beat at high speed until smooth and fluffy. Return to trays; cover and freeze until firm. Allow to soften slightly before serving.

	Per Serving
Calories	58.9
Carbohydrate (g)	13.5
Protein (g)	1.8
Total Fat (g)	0.0
Saturated Fat (g)	0.0
Cholesterol (mg)	0.0
Sodium (mg)	18.6

Nectar Whip

Makes 8 servings

2 envelopes unflavored gelatin
¹/₂ cup cold water
¹/₄ cup honey ▲
12-oz. can unsweetened peach or apricot nectar ▲
2 tsp. lemon juice
3 egg whites

▲ *SUGAR TIP—Replace honey with sugar substitute to taste. Check nectar label for added sugar.*

Combine gelatin and water in a saucepan. Wait 1 minute, then cook over low heat, stirring constantly, until gelatin dissolves. Remove from heat. Stir in honey, peach nectar, and lemon juice. Chill, stirring occasionally until mixture is syrupy-thick. Add egg whites to gelatin. Beat at high speed with electric mixer until light and fluffy. Chill until firm.

	Per Serving
Calories	67.1
Carbohydrate (g)	14.4
Protein (g)	3.1
Total Fat (g)	0.0
Saturated Fat (g)	0.0
Cholesterol (mg)	0.0
Sodium (mg)	20.5

Homemade Fat-Free Strawberry Ice Milk

Makes 8 servings
2 tsp. unflavored gelatin
1 cup cold water
3/4 cup instant dry nonfat milk crystals
1 1/2 cups skim milk
2/3 cup sugar ▲
2 tsp. vanilla
1 tbsp. lemon juice
1 cup fresh or frozen unsweetened strawberries, mashed or pureed

▲ SUGAR TIP—Use equivalent sugar substitute.

Soften the gelatin in 1/2 cup of the cold water. Combine 1/4 cup of the milk crystals with the skim milk and heat gently in a saucepan. Add the gelatin mixture and heat until dissolved. Stir in 1/2 cup sugar until dissolved. Stir in vanilla. Chill until slightly thickened. Beat remaining 1/2 cup milk crystals with remaining 1/2 cup cold water until it begins to thicken slightly. Add the lemon juice and remaining sugar and beat 5 minutes or until the consistency of whipped cream. Fold in the chilled gelatin mixture. Spoon into refrigerator trays. Freeze until the edges are set. Remove to mixer bowl and beat on high speed until fluffy. Cover and freeze until firm. Allow to soften slightly before serving.

Hints: For Vanilla Ice Milk, omit strawberries.

For Banana Ice Milk, substitute 2 very ripe bananas, mashed, for strawberries.

For Chocolate Ice Milk, omit strawberries. Add 3 tbsp. unsweetened cocoa and 3 additional tbsp. sugar (or equivalent sugar substitute) when adding the 1/2 cup sugar to the warm milk mixture.

	Per Serving
Calories	116.5
Carbohydrate (g)	24.6
Protein (g)	4.4
Total Fat (g)	0.0
Saturated Fat (g)	0.0
Cholesterol (mg)	2.3
Sodium (mg)	58.0

Pronto Orange Ice

Makes 4 servings
4-serving envelope regular or low-calorie orange flavored gelatin dessert mix ● ▲
1/2 cup hot water
1 cup orange juice

● SODIUM TIP—Use low-sodium gelatin dessert mix.

▲ SUGAR TIP—Use sugar-free gelatin dessert mix.

Dissolve gelatin mix in hot water. Stir in orange juice. Pour into shallow container; freeze until slushy. Remove to mixer bowl; beat on high speed until fluffy. Cover and freeze firm. Soften slightly before serving.

	Per Serving
Calories	109.3
Carbohydrate (g)	25.9
Protein (g)	2.4
Total Fat (g)	0.1
Saturated Fat (g)	0.0
Cholesterol (mg)	0.0
Sodium (mg)	68.0

Chocolate Pudding

Makes 4 servings
2 cups skim milk
2 tbsp. unsweetened cocoa
3 tbsp. sugar ▲
2 1/2 tbsp. cornstarch
1/4 tsp. salt ● (optional)
2 tsp. vanilla

● SODIUM TIP—Omit added salt.

▲ SUGAR TIP—Use equivalent sugar substitute; add after cooking, along with the vanilla.

Scald 1 1/2 cups of the milk. Combine the cocoa, sugar, cornstarch, and salt. Blend the remaining 1/2 cup cold milk into cocoa mixture. Mix well. Stir into the scalded milk. Cook over very low heat, stirring constantly, until the mixture is thick. Remove from heat. Stir in vanilla. Cool. Spoon into 4 individual dessert dishes and chill.

	Per Serving
Calories	108.3
Carbohydrate (g)	22.4
Protein (g)	5.2
Total Fat (g)	0.3
Saturated Fat (g)	0.1
Cholesterol (mg)	2.5
Sodium (mg)	63.7

Fresh Fruit Bavarian Cream

Makes 8 servings
Graham Cracker Crust, baked (recipe on page 111)
1 cup evaporated skim milk
2 4-serving packages regular or low-calorie gelatin dessert mix (any flavor) ● ▲
Pinch salt ● (optional)
1 1/2 cups boiling water
1 cup sliced fresh strawberries or other fruit

● *SODIUM TIP—Omit added salt. Use low-sodium gelatin dessert mix.*

▲ *SUGAR TIP—Use sugar-free gelatin dessert mix.*

Prepare Graham Cracker Crust in an 8- or 9-inch pie pan. Set aside to cool. Pour evaporated skim milk into ice cube tray or metal mixing bowl. Put in freezer until ice crystals begin to form around edges. (Chill beater blades in freezer also.) Dissolve gelatin mix and salt in boiling water. Chill until syrupy. Beat the chilled skim milk at high speed until stiff, about 8 to 10 minutes. Gently but thoroughly fold milk into gelatin mixture until well blended. Arrange fruit in bottom of pie shell. Cover with filling. Refrigerate several hours until set.

Hint: For Bavarian Cream Parfaits, omit pie crust; layer fruit and filling in 6 parfait glasses. Chill until set.

	Per Serving
Calories	161.8
Carbohydrate (g)	30.0
Protein (g)	5.1
Total Fat (g)	3.1
Saturated Fat (g)	0.6
Cholesterol (mg)	1.3
Sodium (mg)	197.5

Fresh Blueberry Pie

Makes 8 servings
4 cups fresh blueberries
3 tbsp. honey ▲ (optional)
1 1/2 tbsp. cornstarch
Pinch salt ● (optional)
Lean Pie Crust, prebaked (recipe in this section)

● *SODIUM TIP—Omit salt.*

▲ *SUGAR TIP—Use equivalent sugar substitute in place of honey, or omit.*

In a nonstick saucepan, combine 2 cups of the berries with honey, cornstarch, and salt. Simmer over low heat for 10 minutes, stirring occasionally, until berries are soft and slightly thickened. Remove from heat and stir in remaining raw blueberries. Allow to cool. Spoon into crust and chill thoroughly.

	Per Serving
Calories	100.8
Carbohydrate (g)	17.6
Protein (g)	1.3
Total Fat (g)	3.6
Saturated Fat (g)	0.5
Cholesterol (mg)	0.0
Sodium (mg)	133.2

One-Crust Apple Pie

Makes 8 servings
Lean Pie Crust (recipe on page 112)
5 cups thinly-sliced pared cooking apples
3/4 cup white raisins
3 tbsp. honey ▲ (optional)
1 tsp. lemon juice
1 tbsp. cornstarch
Pinch salt ● (optional)
1 tsp. apple pie spice or:
1/2 tsp. ground cinnamon, 1/4 tsp. ground nutmeg, and 1/4 tsp. allspice.

● *SODIUM TIP—Omit added salt.*

▲ *SUGAR TIP—Use equivalent sugar substitute in place of honey, or omit.*

Line an 8-inch nonstick pie pan with pastry. Combine remaining ingredients and mix well. Turn into pastry-lined pie plate. Cut a foil circle large enough to cover apples but not pastry or invert another pie pan over filling. Bake in a preheated 375° oven 1 hour or until apples are tender.

	Per Serving
Calories	130.8
Carbohydrate (g)	26.5
Protein (g)	1.3
Total Fat (g)	3.3
Saturated Fat (g)	0.5
Cholesterol (mg)	0.0
Sodium (mg)	137.0

Slim and Speedy Chocolate Cream Pie

Makes 8 servings
Graham Cracker Crust
(recipe on this page)
2 envelopes unflavored
gelatin
1¹/₂ cups skim milk
¹/₂ cup boiling water
¹/₄ cup sugar ▲
2 tbsp. unsweetened cocoa
2 tsp. vanilla
1 pint chocolate low-fat ice
milk ▲

▲ *SUGAR TIP—Replace sugar with equivalent sugar substitute. Substitute sugar-free dietetic frozen dessert for ice milk.*

Prepare Graham Cracker Crust in an 8- or 9-inch pie plate. Set aside to cool. Combine gelatin and ¹/₃ cup of the skim milk in container of blender. Wait 1 minute, then add boiling water. Cover and blend until gelatin is completely dissolved. Add remaining milk, sugar, cocoa, and vanilla; cover and blend. Add ice milk; cover and blend until smooth and creamy. Refrigerate a few minutes until mixture thickens. Fill pie crust with chilled filling. Chill until completely set.

Hint: For Chocolate Mini-Mousse, omit pie crust; spoon filling into 6 dessert cups or a large bowl. Chill until set.

	Per Serving
Calories	152.9
Carbohydrate (g)	23.0
Protein (g)	5.7
Total Fat (g)	4.9
Saturated Fat (g)	1.6
Cholesterol (mg)	7.4
Sodium (mg)	142.4

Angel Pie Shell

Makes 8 servings
2 egg whites
Pinch salt ● or cream of
tartar
¹/₂ tsp. vanilla
7 tbsp. sugar

● *SODIUM TIP—Use cream of tartar.*

With an electric mixer, beat egg whites in nonplastic bowl until frothy. Add salt or cream of tartar. Beat until soft peaks form. Add vanilla. Beat in sugar, 1 tbsp. at a time. Continue beating until stiff peaks form. Spread meringue on bottom and sides of a 9-inch nonstick pie pan which has been sprayed with cooking spray. Bake in preheated 275° oven 1 hour or until crisp. Turn off oven. Leave shell in the oven 30 minutes; remove and cool. (Pile shell with fresh fruit, frozen yogurt, or low-fat ice milk, or use as a base for refrigerator pie filling.)

	Per Serving
Calories	46.6
Carbohydrate (g)	11.2
Protein (g)	1.0
Total Fat (g)	0.0
Saturated Fat (g)	0.0
Cholesterol (mg)	0.0
Sodium (mg)	45.3

Graham Cracker Crust

Makes 8 servings
³/₄ cup plain graham
cracker crumbs ● ▲
3 tbsp. diet margarine,
softened ● ■

● *SODIUM TIP—Use low-sodium graham crackers or low-sodium cookies to make crumbs. Use unsalted margarine.*

■ *CHOLESTEROL TIP—Use polyunsaturated margarine.*

▲ *SUGAR TIP—Use sugar-free cookies to make crumbs.*

Fork-blend crumbs and margarine thoroughly. Press mixture firmly and evenly onto the bottom and sides of nonstick 8- or 9-inch pie plate for pie crust or 8-inch springform pan for cheesecake crust.

For pie crust, bake in a preheated 400° oven 5 minutes. Cool before filling. For cheesecake, chill un-baked crust about 45 minutes before filling.

	Per Serving
Calories	49.4
Carbohydrate (g)	5.8
Protein (g)	0.6
Total Fat (g)	3.0
Saturated Fat (g)	0.6
Cholesterol (mg)	0.0
Sodium (mg)	94.7

Lean Pie Crust

Makes 8 servings

1/2 **cup sifted all-purpose flour**
1/4 **tsp. salt** ●
1/4 **tsp. baking powder** ●
1/4 **cup diet margarine at room temperature** ● ■

● *SODIUM TIP—Omit added salt and baking powder. Use unsalted margarine.*

■ *CHOLESTEROL TIP—Use polyunsaturated margarine.*

Stir flour, salt, and baking powder together. Add margarine. Cut in with fork or pastry blender and continue mixing until no pastry sticks to the sides of the bowl. Shape into a ball. Wrap and refrigerate to chill for an hour or more. Roll the dough out on a floured board. If prebaking, heat oven to 425° and bake about 12 minutes, until golden. This recipe makes single crust to line an 8- or 9- inch pie plate. For a 2-crust pie, double the recipe.

	Per Serving
Calories	51.3
Carbohydrate (g)	5.5
Protein (g)	0.8
Total Fat (g)	3.1
Saturated Fat (g)	0.5
Cholesterol (mg)	0.0
Sodium (mg)	132.0

Blueberry Topping

Makes about 1 1/2 cups

1 **pint fresh or frozen unsweetened blueberries**
2 **tbsp. sugar** ▲
1 **tsp. cornstarch**
1/4 **tsp. ground cinnamon**

▲ *SUGAR TIP—Omit sugar; after cooking, stir in equivalent sugar substitute.*

Combine all ingredients in small saucepan. Cook and stir 2 minutes over low heat. Cool completely.

	Per Tablespoon
Calories	14.8
Carbohydrate (g)	3.7
Protein (g)	0.1
Total Fat (g)	0.1
Saturated Fat (g)	0.0
Cholesterol (mg)	0.0
Sodium (mg)	0.2

Fruit Glaze for Cheesecake or Pie

Makes 8 servings

1 **tbsp. cornstarch**
1 **cup unsweetened peach juice, or other unsweetened fruit juice**
Sugar to taste ▲ **(optional)**
2 **cups sliced fresh peaches, or other sliced fruit or whole berries**

▲ *SUGAR TIP—Use sugar substitute to taste.*

Blend cornstarch with juice in small saucepan. Cook over low heat, stirring constantly, until clear and thickened. Add sugar; stir until sugar is dissolved. Set aside to cool. Arrange peach slices on top of cheesecake or pie. Spoon sauce over fruit.

	Per Serving
Calories	34.5
Carbohydrate (g)	8.7
Protein (g)	0.3
Total Fat (g)	0.2
Saturated Fat (g)	0.0
Cholesterol (mg)	0.0
Sodium (mg)	0.8

Whipped Milk Topping

Makes 2 cups

2/3 **cup evaporated skim milk**
3 **tbsp. sugar** ▲
2 **tsp. vanilla**

▲ *SUGAR TIP—Use equivalent sugar substitute.*

Pour milk into ice cube tray. Chill in freezer until slushy. Scrape the slushy milk into pre-chilled mixing bowl. Using pre-chilled beaters, beat at high speed until fluffy. Add sugar and vanilla; beat until stiff. (Serve as topping on plain cake, fruit, gelatin, or other desserts.)

	Per Tablespoon
Calories	9.4
Carbohydrate (g)	1.9
Protein (g)	0.4
Total Fat (g)	0.0
Saturated Fat (g)	0.0
Cholesterol (mg)	0.2
Sodium (mg)	5.8

Strawberry Topping

Makes 6 servings

2 cups fresh or frozen whole unsweetened strawberries

3/4 cup water

Combine ingredients in blender and cover. Turn blender on and off repeatedly until coarsely chopped. (Spoon over low-fat cottage cheese, ice milk, or fruit.)

	Per Serving
Calories	18.3
Carbohydrate (g)	4.3
Protein (g)	0.3
Total Fat (g)	0.3
Saturated Fat (g)	0.0
Cholesterol (mg)	0.0
Sodium (mg)	0.3

Quick Dessert Sauce

Makes 2 1/2 cups

2 1/2 cups skim milk

4-serving envelope regular or low-calorie pudding mix, any flavor ● ▲

● *SODIUM TIP—Use low-sodium pudding mix.*

▲ *SUGAR TIP—Use sugar-free pudding mix.*

Stir the milk into the pudding mix in a nonstick saucepan. Cook and stir over low heat until the mixture simmers and thickens. (Use hot or cold over fruit, ice milk, or frozen yogurt.) Store covered in refrigerator.

	Per Tablespoon
Calories	15.8
Carbohydrate (g)	3.3
Protein (g)	0.6
Total Fat (g)	0.1
Saturated Fat (g)	0.1
Cholesterol (mg)	0.3
Sodium (mg)	20.6

Easy Strawberry Preserves

Makes about 2 cups

1 pint strawberries, hulled

1 cup cold water

4-serving envelope regular or low-calorie strawberry gelatin dessert mix ● ▲

● *SODIUM TIP—Use low-sodium gelatin dessert mix.*

▲ *SUGAR TIP—Use sugar-free gelatin dessert mix.*

Crush the strawberries in a saucepan. Add the water and gelatin dessert mix. Cook and stir until gelatin is completely dissolved. Simmer gently, uncovered, for 2 minutes. Pour into 3 jelly jars. Cover and store in refrigerator.

	Per Tablespoon
Calories	13.6
Carbohydrate (g)	3.2
Protein (g)	0.3
Total Fat (g)	0.5
Saturated Fat (g)	0.0
Cholesterol (mg)	0.0
Sodium (mg)	8.5

Cocoa Kisses

Makes about 8 dozen

3 egg whites

1/2 tsp. cream of tartar

1 cup sugar

2 tbsp. unsweetened cocoa

Beat the egg whites until foamy. Add cream of tartar; beat until soft peaks form. Gradually beat in sugar, a few tablespoons at a time. Beat until stiff. Fold in cocoa. Drop batter by level teaspoonful on nonstick cookie sheets which have been sprayed with cooking spray. Bake in a preheated 275° oven 18 to 20 minutes. Cool before removing from pans. Store in a very dry place.

	Per Serving
Calories	8.8
Carbohydrate (g)	2.2
Protein (g)	0.2
Total Fat (g)	0.0
Saturated Fat (g)	0.0
Cholesterol (mg)	0.0
Sodium (mg)	2.6

Maple Baked Pears

Makes 8 servings

4 fresh ripe pears (D'Anjou or Bosc), cored, cut into halves
1 tbsp. lemon juice
1/2 cup water
8 tsp. maple syrup or honey ▲
1/4 tsp. ground cinnamon or apple pie spice

▲ *SUGAR TIP—Use dietetic syrup.*

Place pears cut-side down in baking pan. Add lemon juice and water. Bake in a preheated 350° oven for 10 minutes. Turn pears cut-side up and spoon 1 tsp. maple syrup in center of each pair. Sprinkle with cinnamon and bake 8 to 10 minutes longer, basting occasionally.

	Per Serving
Calories	79.1
Carbohydrate (g)	20.1
Protein (g)	0.7
Total Fat (g)	0.4
Saturated Fat (g)	0.0
Cholesterol (mg)	0.0
Sodium (mg)	2.5

Strawberries a l'Orange

Makes 4 servings

1 pint ripe fresh strawberries
3 oz. frozen unsweetened orange juice concentrate, defrosted, undiluted
1 tbsp. orange liqueur ▲

▲ *SUGAR TIP—Omit liqueur; add a little sugar substitute, if desired.*

Wash and hull the berries; leave whole. Combine with orange juice and liqueur; mix well. Chill. Spoon into 4 stemmed wine glasses.

	Per Serving
Calories	89.0
Carbohydrate (g)	19.1
Protein (g)	1.2
Total Fat (g)	0.4
Saturated Fat (g)	0.0
Cholesterol (mg)	0.0
Sodium (mg)	1.3

Cantaloupe Compote

Makes 6 servings

1 large ripe cantaloupe
1 cup fresh blueberries
6 tbsp. unsweetened frozen pineapple juice concentrate, defrosted, undiluted

Make melon balls with melon ball cutter. Combine with remaining ingredients in a bowl. Cover and chill.

	Per Serving
Calories	72.5
Carbohydrate (g)	17.9
Protein (g)	1.9
Total Fat (g)	0.3
Saturated Fat (g)	0.0
Cholesterol (mg)	0.0
Sodium (mg)	11.3

Cherry Yogurt Jubilee

Makes 8 servings

1 qt. low-fat vanilla frozen yogurt ▲
16-oz. can juice-packed pitted dark red cherries, undrained
2 tsp. cornstarch or arrowroot
Few drops red food coloring (optional)
3 tbsp. brandy

▲ *SUGAR TIP—Substitute low-fat, sugar-free vanilla ice milk for the frozen yogurt.*

Scoop yogurt into 8 sherbet glasses (place in freezer until serving time). Combine cherries, cornstarch, and food coloring in a chafing dish. Stir over moderate flame until sauce simmers and clears. Pour brandy on the sauce. Carefully ignite the vapors with a long match. Spoon flaming cherries over yogurt and serve immediately.

	Per Serving
Calories	123.8
Carbohydrate (g)	21.6
Protein (g)	4.0
Total Fat (g)	2.1
Saturated Fat (g)	0.9
Cholesterol (mg)	5.5
Sodium (mg)	64.6

Peaches Jubilee

Makes 4 servings

16-oz. can juice-packed peach halves, drained, juice reserved
1 tsp. cornstarch or arrowroot
1 jigger heated brandy

Combine reserved peach juice with cornstarch in small saucepan. Cook and stir over low heat until sauce simmers and thickens. Add peach halves and simmer until thoroughly heated through. Arrange peach halves in chafing dish or on platter, cut-side up. Cover with sauce; add heated brandy. Light and serve flaming.

	Per Serving
Calories	83.4
Carbohydrate (g)	13.4
Protein (g)	0.9
Total Fat (g)	0.1
Saturated Fat (g)	0.0
Cholesterol (mg)	0.0
Sodium (mg)	9.3

Blushing Pears

Makes 4 servings

16-oz. can juice-packed pear halves, drained, juice reserved
1/2 cup red Concord wine
1/2 cup unsweetened orange juice
1/4 tsp. apple pie spice

Arrange the pears in 4 individual stemmed glasses. Combine pear juice with remaining ingredients in a saucepan and bring to a boil. Lower heat and simmer, uncovered, until reduced by half. Remove from heat; let cool slightly. Pour liquid over the pears. Chill before serving.

	Per Serving
Calories	95.3
Carbohydrate (g)	19.5
Protein (g)	0.5
Total Fat (g)	0.3
Saturated Fat (g)	0.0
Cholesterol (mg)	0.0
Sodium (mg)	10.4

Baked Apples Stuffed with Raisins

Makes 6 servings

1/2 cup raisins
1/2 cup white wine or unsweetened fruit juice
6 baking apples, cored

Combine wine and raisins in small bowl; let soak 1 hour. Drain raisins and reserve wine. Stuff apples with raisins. Stand apples in baking pan just large enough to hold them. Pour on reserved wine. Bake in preheated 350° oven, basting frequently with wine, about 20 to 25 minutes.

	Per Serving
Calories	131.6
Carbohydrate (g)	30.2
Protein (g)	0.6
Total Fat (g)	0.8
Saturated Fat (g)	0.0
Cholesterol (mg)	0.0
Sodium (mg)	4.9

Honey Glazed Pears

Makes 8 servings

4 fresh ripe pears (D'Anjou or Bosc)
2 tbsp. honey
1/2 cup water

Halve and core pears; don't pare them. Combine honey and water in a skillet. Place pear halves cut-side down in skillet. Cover and simmer for 6 to 8 minutes. Uncover; turn pear halves cut-side up and continue to simmer 10 to 15 minutes, basting often. Serve warm or chilled.

	Per Serving
Calories	77.3
Carbohydrate (g)	19.6
Protein (g)	0.7
Total Fat (g)	0.4
Saturated Fat (g)	0.0
Cholesterol (mg)	0.0
Sodium (mg)	2.2

Fresh Raspberry Jam

Makes about 2 cups

1 tbsp. unflavored gelatin
2 tbsp. cold water
3 pints fresh raspberries, or other fresh berries, crushed
1 cup sugar (or less, to taste) ▲
1¹/₂ tbsp. lemon juice
¹/₂ cup liquid pectin

▲ *SUGAR TIP—Omit sugar; after heating, stir in equivalent sugar substitute.*

Soften the gelatin in the cold water. Combine berries with sugar and lemon juice in a saucepan. Heat to boiling. Cook and stir for 1 minute. Stir in pectin and gelatin. Boil for 3 minutes, stirring constantly. Pour into jelly jars. Cover and store in refrigerator.

	Per Tablespoon
Calories	42.9
Carbohydrate (g)	10.7
Protein (g)	0.6
Total Fat (g)	0.2
Saturated Fat (g)	0.0
Cholesterol (mg)	0.0
Sodium (mg)	0.5

Pureed Pineapple Preserves

Makes about 2 cups

16-oz. can juice-packed crushed pineapple, drained, juice reserved
1 envelope unflavored gelatin

Pour reserved juice into a small saucepan. Sprinkle gelatin on juice. Heat gelatin-juice mixture over low heat, only until gelatin melts. Pour into blender; add crushed pineapple. Cover and blend until smooth. Spoon into jars. Cover and store in refrigerator or freezer.

	Per Tablespoon
Calories	9.5
Carbohydrate (g)	2.2
Protein (g)	0.3
Total Fat (g)	0.1
Saturated Fat (g)	0.0
Cholesterol (mg)	0.0
Sodium (mg)	0.4

Grape Jelly

Makes 1¹/₂ cups

1 envelope unflavored gelatin
³/₄ cup cold water
6-oz. can frozen grape juice concentrate, defrosted, undiluted

Sprinkle gelatin on cold water in a saucepan; wait until softened, about 1 minute. Add grape juice concentrate. Cook and stir until mixture boils. Store in a covered jar in refrigerator.

	Per Tablespoon
Calories	17.5
Carbohydrate (g)	4.2
Protein (g)	0.3
Total Fat (g)	0.0
Saturated Fat (g)	0.0
Cholesterol (mg)	0.0
Sodium (mg)	0.5

Peach Jam

Makes about 4 cups

3 cans (16 oz. each) juice-packed sliced peaches, drained, juice reserved
1 envelope unflavored gelatin
¹/₂ cup sugar ▲

▲ *SUGAR TIP—Omit sugar; add equivalent sugar substitute to gelatin mixture after cooking.*

Puree drained peaches in blender. Measure puree; add enough reserved juice to make 3 cups. Set aside. Measure another ¹/₄ cup reserved juice into a saucepan. Sprinkle gelatin on juice. When gelatin is softened, add sugar and heat to boiling, stirring until gelatin is completely dissolved. Combine with peach puree. Store in covered jars in refrigerator or freezer.

	Per Tablespoon
Calories	16.7
Carbohydrate (g)	4.0
Protein (g)	0.3
Total Fat (g)	0.0
Saturated Fat (g)	0.0
Cholesterol (mg)	0.0
Sodium (mg)	1.8

Cholesterol & Fat Counter

To help you choose low-cholesterol, low-fat foods, we have included this counter. The counter lists the calorie, total fat, and cholesterol content of hundreds of common foods, including generic foods, brand name items, and fast foods.

You will find the individual food items grouped into categories, like "Beverages" and "Poultry," which are listed in alphabetical order. After the description of each item, you will find a specific portion size. The values listed for calories, total fat, and cholesterol are for the portion size listed.

The total fat for each item is listed in grams (g). If you've already figured out how many grams of fat you should be consuming each day using the charts in Chapter 12, you can simply add up the grams of fat contained in all the items you'll be eating to determine if you are within your limit.

If you have not figured out how many grams of fat you should be eating each day, you can use the calorie and fat information provided for a particular food to determine if it is too high in fat for your diet. To do this: 1) multiply the grams of fat by nine; 2) divide the result by the total number of calories in the food; and 3) multiply by 100. This will tell you what percent of that item's calories comes from fat. If the answer is well above 30 percent, the food is high in fat. If you still want to include that product, try to eat other foods that day that are much lower in fat. The main point to remember is that, overall, your diet should provide you with less than 30 percent of your total calories as fat. Cutting out or cutting back on those foods that are high in fat—especially saturated fat—can help you reach your cholesterol-lowering goals.

Keep in mind, too, that decreasing your total fat intake should help you decrease your saturated fat intake and control your weight. Since animal products generally contain more saturated fats than do vegetable products, it's better to cut down on high-fat foods from animal sources and choose more foods from plant sources to reach your dietary fat goals. You'll find more information on cutting back on foods that are high in saturated fat in Chapter 12. For more information on methods designed specifically to help you keep track of the saturated fat content of the foods in your diet, check the program reviews in Chapter 5.

The cholesterol content of food items is listed in milligrams (mg). Remember that in terms of cholesterol, you should limit your total daily intake to less than 300 mg. So when you're planning meals, be sure to pay attention to how both the fat and cholesterol content will fit into your dietary plan.

Values in this counter were obtained from the United States Department of Agriculture and from food labels, manufacturers, and processors. While every effort has been made to ensure that these values are accurate and current at the time of printing, changes in values can occur at the time of food processing. Some food items have an "na" or a "tr" listed in one of the columns. The "na" means that the content was unavailable to us at the time of printing. The "tr" means that the food item contains only trace amounts of the substance.

Baked Goods

FOOD/PORTION SIZE	CAL	FAT (g)	CHOL (mg)
CAKE			
Angelfood, enriched mix, tube cake, 1 piece ($^1/_{12}$ cake)	125	tr	0
Carrot, with cream cheese frosting, home recipe, 1 piece ($^1/_{16}$ cake)	385	21	74
Carrot, with cream cheese frosting, home recipe, whole 10-in. diameter tube cake	6,175	328	1,183
Cheesecake, 1 piece ($^1/_{12}$ cake)	280	18	170
Cheesecake, whole 9-in. diameter cake	3,350	213	2,053
Coffeecake, crumb, 1 piece ($^1/_6$ cake)	230	7	47
Coffeecake, crumb, $7^3/_4 \times 5^5/_8 \times 1^1/_4$-in. cake	1,385	41	279
Devil's food, with chocolate frosting, 1 $2^1/_2$-in. cupcake	120	4	19
Devil's food, with chocolate frosting, 1 piece ($^1/_{16}$ cake)	235	8	37
Devil's food, with chocolate frosting, 2-layer cake	3,755	136	598
Fruitcake, dark, home recipe, 1 piece ($^1/_{32}$ cake)	165	7	20
Fruitcake, dark, home recipe, $7^1/_2$-in. tube cake	5,185	228	640
Gingerbread, 1 piece ($^1/_9$ cake)	175	4	1
Gingerbread, 8-in. square cake	1,575	39	6
Pound, 1 slice ($^1/_{17}$ loaf)	120	5	32
Pound, $8^1/_2 \times 3^1/_2 \times 3^1/_4$-in. loaf	2,025	94	555
Pound, commercial, 1 loaf	1,935	94	1,100
Pound, commercial, 1 slice ($^1/_{17}$ loaf)	110	5	64
Sheet, plain, without frosting, 1 piece ($^1/_9$ cake)	315	12	61
Sheet, plain, without frosting, 9-in. square cake	2,830	108	552
Sheet, plain, with uncooked white frosting, 1 piece ($^1/_9$ cake)	445	14	70
Sheet, plain, with uncooked white frosting, 9-in. square cake	4,020	129	636
Snack, devil's food cream filled, 1 cake (2/pk)	105	4	15
Snack, sponge cream filled, 1 cake (2/pk)	155	5	7
White, with white frosting, commercial, 1 piece ($^1/_{16}$ cake)	260	9	3
White, with white frosting, commercial, 2-layer cake	4,170	148	46
Yellow, with chocolate frosting, commercial, 1 piece ($^1/_{16}$ cake)	245	11	38
Yellow, with chocolate frosting, commercial, 2-layer cake	3,895	175	609
Yellow, with chocolate frosting, enriched mix, 1 piece ($^1/_{16}$ cake)	235	8	36
Yellow, with chocolate frosting, enriched mix, 2-layer cake	3,735	125	576
COOKIES			
Animal Crackers, Barnum's, 11 cookies	130	4	na
Chocolate chip, commercial, 4 cookies	180	9	5
Chocolate chip, home recipe, 4 cookies	185	11	18
Chocolate chip, refrigerated dough, 4 cookies	225	11	22
Oatmeal Chocolate Chip, Almost Home, 2 cookies	130	5	na
Oatmeal, with raisins, 4 cookies	245	10	2
Oreo, 3 cookies	140	6	na
Oreo, Double Stuff, 2 cookies	140	7	na
Peanut Butter Fudge, Almost Home, 2 cookies	140	7	na
Peanut butter, home recipe, 4 cookies	245	14	22
Sandwich (chocolate or vanilla), 4 cookies	195	8	0
Shortbread, commercial, 4 small cookies	155	8	27
Shortbread, home recipe, 2 large cookies	145	8	0
Shortbread, Lorna Doone, 4 cookies	140	7	na
Sugar, refrigerated dough, 4 cookies	235	12	29
Wafers, vanilla, 10 cookies	185	7	25
PASTRY			
Danish, fruit, $4^1/_4$-in. round, 1 pastry	235	13	56
Danish, plain, 1 oz.	110	6	24
Danish, plain, $4^1/_4$-in. round, 1 pastry	220	12	49
Danish, plain, 12-oz. packaged ring, 1 ring	1,305	71	292
Toaster, 1 pastry	210	6	0
PIE			
Apple, crust made with enriched flour and vegetable shortening, 1 piece ($^1/_6$ pie)	405	18	0
Apple, crust made with enriched flour and vegetable shortening, 9-in. pie	2,420	105	0

FOOD/PORTION SIZE	CAL	FAT (g)	CHOL (mg)
Blueberry, crust made with enriched flour and vegetable shortening, 1 piece (1/6 pie)	380	17	0
Blueberry, crust made with enriched flour and vegetable shortening, 9-in. pie	2,285	102	0
Cherry, crust made with enriched flour and vegetable shortening, 1 piece (1/6 pie)	410	18	0
Cherry, crust made with enriched flour and vegetable shortening, 9-in. pie	2,465	107	0
Chocolate Mousse Pie, Jell-O, made with whole milk, 1/8 pie	250	15	30
Coconut Cream Pie, Jell-O, made with whole milk, 1/8 pie	260	17	30
Creme, crust made with enriched flour and vegetable shortening, 1 piece (1/6 pie)	455	23	8
Creme, crust made with enriched flour and vegetable shortening, 9-in. pie	2,710	139	46
Custard, crust made with enriched flour and vegetable shortening, 1 piece (1/6 pie)	330	17	169
Custard, crust made with enriched flour and vegetable shortening, 9-in. pie	1,985	101	1,010
Lemon meringue, crust made with enriched flour and vegetable shortening, 1 piece (1/6 pie)	355	14	143
Lemon meringue, crust made with enriched flour and vegetable shortening, 9-in. pie	2,140	86	857
Peach, crust made with enriched flour and vegetable shortening, 1 piece (1/6 pie)	405	17	0
Peach, crust made with enriched flour and vegetable shortening, 9-in. pie	2,410	101	0
Pecan, crust made with enriched flour and vegetable shortening, 1 piece (1/6 pie)	575	32	95
Pecan, crust made with enriched flour and vegetable shortening, 9-in. pie	3,450	189	569
Piecrust, home recipe, made with enriched flour and vegetable shortening, 9-in. shell	900	60	0
Piecrust, mix, 9-in., 2-crust pie	1,485	93	0
Pumpkin, crust made with enriched flour and vegetable shortening, 1 piece (1/6 pie)	320	17	109
Pumpkin, crust made with enriched flour and vegetable shortening, 9-in. pie	1,920	102	655

FOOD/PORTION SIZE	CAL	FAT (g)	CHOL (mg)
MISCELLANEOUS			
Brownies, Fudge 'n Nut, Almost Home, 1 brownie	160	7	na
Brownies, with nuts and frosting, commercial, 1 brownie	100	4	14
Brownies, with nuts and frosting, home recipe, 1 brownie	95	6	18
Doughnuts, cake, plain, 1 doughnut	210	1	20
Doughnuts, yeast, glazed, 1 doughnut	235	13	21
Fig bars, square/rectangular, 4 cookies	210	4	27

Baking Products & Condiments

FOOD/PORTION SIZE	CAL	FAT (g)	CHOL (mg)
Bacos, 2 tsp.	25	1	0
Baking powder for home use, 1 tsp.	5	0	0
Baking soda for home use, 1 tsp.	5	0	0
Barbecue Sauce, Hickory Smoke Flavor, Kraft, 2 tbsp.	40	1	0
Barbecue Sauce, Hickory Smoke, Open Pit, 1 tbsp.	25	0	0
Barbecue Sauce, Hot, Kraft, 2 tbsp.	40	1	0
Barbecue Sauce, Hot 'n Tangy, Open Pit, 1 tbsp.	25	0	0
Barbecue Sauce, Italian Seasonings, Kraft, 2 tbsp.	45	1	0
Barbecue Sauce, Kansas City Style, 2 tbsp.	45	1	0
Barbecue Sauce, Kraft, 2 tbsp.	40	1	0
Barbecue Sauce, Mesquite 'n Tangy, Open Pit, 1 tbsp.	25	0	0
Barbecue Sauce, Mesquite Smoke, Kraft, 2 tbsp.	45	1	0
Barbecue Sauce, Onion Bits, Kraft, 2 tbsp.	50	1	0
Barbecue Sauce, Original, Open Pit, 1 tbsp.	25	0	0
Barbecue Sauce, Original with Minced Onions, Open Pit, 1 tbsp.	25	0	0
Barbecue Sauce, Sweet 'n Tangy, Open Pit, 1 tbsp.	25	0	0
Barbecue Sauce, Thick'n Spicy, Chunky, Kraft, 2 tbsp.	50	1	0

FOOD/PORTION SIZE	CAL	FAT (g)	CHOL (mg)
Barbecue Sauce, Thick'n Spicy Hickory Smoked, Kraft, 2 tbsp.	50	1	0
Barbecue Sauce, Thick'n Spicy Kansas City Style, Kraft, 2 tbsp.	60	1	0
Barbecue Sauce, Thick'n Spicy Original, Kraft, 2 tbsp.	50	1	0
Barbecue Sauce, Thick'n Spicy with Honey, Kraft, 2 tbsp.	60	1	0
Barbecue Sauce, Thick 'n Tangy Hickory, Open Pit, 1 tbsp.	25	0	0
Barley, pearled, light, uncooked, 1 cup	700	2	0
Bulgur, uncooked, 1 cup	600	3	0
Butterscotch Topping, Artificially Flavored, Kraft, 1 tbsp.	60	1	0
Caramel Topping, Kraft, 1 tbsp.	60	0	0
Catsup, 1 tbsp.	15	tr	0
Catsup, Weight Watchers, 1 tbsp.	8	0	na
Celery seed, 1 tsp.	10	1	0
Chili powder, 1 tsp.	10	tr	0
Chocolate Caramel Topping, Kraft, 1 tbsp.	60	0	0
Chocolate Chips, Real, Semi-Sweet, Baker's, 1/4 cup	200	12	0
Chocolate Flavored Chips, Semi-Sweet, Baker's, 1/4 cup	190	9	0
Chocolate, German's Sweet Chocolate, Baker's, 1 oz.	140	10	0
Chocolate, Semi-Sweet, Baker's, 1 oz.	140	8	0
Chocolate Topping, Kraft, 1 tbsp.	50	0	0
Chocolate, Unsweetened, Baker's, 1 oz.	140	15	0
Cinnamon, 1 tsp.	5	tr	0
Cocktail Sauce, Sauceworks, 1 tbsp.	12	0	0
Coconut, Angel Flake, Baker's, (bag) 1/3 cup	120	8	0
Coconut, Angel Flake, Baker's, (can) 1/3 cup	110	9	0
Coconut, Premium Shred, Baker's, 1/3 cup	140	9	0
Cornmeal, bolted, dry, 1 cup	440	4	0
Cornmeal, degermed, enriched, cooked, 1 cup	120	tr	0
Cornmeal, degermed, enriched, dry, 1 cup	500	2	0
Cornmeal, whole-ground, unbolted, dry, 1 cup	435	5	0
Curry powder, 1 tsp.	5	tr	0
Flour, buckwheat, light; sifted, 1 cup	340	1	0
Flour, cake/pastry, enriched, sifted, spooned, 1 cup	350	1	0
Flour, carob, 1 cup	255	tr	0
Flour, self-rising, enriched, unsifted, spooned, 1 cup	440	1	0

FOOD/PORTION SIZE	CAL	FAT (g)	CHOL (mg)
Flour, wheat, all-purpose, sifted, spooned, 1 cup	420	1	0
Flour, wheat, all-purpose, unsifted, spooned, 1 cup	455	1	0
Flour, whole-wheat from hard wheats, stirred, 1 cup	400	2	0
Garlic powder, 1 tsp.	10	tr	0
Honey, strained or extracted, 1 cup	1,030	0	0
Horseradish, Cream Style Prepared, Kraft, 1 tbsp.	8	0	0
Horseradish, Prepared, Kraft, 1 tbsp.	4	0	0
Horseradish Sauce, Kraft, 1 tbsp.	50	5	5
Horseradish Sauce, Sauceworks, 1 tbsp.	50	5	5
Hot Fudge Topping, Kraft, 1 tbsp.	70	3	0
Jams and preserves, 1 tbsp.	55	tr	0
Jellies, 1 tbsp.	50	tr	0
Marshmallow Creme, Kraft, 1 oz.	90	0	0
Mayonnaise, Hellman's, 1 tbsp.	100	11	5
Mayonnaise, imitation, 1 tbsp.	35	3	4
Mayonnaise, Light, Reduced Calorie, Kraft, 1 tbsp.	45	5	5
Mayonnaise, Real, Kraft, 1 tbsp.	100	12	5
Mayonnaise, regular, 1 tbsp.	100	11	8
Mustard, Dijon, Grey Poupon, 1 tbsp.	18	1	na
Mustard, Horseradish, Kraft, 1 tbsp.	4	0	0
Mustard, prepared yellow, 1 tsp. or individual packet	5	tr	0
Mustard, Pure Prepared, Kraft, 1 tbsp.	4	0	0
Mustard Sauce, Hot, Sauceworks, 1 tbsp.	35	2	5
Mustard, Spicy Brown, Gulden's, .25 oz.	8	0	na
Onion powder, 1 tsp.	5	tr	0
Oregano, 1 tsp.	5	tr	0
Paprika, 1 tsp.	5	tr	0
Pepper, black, 1 tsp.	5	tr	0
Pineapple Topping, Kraft, 1 tbsp.	50	0	0
Red Raspberry Topping, Kraft, 1 tbsp.	50	0	0
Relish, finely chopped sweet, 1 tbsp.	20	tr	0
Salad Dressing, Light, Miracle Whip, 1 tbsp.	45	4	5
Salad Dressing, Miracle Whip, 1 tbsp.	70	7	5
Salsa, Green Chile, Mild/Medium, Ortega, 1 oz.	8	0	na
Salsa, Green Chile, Hot, Ortega, 1 oz.	10	0	na
Salt, 1 tsp.	0	0	0
Sandwich Spread, Kraft, 1 tbsp.	50	5	5

FOOD/PORTION SIZE	CAL	FAT (g)	CHOL (mg)
Shake 'N Bake Oven Fry Coating, Extra Crispy Recipe for Chicken, 1/4 pouch	110	2	0
Shake 'N Bake Oven Fry Coating, Extra Crispy Recipe for Pork, 1/4 pouch	120	3	0
Shake 'N Bake Oven Fry Coating, Homestyle Recipe for Chicken, 1/4 pouch	80	2	0
Shake 'N Bake Seasoning Mixture, Country Mild Recipe, 1/4 pouch	80	4	0
Shake 'N Bake Seasoning Mixture, Italian Herb Recipe, 1/4 pouch	80	1	0
Shake 'N Bake Seasoning Mixture, Original Barbecue Recipe for Chicken, 1/4 pouch	90	2	0
Shake 'N Bake Seasoning Mixture, Original Barbecue Recipe for Pork, 1/4 pouch	80	2	0
Shake 'N Bake Seasoning Mixture, Original Recipe for Chicken, 1/4 pouch	80	2	0
Shake 'N Bake Seasoning Mixture, Original Recipe for Fish, 1/4 pouch	70	1	0
Shake 'N Bake Seasoning Mixture, Original Recipe for Pork, 1/4 pouch	80	1	0
Steak Sauce, A.1., 1 tbsp.	12	0	na
Strawberry Topping, Kraft, 1 tbsp.	50	0	0
Sugar, brown, pressed down, 1 cup	820	0	0
Sugar, powdered, sifted, spooned into cup, 1 cup	385	0	0
Sugar, white, granulated, 1 cup	770	0	0
Sweet'n Sour Sauce, Sauceworks, 1 tbsp.	20	0	0
Syrup, chocolate-flavored syrup or topping, fudge type, 2 tbsp.	125	5	0
Syrup, chocolate-flavored syrup or topping, thin type, 2 tbsp.	85	tr	0
Syrup, molasses, cane, blackstrap, 2 tbsp.	85	0	0
Syrup, table syrup (corn & maple), 2 tbsp.	122	0	0
Tartar sauce, 1 tbsp.	75	8	4
Tartar Sauce, Hellman's, 1 tbsp.	70	8	5
Tartar Sauce, Kraft, 1 tbsp.	70	8	5
Tartar Sauce, Natural Lemon Herb Flavor, Sauceworks, 1 tbsp.	70	8	5
Tartar Sauce, Sauceworks, 1 tbsp.	70	8	5
Vinegar, cider, 1 tbsp.	tr	0	0
Walnut Topping, Kraft, 1 tbsp.	90	5	0

FOOD/PORTION SIZE	CAL	FAT (g)	CHOL (mg)
Yeast, baker's dry active, 1 package	20	tr	0
Yeast, brewer's dry, 1 tbsp.	25	tr	0

Beverages

FOOD/PORTION SIZE	CAL	FAT (g)	CHOL (mg)
ALCOHOL			
Beer, light, 12 fl. oz.	95	0	0
Beer, regular, 12 fl. oz.	150	0	0
Gin, rum, vodka, whiskey, 80-proof, 1 1/2 fl. oz.	95	0	0
Gin, rum, vodka, whiskey, 86-proof, 1 1/2 fl. oz.	105	0	0
Gin, rum, vodka, whiskey, 90-proof, 1 1/2 fl. oz.	110	0	0
Wine, dessert, 3 1/2 fl. oz.	140	0	0
Wine, table, red, 3 1/2 fl. oz.	75	0	0
Wine, table, white, 3 1/2 fl. oz.	80	0	0
BREAKFAST DRINKS			
Carnation Instant Breakfast, Chocolate, 1 envelope	130	1	na
Carnation Instant Breakfast, Strawberry, 1 envelope	130	1	na
Carnation Instant Breakfast, Vanilla, 1 envelope	130	1	na
Tang Breakfast Beverage Crystals, 6 fl. oz.	90	0	0
Tang Sugar Free Breakfast Beverage Crystals, 6 fl. oz.	6	0	0
COFFEE			
Brewed, 6 fl. oz.	tr	tr	0
Cafe Amaretto, General Foods International Coffees, 6 fl. oz.	50	2	0
Cafe Amaretto, General Foods Sugar Free International Coffees, 6 fl. oz.	35	3	0
Cafe Francais, General Foods International Coffees, 6 fl. oz.	50	3	0
Cafe Francais, General Foods Sugar Free International Coffees, 6 fl. oz.	35	2	0
Cafe Irish Cream, General Foods International Coffees, 6 fl. oz.	60	3	0
Cafe Irish Cream, General Foods Sugar Free International Coffees, 6 fl. oz.	30	2	0
Cafe Vienna, General Foods International Coffees, 6 fl. oz.	60	2	0

FOOD/PORTION SIZE	CAL	FAT (g)	CHOL (mg)
Cafe Vienna, General Foods Sugar Free International Coffees, 6 fl. oz.	30	2	0
Double Dutch Chocolate, General Foods International Coffees, 6 fl. oz.	50	2	0
Instant, prepared, 6 fl. oz.	tr	tr	0
Irish Mocha Mint, General Foods International Coffees, 6 fl. oz.	50	2	0
Irish Mocha Mint, General Foods Sugar Free International Coffees, 6 fl. oz.	25	2	0
Orange Capuccino, General Foods International Coffees, 6 fl. oz.	60	2	0
Orange Capuccino, General Foods Sugar Free International Coffees, 6 fl. oz.	30	2	0
Postum Coffee Flavor Instant Hot Beverage, 6 fl. oz.	12	0	0
Swiss Mocha, General Foods International Coffees, 6 fl. oz.	50	2	0
Swiss Mocha, General Foods Sugar Free International Coffees, 6 fl. oz.	30	2	0

JUICE

FOOD/PORTION SIZE	CAL	FAT (g)	CHOL (mg)
Apple, bottled or canned, 1 cup	115	tr	0
Apple/Cranberry, DelMonte Fruit Blends, 8.45 oz.	140	0	na
Apple, Kraft Pure 100%, 6 oz.	80	0	0
Cranberry juice cocktail, bottled, sweetened, 1 cup	145	tr	0
Cranberry Juice Cocktail, Ocean Spray, 6 oz.	110	0	na
Grape, canned or bottled, 1 cup	155	tr	0
Grape, frozen concentrate, sweetened, diluted, 1 cup	125	tr	0
Grape, frozen concentrate, sweetened, undiluted, 6-fl.-oz. can	385	1	0
Grapefruit, canned, sweetened, 1 cup	115	tr	0
Grapefruit, canned, unsweetened, 1 cup	95	tr	0
Grapefruit, frozen concentrate, unsweetened, diluted, 1 cup	100	tr	0
Grapefruit, frozen concentrate, unsweetened, undiluted, 6-oz. can	300	1	0
Grapefruit, Kraft Pure 100% Unsweetened, 6 oz.	70	0	0
Grapefruit, raw, 1 cup	95	tr	0
Lemon, canned or bottled, unsweetened, 1 cup	50	1	0
Lemon, canned or bottled, unsweetened, 1 tbsp.	5	tr	0
Lemon, frozen, single-strength, unsweetened, 6-oz. can	50	1	0
Lemon, raw, 1 cup	60	tr	0

FOOD/PORTION SIZE	CAL	FAT (g)	CHOL (mg)
Lime, canned, unsweetened, 1 cup	50	1	0
Lime, raw, 1 cup	65	tr	0
Orange and grapefruit, canned, 1 cup	105	tr	0
Orange, canned, unsweetened, 1 cup	105	tr	0
Orange, chilled, 1 cup	110	1	0
Orange, frozen concentrate, diluted, 1 cup	110	tr	0
Orange, frozen concentrate, undiluted, 6-oz. can	340	tr	0
Orange/Grapefruit, Kraft Pure 100% Unsweetened, 6 oz.	80	0	0
Orange, Kraft Pure 100% Unsweetened, 6 oz.	90	0	0
Orange/Pineapple, Kraft Pure 100% Unsweetened, 6 oz.	80	0	0
Orange, raw, 1 cup	110	tr	0
Pineapple/Orange, DelMonte Fruit Blends, 8.45 oz.	140	0	na
Pineapple, unsweetened, canned, 1 cup	140	tr	0
Prune, canned or bottled, 1 cup	180	tr	0
Tangerine, canned, sweetened, 1 cup	125	tr	0
V-8, 100% Vegetable, 6 oz.	35	0	na
V-8, Spicey Hot Vegetable, 6 oz.	35	0	na
Vegetable juice cocktail, canned, 1 cup	75	tr	0

MILK

FOOD/PORTION SIZE	CAL	FAT (g)	CHOL (mg)
Buttermilk, 1 cup	100	2	9
Buttermilk, dried, 1 cup	465	7	83
Canned, condensed, sweetened, 1 cup	980	27	104
Canned, evaporated, skim, 1 cup	200	1	9
Canned, evaporated, whole, 1 cup	340	19	74
Chocolate, lowfat (1%), 1 cup	160	3	7
Chocolate, lowfat (2%), 1 cup	180	5	17
Chocolate Malt Flavor, Ovaltine Classic, 3/4 oz.	80	0	0
Chocolate, regular, 1 cup	210	8	31
Cocoa Mix, Carnation, Milk Chocolate, 1 envelope	110	1	na
Cocoa Mix, Carnation, Rich Chocolate, 1 envelope	110	1	na
Cocoa Mix, Carnation, Rich Chocolate with Marshmallows, 1 envelope	110	1	na
Cocoa, powder, prepared with nonfat dry milk, 1 serving	100	1	1
Cocoa, powder, prepared with whole milk, 1 serving	225	9	33
Dried, nonfat, instant, 1 3.2-oz. envelope	325	1	17
Dried, nonfat, instant, 1 cup	245	tr	12
Eggnog (commercial), 1 cup	340	19	149

FOOD/PORTION SIZE	CAL	FAT (g)	CHOL (mg)
Fudge Drink, Slender Chocolate, 10 oz.	220	4	na
Lowfat (2%), milk solids added, 1 cup	105	2	10
Lowfat (2%), no milk solids, 1 cup	120	5	18
Malt Drink, Slender Chocolate, 10 oz.	220	4	na
Malted, chocolate, powder, 3/4 oz.	85	1	1
Malted, chocolate, powder, prepared, 1 serving	235	9	34
Malted Milk Chocolate, Kraft Instant, 3 tsp.	240	9	25
Malted, Natural, Kraft Instant, 3 tsp.	240	10	25
Malted, natural, powdered, 3/4 oz.	85	2	4
Malted, natural, powdered, prepared with milk, 1 serving	235	10	37
Malt Flavor, Ovaltine Classic, 3/4 oz.	80	0	0
Nonfat (skim), milk solids added, 1 cup	90	1	5
Nonfat (skim), no milk solids, 1 cup	85	tr	4
Shake Mix, Alba 77 Fit n' Frosty, Chocolate, 1 envelope	70	0	na
Shake Mix, Alba 77 Fit n' Frosty, Milk Chocolate, 1 envelope	70	0	na
Shake Mix, Alba 77 Fit n' Frosty, Strawberry, 1 envelope	70	0	na
Shake Mix, Alba 77 Fit n' Frosty, Vanilla, 1 envelope	70	0	na
Shakes, thick, chocolate, 10-oz. container	335	8	30
Shakes, thick, vanilla, 10-oz. container	315	9	33
Whole (3.3% fat), 1 cup	150	8	33

SOFT DRINKS, CARBONATED

FOOD/PORTION SIZE	CAL	FAT (g)	CHOL (mg)
7-Up, Diet, 6 oz.	2	0	na
7-Up, Diet Cherry, 6 oz.	2	0	na
Club soda, 12 fl. oz.	0	0	0
Coca-Cola, 6 fl. oz.	77	0	0
Coca-Cola Classic, 6 fl. oz.	72	0	0
Cola, diet, artificially sweetened, 12 fl. oz.	tr	0	0
Cola, regular, 12 fl. oz.	160	0	0
Diet-Rite, Black Cherry, 6 oz.	2	0	na
Diet-Rite, Cola, 6 oz.	2	0	na
Diet-Rite, Pink Grapefruit, 6 oz.	2	0	na
Diet-Rite, Red Raspberry, 6 oz.	2	0	na
Diet-Rite, Tangerine, 6 oz.	2	0	na
Dr. Pepper (Diet), 6 oz.	2	0	na
Fresca, 6 oz.	2	0	na
Ginger ale, 12 fl. oz.	125	0	0
Ginger Ale, Canada Dry, Diet, 6 oz.	2	0	na
Ginger Ale, Schweppes, Diet, 6 oz.	2	0	na
Grape, carbonated, 12 fl. oz.	180	0	0

FOOD/PORTION SIZE	CAL	FAT (g)	CHOL (mg)
Lemon-lime, carbonated, 12 fl. oz.	155	0	0
Orange, carbonated, 12 fl. oz.	180	0	0
Pepper type, carbonated, 12 fl. oz.	160	0	0
Pepsi Cola, Caffeine-Free, Diet, 6 oz.	0	0	na
Pepsi Cola, Diet, 6 oz.	0	0	na
Root beer, 12 fl. oz.	165	0	0
Root Beer, A & W, Diet, 6 oz.	2	0	na
Root Beer, Barrelhead, Diet, 6 oz.	2	0	na
Root Beer, Dad's, Diet, 6 oz.	2	0	na

SOFT DRINKS, NONCARBONATED

FOOD/PORTION SIZE	CAL	FAT (g)	CHOL (mg)
Country Time Drink Mix, Sugar Sweetened, Lemonade/Pink Lemonade, 8 fl. oz.	80	0	0
Country Time Drink Mix, Sugar Sweetened, Lemon-Lime, 8 fl. oz.	80	0	0
Country Time Sugar Free Drink Mix, Lemonade/Pink Lemonade, 8 fl. oz.	4	0	0
Country Time Sugar Free Drink Mix, Lemon-Lime, 8 fl. oz.	4	0	0
Crystal Light Sugar Free Drink Mix, all flavors, 8 fl. oz.	4	0	0
Fruit punch drink, noncarbonated, canned, 6 fl. oz.	85	0	0
Grape drink, noncarbonated, canned, 6 fl. oz.	100	0	0
Hi-C Cherry Drink, 6 oz.	100	0	na
Hi-C Citrus Cooler Drink, 6 oz.	100	0	na
Hi-C Double Fruit Cooler Drink, 6 oz.	90	0	na
Hi-C Fruit Punch Drink, 6 oz.	100	0	na
Hi-C Hula Punch Drink, 6 oz.	80	0	na
Kool-Aid Koolers Juice Drink, all flavors, 8.45 fl. oz.	130	0	0
Kool-Aid Soft Drink Mix Sugar-Sweetened, all flavors, 8 fl. oz.	80	0	0
Kool-Aid Soft Drink Mix Unsweetened, all flavors, 8 fl. oz.	2	0	0
Kool-Aid Soft Drink Mix Unsweetened, all flavors, with sugar added, 8 fl. oz.	100	0	0
Kool-Aid Sugar-Free Soft Drink Mix, all flavors, 8 fl. oz.	4	0	0
Lemonade concentrate, frozen, diluted, 6 fl. oz.	80	tr	0
Lemonade concentrate, frozen, undiluted, 6-fl.-oz. can	425	tr	0
Limeade concentrate, frozen, diluted, 6 fl. oz.	75	tr	0
Limeade concentrate, frozen, undiluted, 6-fl.-oz. can	410	tr	0

FOOD/PORTION SIZE	CAL	FAT (g)	CHOL (mg)
Ocean Spray, Cran-Apple Drink, 6 oz.	130	0	na
Ocean Spray, Cran-Grape Drink, 6 oz.	130	0	na
Ocean Spray, Cran-Raspberry Drink, 6 oz.	110	0	na
Pineapple-grapefruit juice drink, 6 fl. oz.	90	tr	0
Wylers, Bunch O'Berries Punch Mix, Sweetened, 8 oz.	90	0	na
Wylers, Bunch O'Berries Punch Mix, Unsweetened, 8 oz.	2	0	na
Wylers, Lemonade Drink Mix, Sweetened, 8 oz.	90	0	na
Wylers, Lemonade Drink Mix, Unsweetened, 8 oz.	4	0	na
Wylers, Tropical Punch Mix, Sweetened, 8 oz.	90	0	na
Wylers, Tropical Punch Mix, Unsweetened, 8 oz.	2	0	na
Wylers, Wild Cherry Mix, Sweetened, 8 oz.	90	0	na
Wylers, Wild Cherry Mix, Unsweetened, 8 oz.	2	0	na

TEA

FOOD/PORTION SIZE	CAL	FAT (g)	CHOL (mg)
Berry, Crystal Light Fruit-Tea Sugar Free Drink Mix, 8 fl. oz.	4	0	0
Brewed, 8 fl. oz.	tr	tr	0
Citrus, Crystal Light Fruit-Tea Sugar Free Drink Mix, 8 fl. oz.	4	0	0
Iced Tea, Crystal Light Sugar Free Drink Mix, 8 fl. oz.	4	0	0
Instant, powder, sweetened, 8 fl. oz.	85	tr	0
Instant, powder, unsweetened, 8 fl. oz.	tr	tr	0
Natural Brew, Crystal Light Fruit-Tea Sugar Free Drink Mix, 8 fl. oz.	4	0	0
Tropical Fruit, Crystal Light Fruit-Tea Sugar Free Drink Mix, 8 fl. oz.	4	0	0

MISCELLANEOUS

FOOD/PORTION SIZE	CAL	FAT (g)	CHOL (mg)
Gatorade Lemon-Lime, 8.45 oz.	60	0	na
Gatorade Orange, 8.45 oz.	60	0	0
Postum Instant Hot Beverage, 6 fl. oz.	12	0	0

Breads & Cereals

FOOD/PORTION SIZE	CAL	FAT (g)	CHOL (mg)
BISCUITS			
Baking powder, home recipe, 1 biscuit	100	5	tr
Baking powder, mix, 1 biscuit	95	3	tr
Baking powder, refrigerated dough, 1 biscuit	65	2	1
BREAD			
Boston brown, canned, $3^1/4 \times {}^1/2$-in. slice	95	1	3
Cracked-wheat, 1 slice	65	1	0
Crumbs, enriched, dry, grated, 1 cup	390	5	5
French, enriched, $5 \times 2^1/2 \times 1$-in. slice	100	1	0
Italian, enriched, $4^1/2 \times 3^1/4 \times {}^3/4$-in. slice	85	tr	0
Mixed grain, enriched, 1 slice	65	2	0
Oatmeal, enriched, 1 slice	65	1	0
Pita, enriched, white, $6^1/2$-in. diameter, 1 pita	165	1	0
Pumpernickel, $2/3$ rye, $1/3$ wheat, 1 slice	80	1	0
Raisin, enriched, 1 slice,	65	1	0
Roman Meal, 1 slice	70	1	0
Rye, $2/3$ wheat, $1/3$ rye, $4^3/4 \times 3^3/4 \times {}^7/16$-in. slice	65	1	0
Vienna, enriched, $4^3/4 \times 4 \times {}^1/2$-in. slice	70	1	0
Wheat, enriched, 1 slice	65	1	0
Wheat, Home Pride, Buttertop, 1 slice	70	1	na
White, enriched, 1 slice	65	1	0
White, enriched, cubes, 1 cup	80	1	0
White, enriched, soft crumbs, 1 cup	120	2	0
White, Home Pride Buttertop, 1 slice	70	1	na
White, Wonder, 1 slice	70	1	0
Whole-wheat, 16-slice loaf, 1 slice	70	1	0
CEREALS, COLD			
40% Bran Flakes, Kellogg's, 1 oz. ($3/4$ cup)	90	1	0
100% Natural Cereal, 1 oz. ($1/4$ cup)	135	6	tr
All-Bran, 1 oz. ($1/3$ cup)	70	1	0
Alpha-Bits, 1 oz.	110	1	0
Alpha-Bits, with $1/2$ cup whole milk, 1 oz.	190	5	15
Apple Cinnamon Natural, 1 oz.	126	4.9	na
Apple Jacks, 1 oz.	110	0	0
Cap'n Crunch, 1 oz. ($3/4$ cup)	120	3	0

FOOD/PORTION SIZE	CAL	FAT (g)	CHOL (mg)
Cap'n Crunch Peanut Butter, 1 oz.	119	3.0	na
Cheerios, 1 oz. (1¼ cup)	110	2	0
Cheerios, Honey-Nut, 1 oz. (¾ cup)	105	1	0
Cocoa Krispies, 1 oz.	110	0	0
Cocoa Pebbles, 1 oz.	110	1	0
Cocoa Pebbles, with ½ cup whole milk, 1 oz.	190	5	15
Cocoa Puffs, 1 oz.	110	1	0
Corn Chex, 1 oz.	110	0	0
Corn Flakes, Kellogg's, 1 oz. (1¼ cup)	110	tr	0
Corn Flakes, Toasties, 1 oz. (1¼ cup)	110	tr	0
Cracklin' Bran, 1 oz.	110	4	0
Crispy Wheats & Raisins, 1 oz.	110	1	0
Crunchy Bran, 1 oz.	89	1.3	na
Crunchy Nut Ohs, 1 oz.	127	4.2	na
C.W. Post Hearty Granola, 1 oz.	130	4	0
C.W. Post Hearty Granola, with ½ cup whole milk, 1 oz.	200	8	15
C.W. Post Hearty Granola with Raisins, 1 oz.	120	4	0
C.W. Post Hearty Granola with Raisins, with ½ cup whole milk, 1 oz.	200	8	15
Fortified Oat Flakes, 1 oz.	110	1	0
Fortified Oat Flakes, with ½ cup whole milk, 1 oz.	180	5	15
Froot Loops, 1 oz. (1 cup)	110	1	0
Frosted Mini-Wheats, 1 oz.	100	0	0
Fruit & Fibre-Dates, Raisins, Walnuts, 1 oz.	90	1	0
Fruit & Fibre-Dates, Raisins, Walnuts, with ½ cup whole milk, 1 oz.	160	5	15
Fruit & Fibre-Harvest Medley, 1 oz.	90	1	0
Fruit & Fibre-Harvest Medley, with ½ cup whole milk, 1 oz.	170	5	15
Fruit & Fibre-Mountain Trail, 1 oz.	90	1	0
Fruit & Fibre-Mountain Trail, with ½ cup whole milk, 1 oz.	170	5	15
Fruit & Fibre-Tropical Fruit, 1 oz.	90	1	0
Fruit & Fibre-Tropical Fruit, with ½ cup whole milk, 1 oz.	170	5	15
Fruity Pebbles, 1 oz.	110	1	0
Fruity Pebbles, with ½ cup whole milk, 1 oz.	190	5	15
Golden Grahams, 1 oz. (¾ cup)	110	1	tr
Grape-Nuts, 1 oz.	110	0	0
Grape-Nuts, with ½ cup whole milk, 1 oz.	180	4	15
Grape-Nuts Flakes, 1 oz.	100	1	0
Grape-Nuts Flakes, with ½ cup whole milk, 1 oz.	180	5	15
Grape-Nuts, Raisin, with ½ cup whole milk, 1 oz.	170	4	15
Honeycomb, 1 oz.	110	0	0
Honeycomb, with ½ cup whole milk, 1 oz.	190	4	15
Honey Graham Ohs, 1 oz.	122	3.2	na
Just Right Fiber Nuggets, 1 oz.	100	1	0
Just Right Fruit & Nuts, 1 oz.	140	1	0
Kix, 1 oz.	110	0	0
Life, 1 oz.	101	1.7	na
Life, Cinnamon, 1 oz.	101	1.7	na
Lucky Charms, 1 oz. (1 cup)	110	1	0
Malt-O-Meal, 1 cup	120	tr	0
Mueslix Five Grain, 1 oz.	140	1	0
Natural Bran Flakes, 1 oz.	90	0	0
Natural Bran Flakes, with ½ cup whole milk, 1 oz.	160	4	15
Natural Raisin Bran, Post, 1 oz.	80	0	0
Natural Raisin Bran, Post, with ½ cup whole milk, 1 oz.	160	4	15
Nature Valley Granola, 1 oz. (⅓ cup)	125	5	0
Nutri Grain Almonds & Raisins, 1 oz.	140	2	0
Nutri Grain Biscuits, 1 oz.	90	0	0
Nutri Grain Wheat & Raisins, 1 oz.	130	0	0
Oat Squares, 1 oz.	105	1.6	na
Popeye Puffed Rice, ½ oz.	50	0	na
Popeye Puffed Wheat, ½ oz.	50	0	na
Popeye Sweet Crunch, 1 oz.	113	1.8	na
Post Toasties Corn Flakes, 1 oz.	110	0	0
Post Toasties Corn Flakes, with ½ cup whole milk, 1 oz.	180	4	15
Product 19, 1 oz. (¾ cup)	110	tr	0
Puffed Rice, Quaker Oats, 0.50 oz.	54	0.1	0
Puffed Wheat, Quaker Oats, 0.50 oz.	50	0.2	0
Raisin Bran, Kellogg's, 1 oz. (¾ cup)	90	1	0
Raisin Bran, Post, 1 oz. (½ cup)	85	1	0
Raisin Date Natural, 1 oz.	123	5	na
Rice Chex, 1 oz.	110	0	0
Rice Krispies, 1 oz. (1 cup)	110	tr	0
Shredded Wheat, 1 oz. (⅔ cup)	100	1	0
Shredded Wheat, Spoon Size, 1 oz.	90	na	na
Smurf-Berry Crunch, 1 oz.	110	1	0
Smurf-Berry Crunch, with ½ cup whole milk, 1 oz.	190	5	15
Special K, 1 oz. (1⅓ cup)	110	tr	tr
Sugar Frosted Flakes, Kellogg's, 1 oz. (¾ cup)	110	tr	0
Sugar Smacks, 1 oz. (¾ cup)	105	1	0
Sun Country Granola with Almonds, 1 oz.	130	5.3	0
Sun Country Granola with Raisins, 1 oz.	125	4.8	0
Sun Country Granola with Raisins & Dates, 1 oz.	123	4.5	0

FOOD/PORTION SIZE	CAL	FAT (g)	CHOL (mg)
Super Golden Crisp, 1 oz.	110	0	0
Super Golden Crisp, with ½ cup whole milk, 1 oz.	180	4	15
Super Sugar Crisp, 1 oz. (⅞ cup)	105	tr	0
Total, 1 oz. (1 cup)	100	1	0
Total, Whole Wheat, 1 oz.	110	1	0
Trix, 1 oz. (1 cup)	110	tr	0
Wheat Chex, 1 oz.	100	0	0
Wheat Germ, Honey Crunch, Kretschmer, 1 oz.	105	2.8	0
Wheaties, 1 oz. (1 cup)	100	tr	0

CEREALS, HOT

FOOD/PORTION SIZE	CAL	FAT (g)	CHOL (mg)
Corn grits, instant, plain, 1 cup	80	tr	0
Corn grits, regular/quick, enriched, 1 cup	145	tr	0
Cream of Wheat, Mix 'n Eat, plain, 1 packet	100	tr	0
Cream of Wheat, regular/quick/instant, 1 cup	140	tr	0
Malt-O-Meal, Chocolate, 1 oz.	100	0	na
Malt-O-Meal, Quick, 1 oz.	100	0	na
Oatmeal/rolled oats, instant, fortified, flavored, 1 packet	160	2	0
Oatmeal/rolled oats, instant, fortified, plain, 1 packet	105	2	0
Oatmeal/rolled oats, regular/quick/instant, nonfortified, 1 cup	145	2	0
Oats, Instant, Apple Cinnamon, Quaker Oats, 1.25 oz.	118	1.5	0
Oats, Instant, Bananas & Cream, Quaker Oats, 1.25 oz.	131	2.3	0
Oats, Instant, Blueberries & Cream, Quaker Oats, 1.25 oz.	131	2.4	0
Oats, Instant, Cinnamon Spice, Quaker Oats, 1.63 oz.	164	2.1	0
Oats, Instant, Maple & Brown Sugar, Quaker Oats, 1.50 oz.	152	2.1	0
Oats, Instant, Peaches & Cream, Quaker Oats, 1.25 oz.	129	2.2	0
Oats, Instant, Raisin Date Walnut, Quaker Oats, 1.30 oz.	141	3.8	0
Oats, Instant, Raisin Spice, Quaker Oats, 1.50 oz.	149	2	0
Oats, Instant, Regular, Quaker Oats, 1 oz.	94	2	0
Oats, Instant, Strawberries & Cream, Quaker Oats, 1.25 oz.	129	2	0
Oats, Old Fashioned, Quaker Oats, 1 oz.	99	2	0
Oats, Quick, Quaker Oats, 1 oz.	99	2	0
Wheatena, 1 oz.	100	na	na
Whole Wheat Hot Natural, Quaker Oats, 1 oz.	92	0.6	0

CRACKERS

FOOD/PORTION SIZE	CAL	FAT (g)	CHOL (mg)
Cheese, plain, 1-in. square, 10 crackers	50	3	6
Cheese, sandwich/peanut butter, 1 sandwich	40	2	1
Graham, plain, 2½-in. square, 2 crackers	60	1	0
Rye wafers, whole-grain, 2 wafers	55	1	0
Rykrisp, (Natural), ½	40	0	0
Rykrisp, (Sesame), ½	45	1	0
Saltines, 4 crackers	50	1	4
Snack-type, standard, 1 round cracker	15	1	0
Wheat, thin, 4 crackers	35	1	0
Whole-wheat wafers, 2 crackers	35	2	0

MELBA TOAST

FOOD/PORTION SIZE	CAL	FAT (g)	CHOL (mg)
Garlic, Old London, ½ oz.	60	2	na
Onion, Old London, ½ oz.	60	2	na
Plain, 1 piece	20	tr	0
Rye, Old London, ½ oz.	60	2	na
Sesame, Old London, ½ oz.	60	2	na

MUFFINS

FOOD/PORTION SIZE	CAL	FAT (g)	CHOL (mg)
Blueberry, home recipe, enriched flour, 1 muffin	135	5	19
Blueberry, mix, 1 muffin	140	5	45
Blueberry-Streusel Mix, Betty Crocker, 1 muffin	190	6	na
Bran, home recipe, enriched flour, 1 muffin	125	6	24
Bran, mix, 1 muffin	140	4	28
Corn, home recipe, enriched degermed cornmeal, 1 muffin	145	5	23
Corn, mix, 1 muffin	145	6	42
Corn, Mix, Dromedary, 1 muffin	120	4	na
English, Bays, 2 oz.	140	2	na
English, plain, enriched, 1 muffin	140	1	0
English, Wonder, 2 oz.	180	2	na

ROLLS

FOOD/PORTION SIZE	CAL	FAT (g)	CHOL (mg)
Dinner, enriched commercial, 1 roll	85	2	tr
Dinner, home recipe, 1 roll	120	3	12
Frankfurter/hamburger, enriched commercial, 1 roll	115	2	tr
Hard, enriched commercial, 1 roll	155	2	tr
Hoagie/submarine, enriched commercial, 1 roll	400	8	tr

STUFFING MIX

FOOD/PORTION SIZE	CAL	FAT (g)	CHOL (mg)
Americana New England, Stove Top, ½ cup	110	1	0
Americana New England, Stove Top, prepared with butter, ½ cup	180	9	20

FOOD/PORTION SIZE	CAL	FAT (g)	CHOL (mg)
Americana San Francisco, Stove Top, 1/2 cup	110	1	0
Americana San Francisco, Stove Top, prepared with butter, 1/2 cup	170	9	20
Beef, Stove Top, 1/2 cup	110	1	0
Beef, Stove Top, prepared with butter, 1/2 cup	180	9	20
Chicken Flavor Bread, Quaker Oats Golden Grain, as prepared, 1 oz.	180	9	na
Chicken Flavor, Stove Top, prepared with butter, 1/2 cup	180	9	20
Chicken, Stove Top, 1/2 cup	110	1	0
Chicken, Stove Top Flexible Serving, 1/2 cup	120	3	0
Chicken, Stove Top Flexible Serving, prepared with butter, 1/2 cup	170	9	15
Cornbread Rice, Quaker Oats Golden Grain, as prepared, 1 oz.	180	9	na
Cornbread Rice, Quaker Oats Golden Grain, dry mix, 1 oz.	110	1	na
Cornbread, Stove Top, 1/2 cup	110	1	0
Cornbread, Stove Top Flexible Serving, 1/2 cup	120	3	0
Cornbread, Stove Top Flexible Serving, prepared with butter, 1/2 cup	170	8	15
Cornbread, Stove Top, prepared with butter, 1/2 cup	170	9	20
Country Style, Pepperidge Farm, 1 oz.	110	1	na
Enriched bread, dry, 1 cup	500	31	0
Enriched bread, moist, 1 cup	420	26	67
Herb Butter Wild Rice, Quaker Oats Golden Grain, as prepared, 1 oz.	180	9	na
Herb Butter Wild Rice, Quaker Oats Golden Grain, dry mix, 1 oz.	100	1	na
Herb, Pepperidge Farm, 1 oz.	110	1	na
Homestyle Herb, Stove Top Flexible Serving, 1/2 cup	120	3	0
Homestyle Herb, Stove Top Flexible Serving, prepared with butter, 1/2 cup	170	9	15
Long Grain and Wild Rice, Stove Top, 1/2 cup	120	1	0
Long Grain and Wild Rice, Stove Top, prepared with butter, 1/2 cup	180	9	20
Pork, Stove Top, 1/2 cup	110	1	0
Pork, Stove Top, prepared with butter, 1/2 cup	170	9	20
Savory Herbs, Stove Top, 1/2 cup	110	1	0
Savory Herbs, Stove Top, prepared with butter, 1/2 cup	180	9	20
Turkey, Stove Top, 1/2 cup	110	1	0

FOOD/PORTION SIZE	CAL	FAT (g)	CHOL (mg)
Turkey, Stove Top, prepared with butter, 1/2 cup	170	9	20
Wild Rice Bread, Quaker Oats Golden Grain, as prepared, 1 oz.	180	9	0.4
Wild Rice Bread, Quaker Oats Golden Grain, dry mix, 1 oz.	110	1	na
With Rice, Stove Top, 1/2 cup	110	1	0
With Rice, Stove Top, prepared with butter, 1/2 cup	180	9	20

MISCELLANEOUS

FOOD/PORTION SIZE	CAL	FAT (g)	CHOL (mg)
Bagel, plain, Lender's, 2 oz.	150	1	0
Bagel, plain/water, enriched, 1 bagel	200	2	0
Bran, unprocessed, Quaker Oats, 0.25 oz.	8	0.2	na
Croissant, with enriched flour, 1 croissant	235	12	13
Oat Bran, Quaker Oats, 1 oz.	92	2.1	0
Tortilla, corn, 1 tortilla	65	1	0
Wheat Bran, Kretschmer, 1 oz.	57	2.3	0
Wheat Germ, Kretschmer, 1 oz.	103	3.4	0

Candy

FOOD/PORTION SIZE	CAL	FAT (g)	CHOL (mg)
Baby Ruth, 1 oz.	130	6	na
Bonkers! (all flavors), 1 piece	20	0	na
Breath Savers (all flavors), 1 piece	8	0	na
Bubble Yum (all flavors), 1 piece	25	0	na
Bubble Yum, Sugarless (all flavors), 1 piece	20	0	na
Butterfinger, 1 oz.	130	6	na
Butter Mints, Kraft, 1 mint	8	0	0
Caramels, Kraft, 1 caramel	35	1	0
Caramels, plain or chocolate, 1 oz.	115	3	1
Care*Free Sugarless Gum (all flavors), 1 piece	8	0	na
Care*Free Sugarless Bubble Gum (all flavors), 1 piece	10	0	na
Charleston Chew! (all flavors), 1 oz.	120	3	na
Chocolate, bitter or baking, 1 oz.	145	15	0
Chocolate Fudgies, Kraft, 1 fudgie	35	1	0
Chocolate, milk, plain, 1 oz.	145	9	6
Chocolate, milk, with almonds, 1 oz.	150	10	5
Chocolate, milk, with peanuts, 1 oz.	155	11	5

FOOD/PORTION SIZE	CAL	FAT (g)	CHOL (mg)
Chocolate, milk, with rice cereal, 1 oz.	140	7	6
Chocolate, semi-sweet small pieces, 1 cup or 6 oz. (60/oz.)	860	61	0
Chocolate, sweet dark, 1 oz.	150	10	0
Fruit Stripe Gum/Bubble Gum (all flavors), 1 piece	10	0	na
Fudge, chocolate, plain, 1 oz.	115	3	1
Funmallows, Kraft, 1 marshmallow	25	0	0
Gum drops, 1 oz.	100	tr	0
Hard candy, 1 oz.	110	0	0
Jelly beans, 1 oz.	105	tr	0
Jet-Puffed Marshmallows, Kraft, 1 marshmallow	25	0	0
Kisses, Hershey, 9 pieces	220	13	na
Kit Kat, 1.12 oz.	175	9	na
Krackel, 1.65 oz.	250	14	na
Life Savers Roll Candy (all flavors), 1 piece	8	0	na
Marshmallows, 1 oz.	90	0	0
Milk Chocolate Bar, Hershey, 1 bar	220	12	0
Miniature Marshmallows, Kraft, 10 marshmallows	18	0	0
Mr. Goodbar, 1.85 oz.	300	20	na
Party Mints, Kraft, 1 mint	8	0	0
Peanut Brittle, Kraft, 1 oz.	140	5	0
Reese's Peanut Butter Cup, 2 cups	280	17	0
Rolo, 9 pieces	270	12	na
Skor, 1.4 oz.	220	14	na
Special Dark, Hershey, 1 bar	210	12	0
Sugar Babies, 1 pkg.	180	2	na
Sugar Daddy, 1 pop	150	1	na
Toffee, Kraft, 1 piece	30	1	0
Whatchamacallit, 1.8 oz.	270	15	na
Y&S Twizzlers, 1.0 oz.	100	1	na
Y&S Bites, 1.0 oz.	100	1	na

Cheese

FOOD/PORTION SIZE	CAL	FAT (g)	CHOL (mg)
American Flavored, Singles Pasteurized Process Cheese Product, Light n' Lively, 1 oz.	70	4	15
American Flavor, Imitation Pasteurized Process Cheese Food, Golden Image, 1 oz.	90	6	5
American Flavor, Pasteurized Process Cheese Product, Harvest Moon Brand, 1 oz.	70	4	15

FOOD/PORTION SIZE	CAL	FAT (g)	CHOL (mg)
American, pasteurized process cheese, 1 oz.	105	9	27
American, pasteurized process cheese food, 1 oz.	95	7	18
American, Pasteurized Process Cheese Loaf, Deluxe, 1 oz.	110	9	25
American, Pasteurized Process Cheese Slices, Deluxe, 1 oz.	110	9	25
American, pasteurized process cheese spread, 1 oz.	80	6	16
American, Pasteurized Process Cheese Spread, Kraft, 1 oz.	80	6	20
American, Process Cheese, Borden Lite-Line, 4 oz.	50	2	10
American, Sharp, Pasteurized Process Cheese Loaf, Old English, 1 oz.	110	9	30
American, Sharp, Pasteurized Process Slices, Old English, 1 oz.	110	9	30
American, Singles Pasteurized Process Cheese Food, Kraft, 1 oz.	90	7	20
American, Singles Pasteurized Process Cheese Food (white), Kraft, 1 oz.	90	7	20
Bleu, 1 oz.	100	8	21
Bleu, Natural, Kraft, 1 oz.	100	9	30
Brick, Natural, Kraft, 1 oz.	110	9	30
Camembert, 1 wedge (3 wedges/4-oz. container)	115	9	27
Caraway, Natural, Kraft, 1 oz.	100	8	30
Cheddar, 1-in. cube	70	6	18
Cheddar, 1 oz.	115	9	30
Cheddar, Extra Sharp, Cold Pack Cheese Food, Cracker Barrel, 1 oz.	90	7	20
Cheddar Flavored, Sharp, Singles Pasteurized Process Cheese Product, Light n' Lively, 1 oz.	70	4	15
Cheddar, Mild, Imitation, Golden Image, 1 oz.	110	9	5
Cheddar, Natural, Kraft, 1 oz.	110	9	30
Cheddar, Port Wine, Cheese Log with Almonds, Cracker Barrel, 1 oz.	90	6	15
Cheddar, Port Wine, Cold Pack Cheese Food, Cracker Barrel, 1 oz.	90	7	20
Cheddar, Sharp, Cheese Ball with Almonds, Cracker Barrel, 1 oz.	90	6	15
Cheddar, Sharp, Cheese Log with Almonds, Cracker Barrel, 1 oz.	90	6	15
Cheddar, Sharp, Cold Pack Cheese Food, Cracker Barrel, 1 oz.	90	7	20
Cheddar, Sharp, Process Cheese, Borden Lite-Line, 4 oz.	50	2	10

FOOD/PORTION SIZE	CAL	FAT (g)	CHOL (mg)
Cheddar, shredded, 1 cup	455	37	119
Cheddar, Smokey, Cheese Log with Almonds, Cracker Barrel, 1 oz.	90	6	15
Cheese Food, Cold Pack with Real Bacon, Cracker Barrel, 1 oz.	90	7	20
Cheese Food, Pasteurized Process Sharp Singles, Kraft, 1 oz.	100	8	25
Cheese Food, Pasteurized Process, Smokelle, 1 oz.	100	7	20
Cheese Food with Bacon, Pasteurized Process, Kraft, 1 oz.	90	7	20
Cheese Food with Garlic, Pasteurized Process, Kraft, 1 oz.	90	7	20
Cheese Spread with Bacon, Pasteurized Process, Kraft, 1 oz.	80	7	20
Cheese Spread, Hot Mexican, Pasteurized Process, Velveeta, 1 oz.	80	6	20
Cheese Spread, Mild Mexican, Pasteurized Process, Velveeta, 1 oz.	80	6	20
Cheese Spread, Pasteurized Process, Velveeta, 1 oz.	80	6	20
Cheese Spread, Sharp, Pasteurized Process, Old English, 1 oz.	90	7	20
Cheese Spread, Slices, Pasteurized Process, Velveeta, 1 oz.	90	6	20
Cheese Spread with Bacon, Pasteurized Process, Kraft, 1 oz.	90	7	20
Cheese Spread with Bacon, Sharp, Pasteurized Process, Squeez-A-Snak, 1 oz.	90	7	20
Cheese Spread with Garlic, Pasteurized Process, Kraft, 1 oz.	80	6	15
Cheese Spread with Pimentos, Pasteurized Process, Squeez-A-Snak, 1 oz.	90	7	20
Cheez Whiz, Hot Mexican, Pasteurized Process Cheese Spread, 1 oz.	80	6	15
Cheez Whiz, Mild Mexican, Pasteurized Process Cheese Spread, 1 oz.	80	6	15
Cheez Whiz, Pasteurized Process Cheese Spread, 1 oz.	80	6	20
Cheez Whiz, Pimento, Pasteurized Process Cheese Spread, 1 oz.	80	6	15
Cheez Whiz with Jalapeño Pepper, Pasteurized Process Cheese Spread, 1 oz.	80	6	15
Colby, Imitation, Golden Image, 1 oz.	110	9	5

FOOD/PORTION SIZE	CAL	FAT (g)	CHOL (mg)
Colby, Natural, Kraft, 1 oz.	110	9	30
Cottage, Breakstone Low-Fat, 4 oz.	90	3	na
Cottage, creamed, large curd, 1 cup	235	10	34
Cottage, creamed, small curd, 1 cup	215	9	31
Cottage, creamed, with fruit, 1 cup	280	8	25
Cottage, Lite n' Lively, 4 oz.	80	1	15
Cottage, low-fat (2%), 1 cup	205	4	19
Cottage, uncreamed, dry curd, 1 cup	125	1	10
Cream cheese, 1 oz.	100	10	31
Cream Cheese, Philadelphia Brand, 1 oz.	100	10	30
Cream Cheese Product, Pasteurized Process, Light Philadelphia Brand, 1 oz.	60	5	15
Cream Cheese, Soft Philadelphia Brand, 1 oz.	100	10	30
Cream Cheese, Whipped, Philadelphia Brand, 1 oz.	100	10	30
Cream Cheese, Whipped, with Bacon and Horseradish, Philadelphia Brand, 1 oz.	90	9	20
Cream Cheese, Whipped, with Bleu Cheese, Philadelphia Brand, 1 oz.	100	9	25
Cream Cheese, Whipped, with Chives, Philadelphia Brand, 1 oz.	90	9	25
Cream Cheese, Whipped, with Onions, Philadelphia Brand, 1 oz.	90	8	20
Cream Cheese, Whipped, with Pimentos, Philadelphia Brand, 1 oz.	90	9	25
Cream Cheese, Whipped, with Smoked Salmon, Philadelphia Brand, 1 oz.	100	9	25
Cream Cheese with Chives & Onion, Soft Philadelphia Brand, 1 oz.	100	9	30
Cream Cheese with Chives, Philadelphia Brand, 1 oz.	90	9	30
Cream Cheese with Honey, Soft Philadelphia Brand, 1 oz.	100	8	25
Cream Cheese with Olives & Pimento, Soft Philadelphia Brand, 1 oz.	90	8	30
Cream Cheese with Pimentos, Philadelphia Brand, 1 oz.	90	9	30
Cream Cheese with Pineapple, Soft Philadelphia Brand, 1 oz.	90	8	25
Cream Cheese with Smoked Salmon, Soft Philadelphia Brand, 1 oz.	90	8	25
Cream Cheese with Strawberries, Soft Philadelphia Brand, 1 oz.	90	8	25

FOOD/PORTION SIZE	CAL	FAT (g)	CHOL (mg)
Edam, Natural, Kraft, 1 oz.	90	7	20
Feta, 1 oz.	75	6	25
Garlic Flavor Pasteurized Process Cheese Spread, Squeez-A-Snak, 1 oz.	90	7	20
Gouda, Natural, Kraft, 1 oz.	110	9	30
Havarti, Casino, 1 oz.	120	11	35
Hickory Smoke Flavor, Pasteurized Process Cheese Spread, Squeez-A-Snak, 1 oz.	80	7	20
Jalapeño, Pasteurized Process Cheese Spread, Kraft, 1 oz.	80	6	20
Jalapeño Pepper Spread, Kraft, 1 oz.	70	5	15
Jalapeño, Singles Pasteurized Process Cheese Food, Kraft, 1 oz.	90	7	25
Light, Low-Cholesterol, Dorman's, 4 oz.	70	5	3
Limburger, Natural, Little Gem Size, Mohawk Valley, 1 oz.	90	8	25
Limburger, Pasteurized Process Cheese Spread, Mohawk Valley, 1 oz.	70	6	20
Monterey Jack, Natural, Kraft, 1 oz.	110	9	30
Monterey Jack, Natural, with Jalapeño Peppers, Kraft, 1 oz.	110	9	30
Monterey Jack, Natural, with Peppers, Mild, Kraft, 1 oz.	110	9	30
Monterey Jack, Singles Pasteurized Process Cheese Food, Kraft, 1 oz.	90	7	25
Mozzarella, Low Moisture, Casino, 1 oz.	90	7	25
Mozzarella, Part-Skim, Low Moisture, Kraft, 1 oz.	80	5	15
Mozzarella, made with part-skim milk, 1 oz.	80	5	15
Mozzarella, made with whole milk, 1 oz.	80	6	22
Mozzarella String with Jalapeño Pepper, Part-Skim, Low Moisture, Kraft, 1 oz.	80	5	20
Muenster, 1 oz.	105	9	27
Muenster, Natural, Kraft, 1 oz.	110	9	30
Neufchatel, Natural, Kraft, 1 oz.	80	7	25
Olives & Pimento Spread, Kraft, 1 oz.	70	5	15
Parmesan, grated, 1 cup	455	30	79
Parmesan, grated, 1 oz.	130	9	22
Parmesan, grated, 1 tbsp.	25	2	4
Parmesan, Grated, Kraft, 1 oz.	130	9	30
Parmesan, Natural, Kraft, 1 oz.	110	7	20
Peanut Butter 'n Cheese, Handi-Snacks Crackers, 1 package	190	13	0

FOOD/PORTION SIZE	CAL	FAT (g)	CHOL (mg)
Pimento Cheese Spread, Pasteurized Process, Velveeta, 1 oz.	80	6	20
Pimento, Pasteurized Process Cheese Slices, Deluxe, 1 oz.	100	8	25
Pimento, Singles Pasteurized Process Cheese Food, Kraft, 1 oz.	90	7	20
Pimento Spread, Kraft, 1 oz.	70	5	15
Pineapple Spread, Kraft, 1 oz.	70	5	15
Pizza Topping with Vegetable Oil, Lunch Wagon, 1 oz.	80	6	0
Provolone, 1 oz.	100	8	20
Provolone, Natural, Kraft, 1 oz.	100	7	25
Ricotta, made with part-skim milk, 1 cup	340	19	76
Ricotta, made with whole milk, 1 cup	430	32	124
Romano, Grated, Kraft, 1 oz.	130	9	30
Romano, Natural, Casino, 1 oz.	100	7	30
Sandwich Slices with Vegetable Oil, Lunch Wagon, 1 oz.	80	6	5
Scamorze, Part-Skim, Low Moisture, Kraft, 1 oz.	80	5	15
Swiss, 1 oz.	105	8	26
Swiss Flavored, Singles Pasteurized Process Cheese Product, Light n' Lively, 1 oz.	70	4	15
Swiss Flavor, Process Cheese, Borden Lite-Line, 4 oz.	50	2	10
Swiss, Light, No Salt, Dorman's, 4 oz.	100	8	na
Swiss, Natural, Aged, Kraft, 1 oz.	110	8	25
Swiss, Natural, Kraft, 1 oz.	110	8	25
Swiss, pasteurized process cheese, 1 oz.	95	7	24
Swiss, Pasteurized Process Cheese Slices, Deluxe, 1 oz.	90	7	25
Swiss, Singles Pasteurized Process Cheese Food, Kraft, 1 oz.	90	7	25

Creamers & Cream Substitutes

FOOD/PORTION SIZE	CAL	FAT (g)	CHOL (mg)
Coffee Rich, 1/2 oz.	20	2	0
Cool Whip Extra Creamy Dairy Recipe Whipped Topping, Birds Eye, 1 tbsp.	16	1	0
Cool Whip Non-Dairy Whipped Topping, Birds Eye, 1 tbsp.	12	1	0

FOOD/PORTION SIZE	CAL	FAT (g)	CHOL (mg)
Creamer, sweet, imitation, liquid, 1 tbsp.	20	1	0
Creamer, sweet, imitation, powdered, 1 tbsp.	10	1	0
Creamer, sour, 1 cup	495	48	102
Cream, sour, 1 tbsp.	25	3	5
Cream Substitute, Milnot, 1/2 cup	150	8	0
Cream, sweet, half-and-half, 1 cup	315	28	89
Cream, sweet, half-and-half, 1 tbsp.	20	2	6
Cream, sweet, light/coffee/table, 1 cup	470	46	159
Cream, sweet, light/coffee/table, 1 tbsp.	30	3	10
Cream, sweet, whipping, unwhipped, heavy, 1 cup	820	88	326
Cream, sweet, whipping, unwhipped, heavy, 1 tbsp.	50	6	21
Cream, sweet, whipping, unwhipped, light, 1 cup	700	74	265
Cream, sweet, whipping, unwhipped, light, 1 tbsp.	45	5	17
Cream Topping, Real, Kraft, 1/4 cup	25	2	10
Cream, whipped topping, pressurized, 1 cup	155	13	46
Cream, whipped topping, pressurized, 1 tbsp.	10	1	2
Sour dressing, filled cream-type, imitation, 1 cup	415	39	13
Sour dressing, filled cream-type, imitation, 1 tbsp.	20	2	1
Whipped Topping, Kraft, 1/4 cup	35	3	0
Whipped Topping Mix, Dream Whip, prepared with whole milk, 1 tbsp.	10	0	0
Whipped Topping Mix, Reduced Calorie, D-Zerta, 1 tbsp.	8	1	0
Whipped topping, sweet, imitation, frozen, 1 cup	240	19	0
Whipped topping, sweet, imitation, frozen, 1 tbsp.	15	1	0
Whipped topping, sweet, imitation, pressurized, 1 cup	185	16	0
Whipped topping, sweet, imitation, pressurized, 1 tbsp.	10	1	0
Whipped topping, sweet, powdered, prepared with whole milk, 1 cup	150	10	8
Whipped topping, sweet, powdered, prepared with whole milk, 1 tbsp.	10	tr	tr

Eggs

FOOD/PORTION SIZE	CAL	FAT (g)	CHOL (mg)
Egg Substitute, Scramblers, 4 oz.	60	3	0
Large, fried in butter, 1 egg	95	7	278
Large, hard-cooked, shell removed, 1 egg	80	6	274
Large, poached, 1 egg	80	6	273
Large, raw, white only, 1 white	15	tr	0
Large, raw, whole, without shell, 1 egg	80	6	274
Large, raw, yolk only, 1 yolk	65	6	272
Omelet, with milk, cooked in butter, 1 egg	110	8	282
Scrambled, with milk, cooked in butter, 1 egg	110	8	282

Fast Food

FOOD/PORTION SIZE	CAL	FAT (g)	CHOL (mg)
ARBY'S			
Apple Turnover, 1 turnover	303	18.3	0
Bac'n Cheddar Deluxe, 1 sandwich	526	36.5	83
Beef 'N Cheddar, 1 sandwich	455	26.8	63
Cherry Turnover, 1 turnover	280	17.8	0
Chicken Breast Sandwich, 1 sandwich	509	29.1	83
Fish Fillet Sandwich, 1 sandwich	580	31.9	70
French Fries, 1 order (2.5 oz.)	215	9.7	8
Hot Ham 'N Cheese, 1 sandwich	292	13.7	45
Roast Beef, Junior, 1 sandwich	218	8.5	20
Roast Beef, King, 1 sandwich	467	19.2	49
Philly Beef 'N Swiss, 1 sandwich	460	28.4	107
Potato Cakes, 2 cakes (3 oz.)	201	12.9	13
Roast Beef, Giant, 1 sandwich	531	23.1	65
Roast Beef, Regular, 1 sandwich	353	14.8	39
Roast Beef, Super, 1 sandwich	501	22.1	40
Shake, Chocolate, 1 shake (12 oz.)	451	11.6	36
Shake, Jamocha, 1 shake (11.5 oz.)	368	10.5	35
Shake, Vanilla, 1 shake (11 oz.)	330	11.5	32
Turkey Deluxe, 1 sandwich	375	16.6	39
BURGER KING			
Apple Pie, 1 pie	na	12	4
Breakfast Croissan'wich, 1 sandwich	304	19	243
Breakfast Croissan'wich with Bacon, 1 sandwich	355	24	249

FOOD/PORTION SIZE	CAL	FAT (g)	CHOL (mg)
Breakfast Croissan'wich with Ham, 1 sandwich	335	20	261
Breakfast Croissan'wich with Sausage, 1 sandwich	538	41	293
Cheeseburger, 1 cheeseburger	317	15	48
Cheeseburger, Bacon Double, 1 cheeseburger	510	31	104
Chicken Specialty Sandwich, 1 sandwich	688	40	82
French Fries, lightly salted, Regular	227	13	14
French Toast Sticks, 1 order	499	29	74
Great Danish, 1 pastry	500	36	6
Hamburger, 1 hamburger	275	12	37
Ham & Cheese Specialty Sandwich, 1 sandwich	471	27	77
Onion Rings, 1 order	274	16	0
Salad Dressing, 1000 Island, 1 serving	117	12	17
Salad Dressing, Bleu Cheese, 1 serving	156	16	22
Salad Dressing, House, 1 serving	130	13	11
Salad Dressing, Reduced Calorie Italian, 1 serving	14	1	0
Salad, without dressing, 1 salad	28	0	0
Scrambled Egg Platter, 1 platter	468	30	370
Scrambled Egg Platter with Bacon, 1 platter	536	36	378
Scrambled Egg Platter with Sausage, 1 platter	702	52	420
Whaler Fish Sandwich, 1 sandwich	488	27	77
Whopper, 1 sandwich	628	36	90
Whopper with Cheese, 1 sandwich	711	43	113
Whopper Jr., 1 sandwich	322	17	41
Whopper Jr. with Cheese, 1 sandwich	364	20	52

DAIRY QUEEN

FOOD/PORTION SIZE	CAL	FAT (g)	CHOL (mg)
Chicken Breast Fillet, 1 sandwich	608	34	78
Chicken Breast Fillet with Cheese, 1 sandwich	661	38	87
"Chipper" Sandwich, 1 sandwich	318	7	13
Cone, Chocolate, "Queen's Choice," 1 cone	326	16	52
Cone, Vanilla, "Queen's Choice," 1 cone	322	16	52
Fish Fillet, 1 sandwich	430	18	40
Fish Fillet with Cheese, 1 sandwich	483	22	49
"Fudge Nut Bar," 1 bar	406	25	10
"Heath" "Blizzard," 16 oz.	800	24	65
Hounder, 1 sandwich	480	36	80
Hounder with Chili, 1 sandwich	575	41	89
Malt, large, 21 oz.	889	21	60
Shake, large, 21 oz.	831	22	60

DOMINO'S

FOOD/PORTION SIZE	CAL	FAT (g)	CHOL (mg)
Pizza, Cheese, 2 slices	376	10.0	18.5
Pizza, Deluxe, 2 slices	498	20.4	39.8
Pizza, Double Cheese/Pepperoni, 2 slices	545	25.3	47.7
Pizza, Ham, 2 slices	417	11.0	26.0
Pizza, Pepperoni, 2 slices	460	17.5	28.0
Pizza, Sausage/Mushroom, 2 slices	430	15.8	28.1
Pizza, Veggie, 2 slices	498	18.5	36.5

JACK IN THE BOX

FOOD/PORTION SIZE	CAL	FAT (g)	CHOL (mg)
Burger, Ham & Swiss, 1 hamburger	754	49	106
Burger, Monterey, 1 hamburger	865	57	152
Burger, Mushroom, 1 hamburger	470	24	64
Burger, Swiss and Bacon, 1 hamburger	681	47	92
Cheeseburger, 1 cheeseburger	325	17	41
Cheeseburger, Bacon, 1 cheeseburger	667	39	85
Cheesecake, 1 serving	309	17.5	63
Chicken Strip Dinner, 1 serving	689	30	100
Chicken Supreme, 1 sandwich	575	36	62
Crescent, Canadian, 1 serving	452	31	226
Crescent, Sausage, 1 serving	584	43	187
Crescent, Supreme, 1 serving	547	40	178
Dressing, Bleu Cheese, 1 serving	131	11	9.1
Dressing, Buttermilk House, 1 serving	181	18	10.3
Dressing, French, Reduced Calorie, 1 serving	80	4	0
Dressing, Thousand Island, 1 serving	156	15	11.4
Egg Platter, Scrambled, 1 serving	720	44	260
French Fries, large	353	19	13
French Fries, regular	221	12	8
Hamburger, 1 hamburger	288	13	26
Hot Apple Turnover, 1 serving	410	24	15
Jack, Breakfast, 1 serving	307	13	203
Jack, Jumbo, 1 serving	573	34	73
Jack, Jumbo, with Cheese, 1 serving	665	40	102
Jack, Moby, 1 serving	444	25	47
Nachos, Cheese, 1 serving	571	35	37
Nachos, Supreme, 1 serving	639	36	37
Onion Rings, 1 serving	382	23	27
Pancake Platter, 1 serving	630	27	85
Pita Club, without sauce, 1 serving	277	8	43
Pizza Pocket, 1 serving	497	28	32
Salad, Chef, 1 salad	295	18	107
Salad, Pasta & Seafood, 1 salad	394	22	48
Salad, Side, 1 salad	51	3	na
Salad, Taco, 1 salad	377	24	102
Sauce, BBQ, 1 serving	78	<1	0
Sauce, Mayo-Mustard, 1 serving	124	13	10
Sauce, Mayo-Onion, 1 serving	143	15	20

FOOD/PORTION SIZE	CAL	FAT (g)	CHOL (mg)
Sauce, Seafood Cocktail, 1 serving	57	<1	0
Shake, Chocolate Milk, 1 serving	330	7	25
Shake, Strawberry Milk, 1 serving	320	7	25
Shake, Vanilla Milk, 1 serving	320	6	25
Shrimp Dinner, 1 serving	731	37	157
Sirloin Steak Dinner, 1 serving	699	27	75
Taco, 1 serving	191	11	21
Taco, Super, 1 serving	288	17	37

McDONALD'S

FOOD/PORTION SIZE	CAL	FAT (g)	CHOL (mg)
Bacon Bits, 1 serving (3g)	16	1.2	0
Big Mac, 1 sandwich	562	32.4	103
Biscuit with Bacon, Egg, and Cheese, 1 biscuit	449	27.1	336
Biscuit with Biscuit Spread, 1 biscuit	260	12.7	1
Biscuit with Sausage, 1 biscuit	440	29.1	49
Biscuit with Sausage and Egg, 1 biscuit	529	35.3	358
Cheeseburger, 1 sandwich	308	13.8	53
Chicken McNuggets, 1 serving (113g)	288	16.3	65
Chow Mein Noodles, 1 serving (9g)	45	2.21	2
Cookies, Chocolaty Chip, 1 box	325	15.6	4
Cookies, McDonaldland, 1 box	288	9.2	0
Cone, Soft Serve, 1 cone	144	4.5	16
Croutons, 1 serving (11g)	52	2.17	0
Danish, Apple, 1 danish	369	17.9	25
Danish, Cinnamon Raisin, 1 danish	445	21	34
Danish, Iced Cheese, 1 danish	395	21.8	47
Danish, Raspberry, 1 danish	414	15.9	26
Dressing, 1000 Island, 1 packet	390	7.5	8
Dressing, Bleu Cheese, 1 packet	345	6.9	6
Dressing, French, 1 packet	232	5.2	0
Dressing, Lite Vinaigrette, 1 packet	60	.5	0
Dressing, Oriental, 1 packet	96	.1	0
Dressing, Ranch, 1 packet	332	8.6	5
Egg McMuffin, 1 sandwich	293	11.9	299
Eggs, Scrambled, 1 serving (100g)	157	11.1	545
Filet-o-Fish, 1 sandwich	442	26.1	50
French Fries, large	312	16.3	12
French Fries, regular	220	11.5	9
Hamburger, 1 hamburger	257	9.5	37
Hashbrowns, 1 serving (53g)	131	7.3	9
Honey, 1 serving (14g)	46	0	0
Hotcakes, with butter and syrup, 1 serving (176g)	413	9.2	21
McD.L.T., 1 sandwich	674	42.1	112
Muffin, English, with butter, 1 muffin	169	4.6	9
Pie, Apple, 1 pie	262	14.8	6
Quarter Pounder, 1 sandwich	414	20.7	86
Quarter Pounder with Cheese, 1 sandwich	517	29.2	118

FOOD/PORTION SIZE	CAL	FAT (g)	CHOL (mg)
Salad, Chef, 1 salad	231	13.6	152
Salad, Chicken, Oriental, 1 salad	141	3.4	78
Salad, Garden, 1 salad	112	6.8	107
Salad, Shrimp, 1 salad	104	2.8	193
Salad, Side, 1 salad	57	3.4	53
Sauce, Barbeque, 1 serving (32g)	53	0.5	0
Sauce, Hot Mustard, 1 serving (30g)	66	3.6	5
Sauce, Sweet-n-Sour, 1 serving (32g)	57	0.2	0
Sausage McMuffin, 1 serving	372	21.9	64
Sausage McMuffin with Egg, 1 serving	451	27.4	336
Sausage, Pork, 1 serving	180	16.3	48
Shake, Chocolate Milk, 1 shake	388	10.6	41
Shake, Strawberry Milk, 1 shake	384	10.1	41
Shake, Vanilla Milk, 1 shake	354	10.2	41
Sundae, Hot Caramel, 1 sundae	343	9.1	35
Sundae, Hot Fudge, 1 sundae	313	9.4	28
Sundae, Strawberry, 1 sundae	283	7.3	27

TACO BELL

FOOD/PORTION SIZE	CAL	FAT (g)	CHOL (mg)
Bellbeefer, 1 serving	312.1	13.6	56.1
Burrito, Bean, 1 serving	359.6	10.9	13.8
Burrito, Bean, Green, 1 serving	353.9	10.9	58.7
Burrito, Beef, 1 serving	402.1	17.3	58.7
Burrito, Beef, Green, 1 serving	396.5	17.3	58.7
Burrito, Combo, 1 serving	380.9	14.1	36.2
Burrito, Combo, Green, 1 serving	375.2	14.1	36.2
Burrito, Double Beef, Supreme, 1 serving	464.5	22.8	58.7
Burrito, Double Beef, Supreme, Green, 1 serving	458.8	22.8	58.7
Burrito Supreme, 1 serving	422	18.8	35.4
Burrito Supreme, Green, 1 serving	416.3	18.8	35.4
Burrito Supreme Platter, 1 serving	773.7	36.9	79
Burrito Supreme Platter, Green, 1 serving	762.3	37	79
Cheesearito, 1 serving	311.9	12.8	29.2
Crispas, Cinnamon, 1 serving	266.1	15.9	1.8
Dressing, Ranch, 1 serving	235.6	24.8	35.5
Enchirito, 1 serving	381.8	20.1	38.6
Enchirito, Green, 1 serving	370.5	20.1	56.1
Fajita Steak Taco, 1 serving	235.4	10.9	14.3
Fajita Steak Taco with Guacamole, 1 serving	269.4	13.1	14.3
Fajita Steak Taco with Sour Cream, 1 serving	281.1	15.4	14.3
Jalapeño Peppers, 1 serving (100g)	20	.18	.8
Nachos, 1 serving	356.3	19.2	8.6
Pintos & Cheese, 1 serving	194.2	9.5	18.7
Pintos & Cheese, Green, 1 serving	188.6	9.5	18.7
Nachos Bellgrande, 1 serving	719.4	40.7	42.8
Pizza, Mexican, 1 serving	713.9	47.9	80.8

FOOD/PORTION SIZE	CAL	FAT (g)	CHOL (mg)
Salad, Seafood, without dressing, 1 serving	648.3	41.5	81.6
Salad, Seafood, without dressing/shell, 1 serving	216.8	11.4	81
Salad, Taco, without beans, 1 serving	821.8	57.2	80.5
Salad, Taco, without salsa, 1 serving	931.3	62	85.5
Salad, Taco, without shell, 1 serving	524.6	32.1	82.3
Salad, Taco, with Ranch Dressing, 1 serving	1,167.3	86.9	121
Salad, Taco, with Salsa, 1 serving	949.4	62.1	85.5
Salsa, 1 serving (90.7g)	18.1	.09	na
Sauce, Hot Taco, 1 packet,	2.5	.09	na
Sauce, Taco, 1 packet	2.06	.01	na
Taco, 1 serving	183.9	10.9	31.8
Taco Bellgrande, 1 serving	350.5	21.7	55.2
Taco Bellgrande Platter, 1 serving	1,001.5	50.8	80.2
Taco Bellgrande Platter, Green, 1 serving	990.2	50.8	80.2
Taco Light, 1 serving	411.2	28.9	57.3
Taco Light Platter, Green, 1 serving	1,050.9	58.1	82.2
Taco, Soft, 1 serving	228.3	11.8	31.8
Tostada, 1 serving	243.2	10.9	17.9
Tostada, Beefy, 1 serving	322.4	19.6	40.3
Tostada, Beefy, Green, 1 serving	316.5	19.6	40.3
Tostada, Green, 1 serving	237.5	10.9	17.8

WENDY'S

FOOD/PORTION SIZE	CAL	FAT (g)	CHOL (mg)
Big Classic, with Kaiser Bun, 1 sandwich	470	25	80
Biscuit, Buttermilk, 1 biscuit	320	17	tr
Bun, Kaiser, 1 bun	180	2	5
Bun, Multi-Grain, 1 bun	140	3	tr
Bun, White, 1 bun	140	2	tr
Cheese, American, 1 slice	60	6	15
Chicken Breast Filet, 1 sandwich	200	10	60
Chicken Fried Steak, 1 serving	580	41	95
Chicken Nuggets, Crispy, cooked in animal/vegetable oil, 6 pieces	290	21	55
Chicken Nuggets, Crispy, cooked in vegetable oil, 6 pieces	310	21	50
Chili, New, 1 serving	230	9	50
Chili, Regular, 1 serving	240	8	25
Condiments, Pre-Packaged, black pepper, 1 packet	0	0	0
Condiments, Pre-Packaged, creamer, nondairy, 3/8 oz.	14	1	0
Condiments, Pre-Packaged, half & half, 3/8 oz.	14	1	5
Condiments, Pre-Packaged, hot chili seasoning, 1 packet	6	na	na
Condiments, Pre-Packaged, ketchup, 1 packet	12	na	0
Cookie, Chocolate Chip, 1 cookie	320	17	5
Corn Relish, Old Fashion, 1/4 cup	35	na	na

FOOD/PORTION SIZE	CAL	FAT (g)	CHOL (mg)
Danish, Apple, 1 pastry	360	14	na
Danish, Cheese, 1 pastry	430	21	na
Danish, Cinnamon Raisin, 1 pastry	410	18	na
Dressing, Blue Cheese, 1 tbsp.	60	7	10
Dressing, Celery Seed, 1 tbsp.	70	6	5
Dressing, French, 1 tbsp.	70	6	0
Dressing, French Style, 1 tbsp.	70	5	0
Dressing, Golden Italian, 1 tbsp.	50	4	0
Dressing, Oil, 1 tbsp.	120	14	0
Dressing, Ranch, 1 tbsp.	50	6	5
Dressing, Reduced Calorie Bacon/Tomato, 1 tbsp.	45	4	tr
Dressing, Reduced Calorie Creamy Cucumber, 1 tbsp.	50	5	tr
Dressing, Reduced Calorie Italian, 1 tbsp.	25	2	0
Dressing, Reduced Calorie Thousand Island, 1 tbsp.	45	4	5
Dressing, Thousand Island, 1 tbsp.	70	7	5
Dressing, Wine Vinegar, 1 tbsp.	2	na	0
Egg, Fried, 1 egg	90	6	230
Eggs, Scrambled, 2 eggs	190	12	450
Fish Fillet, 1 serving	210	11	45
French Toast, 2 slices	400	19	115
Fries, cooked in animal/vegetable oil, regular	310	15	15
Fries, cooked in vegetable oil, regular	300	15	5
Frosty Dairy Dessert, small	400	14	50
Gravy, Sausage, 6 oz.	440	36	85
Hamburger, 1/4-lb. Single Patty	210	14	75
Hamburger, Kid's Meal, with White Bun, 1 hamburger	200	9	35
Omelet #1, Eggs, Ham, Cheese, 1 serving	290	21	355
Omelet #2, Eggs, Ham, Cheese, Mushrooms, 1 serving	250	17	450
Omelet #3, Eggs, Ham, Cheese, Onion, Green Pepper, 1 serving	280	19	525
Omelet #4, Eggs, Mushrooms, Green Pepper, Onion, 1 serving	210	15	460
Nuggets Sauce, Barbeque, 1 packet	50	na	0
Nuggets Sauce, Honey, 1 packet	45	na	0
Nuggets Sauce, Sweet Mustard, 1 packet	50	1	0
Nuggets Sauce, Sweet & Sour, 1 packet	45	na	0
Potato, Hot Stuffed Baked, Bacon & Cheese, 1 serving	570	30	22
Potato, Hot Stuffed Baked, Broccoli & Cheese, 1 serving	500	25	22
Potato, Hot Stuffed Baked, Cheese, 1 serving	590	34	22
Potato, Hot Stuffed Baked, Chili & Cheese, 1 serving	510	20	22

FOOD/PORTION SIZE	CAL	FAT (g)	CHOL (mg)
Potato, Hot Stuffed Baked, plain, 1 serving	250	2	tr
Potato, Hot Stuffed Baked, Sour Cream & Chives, 1 serving	460	24	15
Potatoes, Breakfast, 1 serving	360	22	20
Pudding, Butterscotch, 1/4 cup	90	4	tr
Salad, Chef (take-out), 1 salad	180	9	120
Salad, Garden (take-out), 1 salad	102	5	0
Salad, Taco, 1 salad	660	37	35
Sandwich, Breakfast, 1 sandwich	370	19	200
Sauce, Special, 1 tbsp.	40	3	5
Sauce, Taco, 1 packet	10	na	0
Sauce, Tartar, 1 tbsp.	90	na	10
Sausage Patty, 1 patty	200	18	45
Topping, Apple, 1 packet	130	na	0
Topping, Blueberry, 1 packet	60	na	0
Topping, Imitation Sour, 1 oz.	45	4	0

Fats & Oils

FOOD/PORTION SIZE	CAL	FAT (g)	CHOL (mg)
Butter Buds, 1 g	4	0	0
Butter, 1 pat	35	4	11
Butter, stick, 1/2 cup	810	92	247
Butter, 1 tbsp. (1/8 stick)	100	11	31
Lard, 1 cup	1,850	205	195
Lard, 1 tbsp.	115	13	12
Margarine, imitation, soft, 1 tbsp.	5	5	0
Margarine, Parkay, 1 tbsp.	100	11	0
Margarine, regular, hard, 1/2 cup (1 stick)	810	91	0
Margarine, regular, hard, 1 pat	35	4	0
Margarine, regular, hard, 1 tbsp. (1/8 stick)	100	11	0
Margarine, regular, soft, 1 tbsp.	100	11	0
Margarine, Soft Diet Parkay Reduced Calorie, 1 tbsp.	50	6	0
Margarine, Soft Parkay, 1 tbsp.	100	11	0
Margarine, Soft Parkay Corn Oil, 1 tbsp.	100	11	0
Margarine, Squeeze Parkay, 1 tbsp.	100	11	0
Margarine, spread, hard, 1/2 cup (1 stick)	610	69	0
Margarine, spread, hard, 1 pat	25	3	0
Margarine, spread, hard, 1 tbsp. (1/8 stick)	75	9	0
Margarine, spread, soft, 1 tbsp.	75	9	0
Margarine, Stick, Corn Oil, Mazola, 1 tbsp.	100	11	0
Margarine, Stick, Soy Oil, Chiffon, 1 tbsp.	100	11	0
Margarine, Stick, Soy Oil, Land O' Lakes, 1 tbsp.	97	4	0

FOOD/PORTION SIZE	CAL	FAT (g)	CHOL (mg)
Margarine, Stick, Soy Oil, Weight Watcher's Reduced-Calorie, 1 tbsp.	60	7	0
Margarine, Stick, Sunflower Oil, Promise, 1 tbsp.	90	10	0
Margarine, Tub, Soy Oil, Chiffon, 1 tbsp.	90	10	0
Margarine, Tub, Soy Oil, Land O' Lakes, 1 tbsp.	97	4	0
Margarine, Tub, Soy Oil, Weight Watchers Reduced Calorie, 1 tbsp.	50	6	0
Margarine, Tub, Sunflower Oil, Promise, 1 tbsp.	90	10	0
Margarine, Whipped, Cup, Parkay, 1 tbsp.	60	7	0
Margarine, Whipped, Miracle Brand, 1 tbsp.	60	7	0
Margarine, Whipped, Stick, Miracle Brand, 1 tbsp.	70	7	0
Margarine, Whipped, Stick, Parkay, 1 tbsp.	60	7	0
Mayonnaise, see BAKING PRODUCTS & CONDIMENTS			
Oil, Corn, Mazola, 1 tbsp.	120	14	0
Oil, salad or cooking, corn, 1 cup	1,925	218	0
Oil, salad or cooking, corn, 1 tbsp.	125	14	0
Oil, salad or cooking, olive, 1 cup	1,910	216	0
Oil, salad or cooking, olive, 1 tbsp.	125	14	0
Oil, salad or cooking, peanut, 1 cup	1,910	216	0
Oil, salad or cooking, peanut, 1 tbsp.	125	14	0
Oil, salad or cooking, safflower, 1 cup	1,925	218	0
Oil, salad or cooking, safflower, 1 tbsp.	125	14	0
Oil, salad or cooking, soybean, hydrogenated, 1 cup	1,925	218	0
Oil, salad or cooking, sunflower, 1 cup	1,925	218	0
Oil, salad or cooking, sunflower, 1 tbsp.	125	14	0
Oil, soybean-cottonseed blend, hydrogenated, 1 cup	1,925	218	0
Oil, salad or cooking, soybean, hydrogenated, 1 tbsp.	125	14	0
Oil, soybean-cottonseed blend, hydrogenated, 1 tbsp.	125	14	0
Oil, Sunflower, Sunlite, 1 tbsp.	120	14	0
Oil, Vegetable, Crisco, 1 tbsp.	120	14	0
Oil, Vegetable, Puritan, 1 tbsp.	120	14	0
Oil, Vegetable, Wesson, 1 tbsp.	120	14	0
Shortening, cooking, vegetable, 1 cup	1,810	205	0
Shortening, cooking, vegetable, 1 tbsp.	115	13	0

FOOD/PORTION SIZE	CAL	FAT (g)	CHOL (mg)
Shortening, Vegetable, Crisco, 1 tbsp.	110	12	0
Spray, Cooking (Vegetable), Pam, 1.25 seconds	7	1	0
Spray, No-Stick (Vegetable), Mazola, 2.5 seconds	6	1	0
Spread, 50% Fat, Parkay, 1 tbsp.	60	7	0
Spread, Cup, Kraft, 1 tbsp.	50	6	0
Spread, Light, Corn Oil, Parkay, 1 tbsp.	70	8	0
Spread, Stick, Kraft, 1 tbsp.	60	7	0
Spread, Tub (Vegetable), Shedd's, 1 tbsp.	70	7	0

Fish & Shellfish

FOOD/PORTION SIZE	CAL	FAT (g)	CHOL (mg)
Clams, canned, drained solids, 3 oz.	85	2	54
Clams, raw, meat only, 3 oz.	65	1	43
Crabmeat, canned, 1 cup	135	3	135
Fish sticks, frozen, reheated, 4 × 1 × 1/2-in. stick	70	3	26
Flounder, baked, with lemon juice, with butter, 3 oz.	120	6	68
Flounder, baked, with lemon juice, with margarine, 3 oz.	120	6	55
Flounder, baked, with lemon juice, without added fat, 3 oz.	80	1	59
Haddock, breaded, fried, 3 oz.	175	9	75
Halibut, broiled, with butter, with lemon juice, 3 oz.	140	6	62
Herring, pickled, 3 oz.	190	13	85
Oysters, breaded, fried, 1 oyster	90	5	35
Oysters, raw, meat only, 1 cup	160	4	120
Perch, ocean, breaded, fried, 1 fillet	185	11	66
Salmon, baked, red, 3 oz.	140	5	60
Salmon, canned, pink, solids and liquid, 3 oz.	120	5	34
Salmon, Pink, Bumble Bee, 3.5 oz.	160	8	na
Salmon, Red, Bumble Bee, 3.5 oz.	180	10	na
Salmon, smoked, 3 oz.	150	8	51
Sardines, canned in oil, drained, 3 oz.	175	9	85
Sardines, (in Vegetable Oil), King Oscar, 3.75 oz.	460	42	na
Scallops, breaded, frozen, reheated, 6 scallops	195	10	70
Shrimp, canned, drained solids, 3 oz.	100	1	128

FOOD/PORTION SIZE	CAL	FAT (g)	CHOL (mg)
Shrimp, French fried, 3 oz. (7 medium)	200	10	168
Sole, baked, with lemon juice, with butter, 3 oz.	120	6	68
Sole, baked, with lemon juice, with margarine, 3 oz.	120	6	55
Sole, baked, with lemon juice, without added fat, 3 oz.	80	1	59
Trout, broiled with butter and lemon juice, 3 oz.	175	9	71
Tuna, Albacore, Chunk (in Water), Starkist, 2 oz.	70	1	na
Tuna, Albacore (in Water), Bumble Bee, 2 oz.	60	1	na
Tuna, Albacore (in Water), Chicken of the Sea, 1 cup	490	32	na
Tuna, canned, drained solids, oil packed, chunk light, 3 oz.	165	7	55
Tuna, canned, drained solids, water packed, solid white, 3 oz.	135	1	48
Tuna, Chunk Light (in Vegetable Oil), Bumble Bee, 2 oz.	160	12	na
Tuna, Chunk Light, (in Vegetable Oil), Chicken of the Sea, 2 oz.	170	13	na
Tuna, Chunk Light (in Vegetable Oil), Starkist, 2 oz.	150	13	na
Tuna, Chunk Light (in Water), Bumble Bee, 2 oz.	60	1	na
Tuna, Chunk Light (in Water), Chicken of the Sea, 2 oz.	60	1	na
Tuna, Chunk Light (in Water), Starkist, 2 oz.	65	1	na
Tuna salad, 1 cup	375	19	80

Frozen Appetizers & Entrees

FOOD/PORTION SIZE	CAL	FAT (g)	CHOL (mg)
APPETIZERS			
Swanson's, Chicken Nuggets Platter, 8 3/4 oz.	460	25	na
Weaver, Chicken Mini Drums, 3 oz.	210	12	na
Weaver, Chicken Nuggets, 3 oz.	170	9	na
Weight Watchers, Baked Cheese Ravioli, 9 oz.	300	12	na
Weight Watchers, Chicken Nuggets, 3 oz.	180	10	na

FOOD/PORTION SIZE	CAL	FAT (g)	CHOL (mg)
COMBINATION ENTREES			
Swanson's, Mexican Style Combination Dinner, 14¼ oz.	500	25	na
MEAT ENTREES			
La Choy, Fresh & Lite, Beef & Broccoli, 11 oz.	290	7	na
Lean Cuisine, Oriental Beef, 8⅝ oz.	270	5	na
Lean Cuisine, Salisbury Steak, 9½ oz.	270	13	na
Swanson's, Salisbury Steak Dinner, 10¾ oz.	410	18	na
Swanson's, Veal Parmigiana, 12¼ oz.	450	22	na
Weight Watchers, Lasagna with Meat Sauce, 11 oz.	330	13	na
POULTRY ENTREES			
La Choy, Fresh & Lite, Chicken Chow Mein, 11 oz.	270	9	na
La Choy, Fresh & Lite, Sweet & Sour Chicken, 10 oz.	280	4	na
Lean Cuisine, Breast of Chicken Marsala, 8⅛ oz.	190	5	na
Lean Cuisine, Chicken Cacciatore, 10⅞ oz.	280	10	na
Swanson's, Turkey White Meat Dinner, 11½ oz.	360	11	na
Weaver, Chicken Italian Style, 3 oz.	205	11	na
Weight Watchers, Chicken a la King, 9 oz.	220	7	na
Weight Watchers, Chicken Burritos, 5 oz.	300	11	na
SEAFOOD ENTREES			
Booth, Light Entree, Filet of Cod Au Gratin, 9½ oz.	280	11	na
Booth, Light Entree, Filet of Cod Mushroom, 9½ oz.	280	11	na
Booth, Light Entree, Shrimp Fettucine Alfredo, 10 oz.	260	8	na
Booth, Light Entree, Shrimp Oriental, 10 oz.	190	3	na
Booth, Light Entree, Shrimp New Orleans, 10 oz.	230	5	na
Lean Cuisine, Filet of Fish Divan, 12⅜ oz.	270	9	na
Lean Cuisine, Tuna Lasagna, 9¾ oz.	280	10	na
La Choy, Fresh & Lite, Shrimp with Lobster Sauce, 10 oz.	210	7	na
Mrs. Pauls, Light Entree, Fish Dijon, 8.75 oz.	220	9	na

FOOD/PORTION SIZE	CAL	FAT (g)	CHOL (mg)
Mrs. Pauls, Light Entree, Fish Mornay, 9 oz.	250	10	na
Mrs. Pauls, Light Entree, Shrimp Primavera, 9.5 oz.	190	4	na
Weight Watchers, Seafood Linguini, 9 oz.	220	7	na

Frozen Desserts

FOOD/PORTION SIZE	CAL	FAT (g)	CHOL (mg)
DAIRY			
Ice Cream, Butter Pecan, Breyers, 1 cup	150	8	na
Ice Cream, Chocolate, Breyers, 1 cup	160	8	na
Ice Cream, Chocolate, Sealtest, ½ cup	140	7	na
Ice Cream, Peach, Natural, Breyers, 1 cup	140	12	na
Ice Cream, Strawberry, Natural, Breyers, 1 cup	130	6	na
Ice Cream, Vanilla/Chocolate/ Strawberry, Sealtest, ½ cup	140	6	na
Ice Cream, Vanilla, Natural, Breyers, 1 cup	180	12	na
Ice cream, vanilla, regular, hardened, 1 cup	270	14	59
Ice cream, vanilla, rich, hardened, 1 cup	350	24	88
Ice Cream, Vanilla, Sealtest, ½ cup	140	7	na
Ice cream, vanilla, soft serve, 1 cup	375	23	153
Ice Milk, Chocolate, Weight Watchers, ½ cup	100	3	na
Ice Milk, Neapolitan, Weight Watchers, ½ cup	100	3	na
Ice milk, vanilla, hardened, 1 cup	185	6	18
Ice milk, vanilla, soft serve, 1 cup	225	5	13
Ice milk, Vanilla, Weight Watchers, ½ cup	100	3	na
Sherbet, 1 cup	270	4	14
SPECIALTY BARS			
Fruit Bars, all flavors, Jell-O, 1 bar	45	0	0
Fruit n' Juice Bars, Pineapple, Dole, 1 bar	70	1	na
Fruit n' Juice Bars, Raspberry-Pineapple, Dole Freshlites, 1 bar	25	1	na

FOOD/PORTION SIZE	CAL	FAT (g)	CHOL (mg)
Gelatin Pops, all flavors, Jell-O, 1 bar	35	0	0
Popsicle, 3-fl.-oz. size, 1 popsicle	70	0	0
Pudding Pops, Chocolate-Caramel Swirl, Jell-O, 1 bar	80	2	0
Pudding Pops, Chocolate-Covered Chocolate, Jell-O, 1 bar	130	7	0
Pudding Pops, Chocolate-Covered Vanilla, Jell-O, 1 bar	130	7	0
Pudding Pops, Chocolate, Jell-O, 1 bar	80	2	0
Pudding Pops, Chocolate-Vanilla Swirl, Jell-O, 1 bar	70	2	0
Pudding Pops, Chocolate with Chocolate Chips, Jell-O, 1 bar	80	3	0
Pudding Pops, Vanilla, Jell-O, 1 bar	70	2	0
Pudding Pops, Vanilla with Chocolate Chips, Jell-O, 1 bar	80	3	0

Fruit

FOOD/PORTION SIZE	CAL	FAT (g)	CHOL (mg)
Applesauce, canned, sweetened, 1 cup	195	tr	0
Applesauce, canned, unsweetened, 1 cup	105	tr	0
Apples, dried, sulfured, 10 rings	155	tr	0
Apples, raw, peeled, sliced, 1 cup	65	tr	0
Apples, raw, unpeeled, 3¼-in. diameter, 1 apple	125	1	0
Apricot nectar, canned, 1 cup	140	tr	0
Apricots, canned, heavy syrup pack, 3 halves	70	tr	0
Apricots, canned, juice pack, 3 halves	40	tr	0
Apricots, dried, cooked, unsweetened, 1 cup	210	tr	0
Apricots, dried, uncooked, 1 cup	310	1	0
Apricots, raw, 3 apricots	50	tr	0
Avocados, California, raw, whole, 1 avocado	305	30	0
Avocados, Florida, raw, whole, 1 avocado	340	27	0
Bananas, raw without peel, whole, 1 banana	105	1	0
Blackberries, raw, 1 cup	75	1	0
Blueberries, frozen, sweetened, 10 oz.	230	tr	0
Blueberries, raw, 1 cup	80	1	0
Cantaloupe, raw, ½ melon	95	1	0

FOOD/PORTION SIZE	CAL	FAT (g)	CHOL (mg)
Cherries, sour, red, pitted, canned, waterpack, 1 cup	90	tr	0
Cherries, sweet, raw, 10 cherries	50	1	0
Cranberry sauce, sweetened, canned, strained, 1 cup	420	tr	0
Dates, chopped, 1 cup	490	1	0
Dates, whole, without pits, 10 dates	230	tr	0
Figs, dried, 10 figs	475	2	0
Fruit cocktail, canned, heavy syrup, 1 cup	185	tr	0
Fruit cocktail, canned, juice pack, 1 cup	115	tr	0
Fruit Cocktail, DelMonte, ½ cup	80	0	na
Fruit Cocktail, DelMonte Lite, ½ cup	50	0	na
Fruit Cocktail, Libby's Lite, ½ cup	50	0	na
Fruit, Mixed, Chunky, Lite, Libby's, ½ cup	50	0	na
Fruit, Mixed, in Syrup, Birds Eye Quick Thaw Pouch, 5 oz.	120	0	0
Fruit Salad, Kraft Pure Chilled, ½ cup	50	0	0
Grapefruit, canned, with syrup, 1 cup	150	tr	0
Grapefruit, raw, ½ grapefruit	40	tr	0
Grapefruit Sections, Kraft, Pure, Chilled Unsweetened, ½ cup	50	0	0
Grapes, Thompson seedless, 10 grapes	35	tr	0
Grapes, Tokay/Emperor, seeded, 10 grapes	40	tr	0
Honeydew melon, raw, 1/10 melon	45	tr	0
Kiwifruit, raw, without skin, 1 kiwifruit	45	tr	0
Lemons, raw, without peel and seeds, 1 lemon	15	tr	0
Mangos, raw, 1 mango	135	1	0
Nectarines, raw, 1 nectarine	65	1	0
Olives, canned, green, 4 medium or 3 extra large	15	2	0
Olives, ripe, mission, pitted, 3 small or 2 large	15	2	0
Oranges, raw, whole, without peel and seeds, 1 orange	60	tr	0
Papayas, raw, ½-in. cubes, 1 cup	65	tr	0
Peaches, canned, heavy syrup, ½ peach	60	tr	0
Peaches, canned, juice pack, ½ peach	35	tr	0
Peaches, dried, uncooked, 1 cup	380	1	0
Peaches, frozen, sliced, sweetened, 1 cup	235	tr	0
Peaches, raw, whole, 2½-in. diameter, 1 peach	35	tr	0
Peaches, Sliced, Lite, Libby's, ½ cup	50	0	na

FOOD/PORTION SIZE	CAL	FAT (g)	CHOL (mg)
Pears, Bartlett raw, with skin, 1 pear	100	1	0
Pears, Bosc raw, with skin, 1 pear	85	1	0
Pears, canned, heavy syrup, 1/2 pear	60	tr	0
Pears, canned, juice pack, 1/2 pear	40	tr	0
Pears, D'Anjou raw, with skin, 1 pear	120	1	0
Pears, Halves, Lite, Libby's, 1/2 cup	60	0	na
Pineapple, canned, heavy syrup, crushed/chunks, 1 cup	200	tr	0
Pineapple, canned, heavy syrup, slices, 1 slice	45	tr	0
Pineapple, canned, juice pack, crushed/chunks, 1 cup	150	tr	0
Pineapple, canned, juice pack, slices, 1 slice	35	tr	0
Pineapple, raw, diced, 1 cup	75	1	0
Plantains, without peel, cooked/boiled, sliced, 1 cup	180	tr	0
Plantains, without peel, raw, 1 plantain	220	1	0
Plums, canned, purple, heavy syrup, 3 plums	120	tr	0
Plums, canned, purple, juice pack, 3 plums	55	tr	0
Plums, raw, 1 1/2-in. diameter, 1 plum	15	tr	0
Plums, raw, 2 1/8-in. diameter, 1 plum	35	tr	0
Prunes, dried, cooked, unsweetened, 1 cup	225	tr	0
Prunes, dried, uncooked, 4 extra large or 5 large	115	tr	0
Raisins, seedless, 1/2-oz. packet, 1 packet	40	tr	0
Raisins, seedless, 1 cup	435	1	0
Raspberries, frozen, sweetened, 1 cup	255	tr	0
Raspberries, frozen, sweetened, 10 oz.	295	tr	0
Raspberries, in Lite Syrup, Birds Eye Quick Thaw Pouch, 5 oz.	100	1	0
Raspberries, raw, 1 cup	60	1	0
Rhubarb, cooked, added sugar, 1 cup	280	tr	0
Strawberries, frozen, sweetened, sliced, 1 cup	245	tr	0
Strawberries, frozen, sweetened, sliced, 10 oz.	275	tr	0
Strawberries, Halved, in Syrup, Birds Eye Quick Thaw Pouch, 5 oz.	90	0	0
Strawberries, raw, capped, whole, 1 cup	45	1	0
Strawberries, Whole, Lite Syrup, Birds Eye, 4 oz.	80	0	0

FOOD/PORTION SIZE	CAL	FAT (g)	CHOL (mg)
Tangerines, canned, light syrup, 1 cup	155	tr	0
Tangerines, raw, 2 3/8-in. diameter, 1 tangerine	35	tr	0
Watermelon, raw, 4 × 8-in. wedge, 1 piece	155	2	0
Watermelon, raw, diced, 1 cup	50	1	0

Gelatins, Puddings, & Pie Fillings

FOOD/PORTION SIZE	CAL	FAT (g)	CHOL (mg)
All flavors, Gelatin, Jell-O, 1/2 cup (average)	80	0	0
All flavors, Gelatin, Low Calorie, D-Zerta, 1/2 cup (average)	8	0	0
All flavors, Gelatin, Sugar Free, Jell-O, 1/2 cup (average)	8	0	0
Banana Cream, Pudding & Pie Filling, Instant, Jell-O, with whole milk, 1/2 cup	160	4	15
Banana Cream, Pudding & Pie Filling, Jell-O, with whole milk, 1/6 pie (excluding crust)	100	3	10
Banana, Pudding & Pie Filling, Instant, Sugar Free Jell-O, with 2% milk, 1/2 cup	90	2	10
Butter Pecan, Pudding & Pie Filling, Instant, Jell-O, with whole milk, 1/2 cup	170	5	15
Butterscotch, Pudding & Pie Filling, Instant, Jell-O, with whole milk, 1/2 cup	160	4	15
Butterscotch, Pudding & Pie Filling, Instant, Sugar Free, Jell-O, with 2% milk, 1/2 cup	90	2	10
Butterscotch, Pudding & Pie Filling, Jell-O, with whole milk, 1/2 cup	170	4	15
Butterscotch, Pudding, Reduced Calorie, D-Zerta, with skim milk, 1/2 cup	70	0	0
Chocolate Fudge, Pudding & Pie Filling, Instant, Jell-O, with whole milk, 1/2 cup	180	5	15
Chocolate Fudge, Pudding & Pie Filling, Instant, Sugar Free, Jell-O, with 2% milk, 1/2 cup	100	3	10
Chocolate Fudge, Pudding & Pie Filling, Jell-O, with whole milk, 1/2 cup	160	4	15

FOOD/PORTION SIZE	CAL	FAT (g)	CHOL (mg)
Chocolate Fudge, Rich & Luscious Mousse, Jell-O, with whole milk, 1/2 cup	150	6	10
Chocolate, pudding, canned, 5-oz. can	205	11	1
Chocolate, pudding, instant, dry mix made with whole milk, 1/2 cup	155	4	14
Chocolate, Pudding & Pie Filling, Instant, Jell-O, with whole milk, 1/2 cup	180	4	15
Chocolate, Pudding & Pie Filling, Instant, Sugar Free, Jell-O, with 2% milk, 1/2 cup	100	3	10
Chocolate, Pudding & Pie Filling, Jell-O, with whole milk, 1/2 cup	160	4	15
Chocolate, Pudding & Pie Filling, Sugar Free, Jell-O, with 2% milk, 1/2 cup	90	3	10
Chocolate, Pudding, Reduced Calorie, D-Zerta, with skim milk, 1/2 cup	60	0	0
Chocolate, pudding, regular (cooked), dry mix made with whole milk, 1/2 cup	150	4	15
Chocolate, Rich & Luscious Mousse, Jell-O, with whole milk, 1/2 cup	150	6	10
Chocolate Tapioca Pudding, Jell-O Americana, with whole milk, 1/2 cup	170	5	15
Coconut Cream, Instant Pudding & Pie Filling, Jell-O, with whole milk, 1/2 cup	180	6	15
Coconut Cream, Pudding & Pie Filling, Jell-O, with whole milk, 1/6 pie (excluding crust)	110	4	10
Custard, baked, 1 cup	305	5	278
Custard, Golden Egg, Mix, Jell-O Americana, with whole milk, 1/2 cup	160	5	80
Fruit Punch, Gelatin, Royal, 1/2 cup	80	0	0
Gelatin dessert, prepared with water, 1/2 cup	70	0	0
Gelatin, dry, 1 envelope	25	tr	0
Lemon, Gelatin, Royal, 1/2 cup	80	0	0
Lemon, Pudding & Pie Filling, Instant, Jell-O, with whole milk, 1/2 cup	170	4	15
Lemon, Pudding & Pie Filling, Jell-O, with whole milk, 1/6 pie (excluding crust)	170	2	90
Lime, Gelatin, Royal, 1/2 cup	80	0	0
Milk Chocolate, Pudding & Pie Filling, Instant, Jell-O, with whole milk, 1/2 cup	180	5	15
Milk Chocolate, Pudding & Pie Filling, Jell-O, whole milk, 1/2 cup	160	4	15
Orange, Gelatin, Royal, 1/2 cup	80	0	0
Pineapple Cream, Pudding & Pie Filling, Instant, Jell-O, with whole milk, 1/2 cup	160	4	15
Pistachio, Pudding & Pie Filling, Instant, Jell-O, with whole milk, 1/2 cup	170	5	15
Pistachio, Pudding & Pie Filling, Instant, Sugar Free, Jell-O, with 2% milk, 1/2 cup	100	3	10
Raspberry, Gelatin, Royal, 1/2 cup	80	0	0
Rice, pudding, prepared with whole milk, 1/2 cup	155	4	15
Strawberry/Banana, Gelatin, Royal, 1/2 cup	80	0	0
Strawberry, Gelatin, Royal, 1/2 cup	80	0	0
Strawberry/Orange, Gelatin, Royal, 1/2 cup	80	0	0
Tapioca, pudding, canned, 5-oz. can	160	5	tr
Tapioca, pudding, prepared with whole milk, 1/2 cup	145	4	15
Vanilla, French, Pudding & Pie Filling, Instant, Jell-O, with whole milk, 1/2 cup	160	4	15
Vanilla, French, Pudding & Pie Filling, Jell-O, with whole milk, 1/2 cup	170	4	15
Vanilla, pudding, canned, 5-oz. can	220	10	1
Vanilla, pudding, instant dry mix made with whole milk, 1/2 cup	150	4	15
Vanilla, Pudding & Pie Filling, Instant, Jell-O, with whole milk, 1/2 cup	170	4	15
Vanilla, Pudding & Pie Filling, Instant, Sugar Free, Jell-O, with 2% milk, 1/2 cup	90	2	10
Vanilla, Pudding & Pie Filling, Jell-O, with whole milk, 1/2 cup	160	4	15
Vanilla, Pudding & Pie Filling, Sugar Free, Jell-O, with 2% milk, 1/2 cup	80	2	10
Vanilla, Pudding, Reduced Calorie, D-Zerta, with skim milk, 1/2 cup	70	0	0
Vanilla, pudding, regular (cooked) dry mix, made with whole milk, 1/2 cup	145	4	15
Vanilla, Tapioca, Pudding, Jell-O Americana, with whole milk, 1/2 cup	160	4	15

Gravies & Sauces

FOOD/PORTION SIZE	CAL	FAT (g)	CHOL (mg)
GRAVIES			
Beef, canned, 1 cup	125	5	7
Brown, from dry mix, 1 cup	80	2	2
Chicken, canned, 1 cup	190	14	5
Chicken, from dry mix, 1 cup	85	2	3
Mushroom, canned, 1 cup	120	6	0
SAUCES			
Barbeque sauce, *see* BAKING PRODUCTS AND CONDIMENTS			
Cheese, from dry mix, prepared with milk, 1 cup	305	17	53
Hollandaise, prepared with water, 1 cup	240	20	52
Soy sauce, *see* BAKING PRODUCTS AND CONDIMENTS			
Spaghetti, Extra Chunky, Mushroom and Green Pepper, Prego, 4 oz.	110	6	na
Spaghetti, Extra Chunky, Tomato and Onion, Prego, 4 oz.	140	6	na
Spaghetti, Plain, Prego, 4 oz.	140	6	na
Spaghetti, Ragu, 4 oz.	80	3	0
Spaghetti, Thick & Hearty, Ragu, 4 oz.	140	5	0
Spaghetti, with Meat, Homestyle, Ragu, 4 oz.	70	2	2
Spaghetti, with Meat, Prego, 4 oz.	150	6	na
Spaghetti, with Meat, Ragu, 4 oz.	80	3	0
Spaghetti, with Mushrooms, Prego, 4 oz.	140	5	na
Spaghetti, with Mushrooms, Ragu, 4 oz.	80	4	0
Spaghetti, with Mushrooms, Thick & Hearty, Ragu, 4 oz.	140	5	2
White, medium, from home recipe, 1 cup	395	30	32
White, prepared with milk, 1 cup	240	13	34

Legumes

FOOD/PORTION SIZE	CAL	FAT (g)	CHOL (mg)
BEANS			
Black, dry cooked, drained, 1 cup	225	1	0
Chickpeas, cooked, drained, 1 cup	270	4	0

FOOD/PORTION SIZE	CAL	FAT (g)	CHOL (mg)
Great Northern, dry, cooked, drained, 1 cup	210	1	0
Lentils, dry, cooked, 1 cup	215	1	0
Lima, dry, cooked, drained, 1 cup	260	1	0
Lima, Giant, Seasoned with Pork, Luck's, 7 oz.	230	7	na
Lima, immature seeds, frozen, cooked, drained: thick-seeded types (Ford-hooks), 1 cup	170	1	0
Lima, immature seeds, frozen cooked, drained: thin-seeded types (baby limas) 1 cup	190	1	0
Lima, Small Green, Seasoned with Pork, Luck's, 7.5 oz.	220	7	na
Mixed (Pinto & Great Northerns), Seasoned with Pork, Luck's, 7.25 oz.	200	5	na
Navies, Ole Fashion, Ranch Style, 7.5 oz.	160	2	na
Navy, Seasoned with Pork, Luck's, 7.5 oz.	230	7	na
October, Seasoned with Pork, Luck's, 7.5 oz.	220	7	na
Pea, (Navy), dry, cooked, drained, 1 cup	225	1	0
Pinto, dry, cooked, drained, 1 cup	225	1	0
Pinto, Premium, Ranch Style, 7.5 oz.	160	1	na
Pinto, Seasoned with Pork, Luck's, 7.5 oz.	220	6	na
Pinto, with Onions, Seasoned with Pork, Luck's, 7.5 oz.	220	6	na
Red kidney, canned, 1 cup	265	1	0
Red Kidney, Dark, Ranch Style, 7.5 oz.	170	1	na
Red Kidney, Seasoned with Pork, Luck's, 7.5 oz.	220	6	na
Red Kidney, Special Cook, Luck's, 7.5 oz.	190	4	na
Refried, canned, 1 cup	295	3	0
Snap, canned, drained, solids (cut), 1 cup	25	tr	0
Snap, cooked, drained, from frozen (cut), 1 cup	25	tr	0
Snap, cooked, drained, from raw (cut and French style), 1 cup	45	tr	0
Speckled Butter, Seasoned with Pork, Luck's, 7.5 oz.	230	8	na
Sprouts, (mung) raw, 1 cup	30	tr	0
Tahini, 1 tbsp.	90	8	0
White, with pork and sweet sauce, canned, 1 cup	385	12	10
White, with pork and tomato sauce, canned, 1 cup	310	7	10
White, with sliced frankfurters, canned, 1 cup	365	18	30

NUTS

FOOD/PORTION SIZE	CAL	FAT (g)	CHOL (mg)
Almonds, Blanched/Slivered/Whole/Sliced, Planters, 1 oz.	170	15	0
Almonds, Dry Roasted, Planters, 1 oz.	170	15	0
Almonds, Honey Roasted, Planters, 1 oz.	170	13	0
Almonds, shelled, slivered, packed, 1 cup	795	70	0
Almonds, shelled, whole, 1 cup	165	15	0
Brazil, shelled, 1 oz.	185	19	0
Cashew Halves, Oil Roasted, Planters, 1 oz.	170	14	0
Cashew Halves, Oil Roasted, Unsalted, Planters, 1 oz.	170	14	0
Cashew, salted, dry roasted, 1 cup	785	63	0
Cashew, salted, roasted in oil, 1 cup	750	63	0
Cashews, Dry Roasted, Planters, 1 oz.	160	13	0
Cashews, Dry Roasted, Unsalted, Planters, 1 oz.	160	13	0
Cashews, Fancy, Oil Roasted, Planters, 1 oz.	170	14	0
Cashews, Honey Roasted, Planters, 1 oz.	170	12	0
Cashews & Peanuts, Honey Roasted, Planters, 1 oz.	170	12	0
Chestnuts, European, roasted, shelled, 1 cup	350	3	0
Coconut, dried, sweetened, shredded, 1 cup	470	33	0
Coconut, raw, 2 × 2 × ½-in. piece	160	15	0
Coconut, raw, shredded or grated, 1 cup	285	27	0
Filberts (hazelnuts), chopped, 1 cup	725	72	0
Macadamia, roasted in oil, salted, 1 cup	960	103	0
Mixed, Deluxe, Oil Roasted, Planters, 1 oz.	180	17	0
Mixed, Dry Roasted, Planters, 1 oz.	160	14	0
Mixed, Dry Roasted, Unsalted, Planters, 1 oz.	170	15	0
Mixed, Oil Roasted, Planters, 1 oz.	180	16	0
Mixed, Oil Roasted, Unsalted, Planters, 1 oz.	180	16	0
Mixed, with peanuts, salted, dry roasted, 1 oz.	170	15	0
Mixed, with peanuts, salted, roasted in oil, 1 oz.	175	16	0
Nut Topping, Planters, 1 oz.	180	16	0
Peanuts, Cocktail, Oil Roasted, Planters, 1 oz.	170	15	0
Peanuts, Cocktail, Oil Roasted, Unsalted, Planters, 1 oz.	170	15	0
Peanuts, Dry Roasted, Planters, 1 oz.	160	14	0
Peanuts, Dry Roasted, Unsalted, Planters, 1 oz.	170	15	0
Peanuts, Honey Roasted, Dry Roasted, Planters, 1 oz.	160	13	0
Peanuts, Honey Roasted, Planters, 1 oz.	170	13	0
Peanuts, Oil Roasted, Salted, Planters, 1 oz.	170	15	0
Peanuts, Redskin, Oil Roasted, Planters, 1 oz.	167	15	0
Peanuts, roasted in oil, salted, 1 cup	840	71	0
Peanuts, Roasted-in-shell, Salted, Planters, 1 oz.	160	14	0
Peanuts, Roasted-in-shell, Unsalted, Planters, 1 oz.	160	14	0
Peanuts, Spanish, Dry Roasted, Planters, 1 oz.	160	14	0
Peanuts, Spanish, Oil Roasted, Planters, 1 oz.	170	15	0
Peanuts, Spanish, Raw, Planters, 1 oz.	150	12	0
Peanuts, Sweet 'N Crunchy, Planters, 1 oz.	140	8	0
Pecans, Chips/Halves/Pieces, Planters, 1 oz.	190	20	0
Pecans, halves, 1 cup	720	73	0
Pine, (pinyons), shelled, 1 oz.	160	17	0
Pistachio, dried, shelled, 1 oz.	165	14	0
Pistachios, Dry Roasted, Planters, 1 oz.	170	15	0
Pistachios, Natural, Planters, 1 oz.	170	5	0
Pistachios, Red, Planters, 1 oz.	170	15	0
Sesame Nut Mix, Dry Roasted, Planters, 1 oz.	160	12	0
Tavern, Planters, 1 oz.	170	15	0
Walnuts, black, chopped, 1 cup	760	71	0
Walnuts, Black, Planters, 1 oz.	180	17	0
Walnuts, English or Persian, pieces/chips, 1 cup	770	74	0
Walnuts, English, Whole/Halves/Pieces, Planters, 1 oz.	190	20	0

PEAS

FOOD/PORTION SIZE	CAL	FAT (g)	CHOL (mg)
Black-eyed, dry, cooked, 1 cup	190	1	0
Split, dry, cooked, 1 cup	230	1	0

SEEDS

FOOD/PORTION SIZE	CAL	FAT (g)	CHOL (mg)
Pumpkin/squash kernels, dry, hulled, 1 oz.	155	13	0
Sesame, dry, hulled, 1 tbsp.	45	4	0
Sunflower, dry, hulled, 1 oz.	160	14	0
Sunflower Nuts, Dry Roasted, Planters, 1 oz.	160	14	0
Sunflower Nuts, Dry Roasted, Unsalted, Planters, 1 oz.	170	15	0

FOOD/PORTION SIZE	CAL	FAT (g)	CHOL (mg)
Sunflower Nuts, Oil Roasted, Planters, 1 oz.	170	15	0
Sunflower Seeds, Planters, 1 oz.	160	14	0

SOY PRODUCTS			
Miso, 1 cup	470	13	0
Soybeans, dry, cooked, drained, 1 cup	235	10	0
Tofu, $2^1/_2 \times 2^3/_4 \times 1$-in. piece	85	5	0

Meat

FOOD/PORTION SIZE	CAL	FAT (g)	CHOL (mg)
BEEF			
Braised/simmered/pot roasted, bottom round, lean and fat, 3 oz.	220	13	81
Braised/simmered/pot roasted, bottom round, lean only, 2.8 oz.	75	8	75
Braised/simmered/pot roasted, chuck blade, lean and fat, 3 oz.	325	26	87
Braised/simmered/pot roasted, chuck blade, lean only, 2.2 oz.	170	9	66
Canned, corned, 3 oz.	185	10	80
Dried, chipped, 2.5 oz.	145	4	46
Ground, broiled, patty, lean, 3 oz.	230	16	74
Ground, broiled, patty, regular, 3 oz.	245	18	76
Heart, lean, braised, 3 oz.	150	5	164
Liver, fried, $6^1/_2 \times 2^3/_8 \times ^3/_8$-in. slice, 3 oz.	185	7	410
Roast, oven cooked, eye of round, lean and fat, 3 oz.	205	12	62
Roast, oven cooked, eye of round, lean only, 2.6 oz.	135	5	52
Roast, oven cooked, rib, lean and fat, 3 oz.	315	26	72
Roast, oven cooked, rib, lean only, 2.2 oz.	150	9	49
Steak, sirloin, broiled, lean and fat, 3 oz.	240	15	77
Steak, sirloin, broiled, lean only, 2.5 oz.	185	10	64

FRANKS & SAUSAGES			
Frankfurter, chicken, 1 frank	115	9	45
Franks, Beef, Oscar Mayer, 1 link	150	14	30

FOOD/PORTION SIZE	CAL	FAT (g)	CHOL (mg)
Franks, Eckrich, 1 frank	190	17	na
Franks, Jumbo Beef, Eckrich, 1 frank	190	17	na
Sausage, pork, brown/serve, browned, 1 link	50	5	9
Sausage, pork, frankfurters, cooked, 1 frank	145	13	23
Sausage, Pork, Jimmy Dean, 33g	140	13	na
Sausage, pork, links, 1 1-oz. pork link	50	4	11
Weiners, Oscar Mayer, 1 link	140	13	30

LAMB			
Chops, arm, braised, lean and fat, 2.2 oz.	220	15	77
Chops, arm, braised, lean only, 1.7 oz.	135	7	59
Leg, roasted, lean and fat, 3 oz.	205	13	78
Leg, roasted, lean only, 2.6 oz.	140	6	65
Loin, broiled, lean and fat, 2.8 oz.	235	16	78
Loin, broiled, lean only, 2.3 oz.	140	6	60
Rib, roasted, lean and fat, 3 oz.	315	26	77
Rib, roasted, lean only, 2 oz.	130	7	50

LUNCHEON MEATS			
Chicken, roll, light, 2 slices (1 slice = 1 oz.)	90	4	28
Bologna, Beef, Oscar Mayer, 28g	90	8	15
Bologna, Oscar Mayer, 15g	50	4	na
Bologna sausage, 2 1-oz. slices	180	16	31
Braunschweiger sausage, 2 1-oz. slices	205	18	89
Ham, chopped, 8-slice (6-oz.) pack, 2 slices	95	7	21
Ham, cooked, extra lean, 8-slice (8-oz.) pack, 2 slices	75	3	27
Ham, cooked, regular, 8-slice (8-oz.) pack, 2 slices	105	6	32
Pork, canned lunch meat, spiced/unspiced, $2\ 3 \times 2 \times ^1/_2$-in. slices	140	13	26
Salami sausage, cooked, 2 1-oz. slices	145	11	37
Salami sausage, dry, 12-slice (4-oz.) pack, 2 slices	85	7	16
Sandwich spread, pork/beef, 1 tbsp.	35	3	6
Turkey, ham cured thigh meat, 2 slices (1 oz. each)	75	3	32
Turkey Bologna, Louis Rich Turkey Coldcuts, 28g	60	5	na
Turkey, ham cured thigh meat, 2 slices (1 oz. each)	75	3	32
Turkey Ham, Louis Rich Turkey Coldcuts, 21g	25	1	na
Turkey Ham, Smoked, Louis Rich Turkey Coldcuts, 28g	35	2	na

FOOD/PORTION SIZE	CAL	FAT (g)	CHOL (mg)
Turkey, loaf, breast meat, 8-slice (6-oz.) pack, 2 slices	45	1	17
Turkey, Oscar Mayer, 21g	21	1	10
Turkey Pastrami, Louis Rich Turkey Coldcuts, 23g	25	1	na
Vienna sausage, 7 per 4-oz. can, 1 sausage	45	4	8

PORK

FOOD/PORTION SIZE	CAL	FAT (g)	CHOL (mg)
Bacon, cured, cooked, Canadian, 2 slices	85	4	27
Bacon, cured, cooked, regular, 3 medium slices	110	9	16
Ham, Boiled, Oscar Mayer, 21g	25	1	15
Ham, canned, roasted, 3 oz.	140	7	35
Ham (leg), fresh, roasted, lean and fat, 3 oz.	250	18	79
Ham (leg), fresh, roasted, lean only, 2.5 oz.	160	8	68
Ham, light cure, roasted, lean and fat, 3 oz.	205	14	53
Ham, light cure, roasted, lean only, 2.4 oz.	105	4	37
Loin chop, fresh, broiled, lean and fat, 3.1 oz.	275	19	84
Loin chop, fresh, broiled, lean only, 2.5 oz.	165	8	71
Loin chop, fresh, pan fried, lean and fat, 3.1 oz.	335	27	92
Loin chop, fresh, pan fried, lean only, 2.4 oz.	180	11	72
Rib, fresh, roasted, lean and fat, 3 oz.	270	20	69
Rib, fresh, roasted, lean only, 2.5 oz.	175	10	56
Shoulder cut, fresh, braised, lean and fat, 3 oz.	295	22	93
Shoulder cut, fresh, braised, lean only, 2.4 oz.	165	8	76

VEAL

FOOD/PORTION SIZE	CAL	FAT (g)	CHOL (mg)
Medium fat, cutlet, braised/broiled, 3 oz.	185	9	109
Medium fat, rib, roasted, 3 oz.	230	14	109

Mixed Dishes

FOOD/PORTION SIZE	CAL	FAT (g)	CHOL (mg)
ABC's & 1, 2, 3's with Mini Meatballs, Chef Boy-ar-dee, 7.5 oz.	240	9	na

FOOD/PORTION SIZE	CAL	FAT (g)	CHOL (mg)
Beefaroni, Chef Boy-ar-dee, 7.5 oz.	220	8	na
Chicken a la king, cooked, home recipe, 1 cup	470	34	221
Chicken and noodles, cooked, home recipe, 1 cup	365	18	103
Chicken Stew, Chef Boy-ar-dee, EZO, 7.5 oz.	140	5	na
Chicken, Sweet & Sour, La Choy, 3/4 cup	120	2	na
Chili con carne with beans, canned, 1 cup	340	16	28
Chop suey with beef and pork, home recipe, 1 cup	300	17	68
Chow Mein, Beef, La Choy, 3/4 cup	70	1	na
Chow mein, chicken, canned, 1 cup	95	tr	9
Chow mein, chicken, home recipe, 1 cup	255	10	75
Chow Mein, Chicken, La Choy, 3/4 cup	80	3	na
Chow Mein with Beef, Chun King Stir-Fry Entrees, 6 oz.	290	19	50
Chow Mein with Chicken, Chun King Stir-Fry Entrees, 6 oz.	220	11	45
Egg Foo Young, Chun King Stir-Fry Entrees, 5 oz.	140	8	140
Egg Noodle and Cheese Dinner, Kraft, 3/4 cup	340	17	50
Egg Noodle with Chicken Dinner, Kraft, 3/4 cup	240	9	35
Hamburger Helper, Beef Noodle, without meat, 1/5 pkg.	140	2	na
Hamburger Helper, Cheeseburger Macaroni, without meat, 1/5 pkg.	180	5	na
Hamburger Helper, Lasagna, without meat, 1/5 pkg.	160	1	na
Lasagna Dinner, Chef Boy-ar-dee, 5.97 oz.	280	8	na
Macaroni and Cheese Deluxe Dinner, Kraft, 3/4 cup	260	8	20
Macaroni and Cheese Dinner, Kraft, 3/4 cup	290	13	5
Macaroni and Cheese Dinner, Spiral, Kraft, 3/4 cup	330	17	10
Macaroni and Cheese Family Size Dinner, Kraft, 3/4 cup	290	13	5
Macaroni & Cheese, Golden Grain, Quaker Oats, dry mix, 1.81 oz.	190	2	na
Macaroni & Cheese, Golden Grain, Quaker Oats, prepared, 1.81 oz.	190	2.1	3.7
Macaroni (enriched) and cheese, canned, 1 cup	230	10	24
Macaroni (enriched) and cheese, home recipe, 1 cup	430	22	44

FOOD/PORTION SIZE	CAL	FAT (g)	CHOL (mg)
Quiche Lorraine, 1 slice (¹/₈ 8-in. diameter quiche)	600	48	285
Potpie, beef, home recipe, baked, 1 piece (¹/₃ 9-in. pie)	515	30	42
Potpie, chicken, home recipe, baked, 1 piece (¹/₃ 9-in. pie)	545	31	56
Ravioli, Hearty Beef, Franco-American, 7¹/₂ oz.	290	11	na
RavioliO's, Beef, Franco-American, 7¹/₂ oz.	250	7	na
Shells and Cheese Dinner, Velveeta, ³/₄ cup	260	10	25
Spaghetti, American Style Dinner, Kraft, 1 cup	310	8	0
Spaghetti Dinner, Tangy Italian Style, Kraft, 1 cup	310	8	5
Spaghetti in tomato sauce with cheese, canned, 1 cup	190	2	3
Spaghetti in tomato sauce with cheese, home recipe, 1 cup	260	9	8
SpaghettiO's, Franco-American, 7¹/₂ oz.	170	2	na
Spaghetti with meatballs and tomato sauce, canned, 1 cup	260	10	23
Spaghetti with meatballs and tomato sauce, home recipe, 1 cup	330	12	89
Spaghetti with Meatballs, Franco-American, 7³/₈ oz.	220	8	na
Spaghetti with Meat Sauce Dinner, Kraft, 1 cup	360	14	15
Spaghetti with Tomato Sauce, Franco-American, 7³/₈ oz.	190	2	na
Stew, beef/vegetable, home recipe, 1 cup	220	11	71

Pasta

FOOD/PORTION SIZE	CAL	FAT (g)	CHOL (mg)
Macaroni and cheese dishes, see MIXED DISHES			
Macaroni, enriched, cooked, firm, hot, 1 cup	190	1	0
Macaroni, enriched, cooked, tender, cold	115	tr	0
Macaroni, enriched, cooked, tender, hot	155	1	0
Noodle Roni Chicken Mushroom, Quaker Oats, dry mix, 1.20 oz.	130	2	na
Noodle Roni Chicken Mushroom, Quaker Oats, prepared, 1.20 oz.	134	2.4	19.4

FOOD/PORTION SIZE	CAL	FAT (g)	CHOL (mg)
Noodle Roni Fettucini, Quaker Oats, dry mix, 1.50 oz.	180	5	na
Noodle Roni Fettucini, Quaker Oats, prepared, 1.50 oz.	181	5.1	26.8
Noodle Roni Garlic Butter, Quaker Oats, dry mix, 1.50 oz.	170	4	na
Noodle Roni Garlic Butter, Quaker Oats, prepared, 1.50 oz.	172	4.2	29.2
Noodle Roni Herb Butter, Quaker Oats, dry mix, 1 oz.	110	3	na
Noodle Roni Herb Butter, Quaker Oats, prepared, 1 oz.	114	2.7	19.0
Noodle Roni Parmesano, Quaker Oats, dry mix, 1.20 oz.	140	3	na
Noodle Roni Parmesano, Quaker Oats, prepared, 1.20 oz.	135	2.9	18.9
Noodle Roni Pesto, Quaker Oats, dry mix, 1.20 oz.	130	2	na
Noodle Roni Pesto, Quaker Oats, prepared, 1.20 oz.	131	2.1	na
Noodle Roni Romanoff, Quaker Oats, dry mix, 1.50 oz.	170	4	na
Noodle Roni Romanoff, Quaker Oats, prepared, 1.50 oz.	168	4.1	22.6
Noodle Roni Stroganoff, Quaker Oats, dry mix, 2 oz.	220	6	na
Noodle Roni Stroganoff, Quaker Oats, prepared, 2 oz.	225	6.4	42.3
Noodles, chow mein, canned, 1 cup	220	11	5
Noodles, egg, enriched, cooked, 1 cup	200	2	50
Spaghetti, enriched, cooked, firm, hot, 1 cup	190	1	0
Spaghetti, enriched, cooked, tender, hot, 1 cup	155	1	0
Spaghetti with sauce/meat, see MIXED DISHES			

Poultry

FOOD/PORTION SIZE	CAL	FAT (g)	CHOL (mg)
Chicken, canned, boneless, 5 oz.	235	11	88
Chicken, liver, cooked, 1 liver	30	1	126
Chicken, roasted, flesh only, breast, 3 oz.	140	3	73
Chicken, roasted, flesh only, drumstick, 1.6 oz.	75	2	41
Chicken, stewed, flesh only, light and dark meat, 1 cup	250	9	116

FOOD/PORTION SIZE	CAL	FAT (g)	CHOL (mg)
Coldcuts, chicken or turkey, *see* LUNCHEON MEATS *in* MEAT			
Duck, roasted, flesh only, 1/2 duck	445	25	197
Frankfurters, chicken or turkey, *see* FRANKFURTERS & SAUSAGES *in* MEAT			
Turkey, gravy and turkey, frozen, 5-oz. pkg.	95	4	26
Turkey, patties, breaded, batter fried, 1 patty	180	12	40
Turkey, roasted, boneless, frozen, seasoned, light and dark meat, chunked, 3 oz.	130	5	45
Turkey, roasted, flesh only, 1 light and 2 dark, 3 pieces	145	4	65
Turkey, roasted, flesh only, dark meat, 4 pieces	160	6	72
Turkey, roasted, flesh only, light and dark meat, 1 cup	240	7	106
Turkey, roasted, flesh only, light meat, 2 pieces	135	3	59

Rice

FOOD/PORTION SIZE	CAL	FAT (g)	CHOL (mg)
Beef Flavor, Rice-A-Roni, Quaker Oats, prepared, 1.33 oz.	135	0.9	0.8
Brown, cooked, hot, 1 cup	230	1	0
Brown & Wild, Mushroom Recipe, Uncle Ben's, 1/2 cup	130	1	na
Brown & Wild, Rice-A-Roni, Quaker Oats, prepared, 1.16 oz.	121	1.5	0.7
Chicken Flavor, Rice-A-Roni, Quaker Oats, prepared, 1.33 oz.	136	0.9	0.8
Chicken Mushroom, Rice-A-Roni, Quaker Oats, prepared, 1.25 oz.	129	1.2	0.9
Chicken Vegetable, Rice-A-Roni, Quaker Oats, prepared, 1.20 oz.	124	0.9	na
Drumstick, Minute Rice Mix, 1/2 cup	120	0	0
Drumstick, Minute Rice Mix, with butter, 1/2 cup	150	4	10
Extra-long grain, Riceland, 1/2 cup	85	0	na
French Style, Birds Eye International Rice Recipes, 3.3 oz.	110	0	0

FOOD/PORTION SIZE	CAL	FAT (g)	CHOL (mg)
Fried Chinese, Rice-A-Roni, Quaker Oats, prepared, 1.04 oz.	106	0.9	0.3
Fried Rice, Minute Rice Mix, 1/2 cup	120	0	0
Fried Rice, Minute Rice Mix, with oil, 1/2 cup	160	5	0
Herb Butter, Rice-A-Roni, Quaker Oats, prepared, 1.04 oz.	105	0.8	1.2
Instant, ready-to-serve, hot, 1 cup	180	0	0
Italian Style, Birds Eye International Rice Recipes, 3.3 oz.	120	1	0
Long Grain & Wild, Minute Rice Mix, 1/2 cup	120	0	0
Long Grain & Wild, Minute Rice Mix, with butter, 1/2 cup	150	4	10
Long Grain & Wild, Original Recipe, Uncle Ben's, 1/2 cup	100	0	na
Long Grain & Wild, Rice-A-Roni, Quaker Oats, prepared, 1 oz.	100	0.3	0.3
Minute Rice, without salt or butter, 2/3 cup	120	0	0
Parboiled, cooked, hot, 1 cup	185	tr	0
Parboiled, raw, 1 cup	685	1	0
Rib Roast, Minute Rice Mix, 1/2 cup	120	0	0
Rib Roast, Minute Rice Mix, with butter, 1/2 cup	150	4	10
Risotto, Rice-A-Roni, Quaker Oats, prepared, 1.50 oz.	157	1.4	2.0
Savory Broccoli AuGratin, Rice-A-Roni, Quaker Oats, prepared, 1.12 oz.	129	3.4	4.0
Savory Cauliflower AuGratin, Rice-A-Roni, Quaker Oats, prepared, 1.20 oz.	141	3.6	4.7
Savory Chicken Florentine, Rice-A-Roni, Quaker Oats, prepared, 1.07 oz.	108	0.8	0.5
Savory Creamy Parmesan & Herb, Rice-A-Roni, Quaker Oats, prepared, 1.22 oz.	145	4.2	6.9
Savory Garden Pilaf, Rice-A-Roni, Quaker Oats, prepared, 1.12 oz.	113	0.8	1.1
Savory Rice Pilaf, Rice-A-Roni, Quaker Oats, prepared, 1.45 oz.	147	0.9	0.7
Savory Spring Vegetable & Cheese, Rice-A-Roni, Quaker Oats, prepared, 1.22 oz.	141	3.5	5.5
Spanish Style, Birds Eye International Rice Recipes, 3.3 oz.	110	0	0
Spanish Style, Rice-A-Roni, Quaker Oats, prepared, 1.07 oz.	107	0.6	0.5

FOOD/PORTION SIZE	CAL	FAT (g)	CHOL (mg)
Stroganoff, Rice-A-Roni, Quaker Oats, prepared, 1.35 oz.	150	3	4.9
White, enriched, cooked, hot, 1 cup	225	tr	0
White, enriched, raw, 1 cup	670	1	0
Yellow, Rice-A-Roni, Quaker Oats, prepared, 2 oz.	196	0.5	0.6

Salad Dressing

FOOD/PORTION SIZE	CAL	FAT (g)	CHOL (mg)
Bacon & Buttermilk, Kraft, 1 tbsp.	80	8	0
Bacon, Creamy, Reduced Calorie, Kraft, 1 tbsp.	30	2	0
Bacon & Tomato, Kraft, 1 tbsp.	70	7	0
Bleu Cheese, 1 tbsp.	75	8	3
Bleu Cheese and Herb, Good Seasons Mix, prepared with oil and vinegar, 1 tbsp.	80	9	0
Bleu Cheese, Chunky, Kraft, 1 tbsp.	70	6	0
Bleu Cheese, Chunky, Reduced Calorie, Kraft, 1 tbsp.	30	2	0
Bleu Cheese, Lite, Less Oil, Wishbone, 1 tbsp.	40	4	5
Bleu Cheese, Reduced Calorie, Roka Brand, 1 tbsp.	14	1	5
Bleu Cheese, Roka Brand, 1 tbsp.	60	6	10
Buttermilk & Chives, Creamy, Kraft, 1 tbsp.	80	8	5
Buttermilk, Creamy, Kraft, 1 tbsp.	80	8	5
Buttermilk, Creamy, Reduced Calorie, Kraft, 1 tbsp.	30	3	0
Buttermilk, Farm Style, Good Seasons Salad Dressing Mix, made with whole milk and mayonnaise, 1 tbsp.	60	6	0
Caesar, Weight Watchers, 1 tbsp.	4	0	na
Cheese Garlic, Good Seasons Mix, prepared with vinegar and oil, 1 tbsp.	80	9	0
Cheese Italian, Good Seasons Mix, prepared with vinegar and oil, 1 tbsp.	80	9	0
Coleslaw, Kraft, 1 tbsp.	70	6	10
Creamy, Reduced Calorie, Rancher's Choice, 1 tbsp.	30	3	5
Cucumber, Creamy, Kraft, 1 tbsp.	70	8	0
Cucumber, Creamy, Reduced Calorie, Kraft, 1 tbsp.	30	3	0
Creamy, Rancher's Choice, 1 tbsp.	80	8	5

FOOD/PORTION SIZE	CAL	FAT (g)	CHOL (mg)
French, Catalina Brand, 1 tbsp.	70	6	0
French, Kraft, 1 tbsp.	60	6	0
French, Lite, Less Oil, Wishbone, 1 tbsp.	18	1	na
French, low calorie, 1 tbsp.	25	2	0
French, No Oil, Pritikin, 1 tbsp.	10	0	na
French, Reduced Calorie, Kraft, 1 tbsp.	25	2	0
French, regular, 1 tbsp.	85	9	0
French, Weight Watchers, 1 tbsp.	10	0	na
Garlic and Herbs, Good Seasons Mix, made with oil and vinegar, 1 tbsp.	80	9	0
Garlic, Creamy, Kraft, 1 tbsp.	50	5	10
Golden Caesar, Kraft, 1 tbsp.	70	7	0
Herb, Classic, Good Seasons Mix, made with vinegar and oil, 1 tbsp.	80	9	0
Home prepared, cooked type, 1 tbsp.	25	2	9
Italian, Creamy, Lite, Less Oil, Wishbone, 1 tbsp.	25	2	10
Italian, Creamy, Reduced Calorie, Kraft, 1 tbsp.	25	2	0
Italian, Creamy, with Real Sour Cream, Kraft, 1 tbsp.	60	6	0
Italian, Good Seasons Mix, made with oil and vinegar, 1 tbsp.	80	9	0
Italian, Lite, Good Seasons Mix, made with oil and vinegar, 1 tbsp.	25	3	0
Italian, Lite, Zesty, Good Seasons Mix, made with oil and vinegar, 1 tbsp.	25	3	0
Italian, low calorie, 1 tbsp.	5	tr	0
Italian, Mild, Good Seasons Mix, made with oil and vinegar, 1 tbsp.	90	9	0
Italian, No Oil, Good Seasons Mix, prepared with vinegar and water, 1 tbsp.	6	0	0
Italian, No Oil, Pritikin, 1 tbsp.	6	0	na
Italian, Oil-Free, Kraft, 1 tbsp.	4	0	0
Italian, Presto, 1 tbsp.	70	7	0
Italian, Reduced Calorie, Kraft, 1 tbsp.	6	0	0
Italian, regular, 1 tbsp.	80	9	0
Italian, Weight Watchers, 1 tbsp.	6	0	na
Italian, Zesty, Good Seasons Mix, made with oil and vinegar, 1 tbsp.	80	9	0
Italian, Zesty, Kraft, 1 tbsp.	70	8	0
Lemon Herb, Good Seasons Mix, made with oil and vinegar, 1 tbsp.	80	9	0
Mayonnaise type, 1 tbsp.	60	5	4
Miracle Whip, 1 tbsp.	70	7	5
Miracle Whip Light, Reduced Calorie, 1 tbsp.	45	4	5

FOOD/PORTION SIZE	CAL	FAT (g)	CHOL (mg)
Oil & Vinegar, Kraft, 1 tbsp.	70	7	0
Onion & Chives, Creamy, Kraft, 1 tbsp.	70	7	0
Reduced Calorie, Catalina Brand, 1 tbsp.	16	0	0
Red Wine Vinegar and Oil, Kraft, 1 tbsp.	50	4	0
Russian, Reduced Calorie, Kraft, 1 tbsp.	30	1	0
Thousand Island & Bacon, Kraft, 1 tbsp.	60	6	0
Thousand Island, Kraft, 1 tbsp.	60	5	5
Thousand Island, Lite, Less Oil, Wishbone, 1 tbsp.	40	3	10
Thousand island, low calorie, 1 tbsp.	25	2	2
Thousand Island, Reduced Calorie, Kraft, 1 tbsp.	30	2	5
Thousand island, regular, 1 tbsp.	60	6	4
Tomato Vinaigrette, Weight Watchers, 1 tbsp.	8	0	na
Tomato, Zesty, No Oil, Pritikin, 1 tbsp.	18	0	na
Vinegar and oil, home prepared, 1 tbsp.	70	8	0

Snacks

BARS

FOOD/PORTION SIZE	CAL	FAT (g)	CHOL (mg)
Breakfast, Peanut Butter Chocolate Chip, Carnation, 1 bar	200	11	na
Breakfast, Peanut Butter Crunch, Carnation, 1 bar	190	10	na
Dipps, Caramel Nut, Quaker Oats, 1.10 oz.	148	6.4	1.8
Dipps, Chocolate Chip, Quaker Oats, 1 oz.	139	6.3	1.4
Dipps, Chocolate Fudge, Quaker Oats, 1.10 oz.	160	7.9	na
Dipps, Peanut Butter & Chocolate Chip, Quaker Oats, 1.15 oz.	174	10	na
Dipps, Peanut Butter, Quaker Oats, 1.15 oz.	170	9.1	1.8
Slender, Chocolate, Carnation, 2 bars	270	14	na
Slender, Chocolate Chip, Carnation, 2 bars	270	14	na
Slender, Vanilla, Carnation, 2 bars	270	15	na

FOOD/PORTION SIZE	CAL	FAT (g)	CHOL (mg)
CORN CHIPS			
Bugles, 1 oz.	150	8	na
Corn chips, 1-oz. package	155	9	0
Doritos, Cool Ranch, 1 oz.	140	7	0
Doritos, Nacho Cheese, 1 oz.	140	7	0
Doritos, Salsa Rio, 1 oz.	140	7	0
Doritos, Toasted Corn, 1 oz.	140	6	0
Fritos Corn Chips, 1 oz.	150	9	0
Fritos Corn Chips, Crisp n' Thin, 1 oz.	160	10	0
Tostitos, Sharp Nacho Cheese, 1 oz.	150	9	0
Tostitos, Traditional, 1 oz.	140	8	0
DIPS			
Acapulco, Ortega, 1oz.	8	0	0
Avocado (guacamole), Kraft, 2 tbsp.	50	4	0
Bacon & Horseradish, Kraft, 2 tbsp.	60	5	0
Bacon & Horseradish, Kraft Premium, 2 tbsp.	50	5	10
Blue Cheese, Kraft Premium, 2 tbsp.	45	4	10
Clam, Kraft, 2 tbsp.	60	4	10
Clam, Kraft Premium, 2 tbsp.	45	4	20
Cucumber, Creamy, Kraft Premium, 2 tbsp.	50	4	10
French Onion, Kraft, 2 tbsp.	60	4	0
French Onion, Kraft Premium, 2 tbsp.	45	4	10
Garlic, Kraft, 2 tbsp.	60	4	0
Green Onion, Kraft, 2 tbsp.	60	4	0
Jalapeño Pepper, Kraft, 2 tbsp.	50	4	0
Jalapeño Pepper, Kraft Premium, 2 tbsp.	60	5	15
Nacho Cheese, Kraft Premium, 2 tbsp.	50	4	10
Onion, Creamy, Kraft Premium, 2 tbsp.	45	4	10
FRUIT SNACKS			
Fruit Roll-Ups, Banana, 1/2 oz.	50	1	na
Fruit Roll-Ups, Cherry, 1/2 oz.	50	1	na
Fruit Roll-Ups, Grape, 1/2 oz.	50	1	na
Fruit Roll-Ups, Strawberry, 1/2 oz.	50	1	na
Fruit Roll-Ups, Watermelon, 1/2 oz.	60	1	na
Fruit Wrinkles, Orange, 1 pouch	100	2	na
Fruit Wrinkles, Strawberry, 1 pouch	100	2	na
Fun Fruits, all shapes, 9 oz.	100	1	na
Fun Fruits, Fantastic Fruit Punch, 9 oz.	100	1	na
Fun Fruits, Grape, 9 oz.	100	1	na

FOOD/PORTION SIZE	CAL	FAT (g)	CHOL (mg)
GRANOLA			
Chocolate Chip, Chewy Granola Bar, Quaker Oats, 1 oz.	128	4.7	0.3
Chocolate Graham & Marshmallow, Chewy Granola Bar, Quaker Oats, 1 oz.	126	4.4	0.3
Honey & Oats, Chewy Granola Bar, Quaker Oats, 1 oz.	125	4.4	0.3
Nut & Raisin, Chunky, Chewy Granola Bar, Quaker Oats, 1 oz.	131	5.8	0.2
Oats n' Honey, Granola Bar, Nature Valley, 1 bar	120	5	na
Peanut Butter, Chewy Granola Bar, Quaker Oats, 1 oz.	128	4.9	0.3
Peanut Butter Chocolate Chip, Chewy Granola Bar, Quaker Oats, 1 oz.	131	5.7	0.3
Raisin Cinnamon, Chewy Granola Bar, Quaker Oats, 1 oz.	128	5.0	0.3
POPCORN			
Air-popped, unsalted, 1 cup	30	tr	0
Microwave, Butter Flavor, Jiffy Pop, 4 cups (popped)	140	7	0
Microwave, Butter, Orville Redenbacher, 4 cups	110	6	na
Microwave, Butter, Planters, 3 cups (popped)	140	10	0
Microwave, Natural, Orville Redenbacher, 4 cups	110	7	na
Microwave, Natural, Planters, 3 cups (popped)	140	9	0
Microwave, Regular, Jiffy Pop, 4 cups (popped)	140	7	0
Pan, Butter Flavor, Jiffy Pop, 4 cups (popped)	130	6	0
Pan, Regular, Jiffy Pop, 4 cups (popped)	130	6	0
Planters, 3 cups (popped)	20	0	0
Popped in vegetable oil, salted, 1 cup	55	3	0
Sugar syrup coated, 1 cup	135	1	0
POTATO CHIPS			
Lays, 1 oz.	150	10	0
Lays, Bar-B-Que, 1 oz.	150	9	0
O'Grady's, 1 oz.	150	9	0
O'Grady's, Au Gratin, 1 oz.	150	8	0
O'Grady's, Hearty Seasoning, 1 oz.	140	8	0
Potato chips, 10 chips	105	7	0
Pringles, 1 oz.	170	13	na
Pringles Light, Bar-B-Que, 1 oz.	150	8	na
Pringles Light, Ranch, 1 oz.	150	8	na
Pringles, Sour Cream n' Onion, 1 oz.	170	12	na

FOOD/PORTION SIZE	CAL	FAT (g)	CHOL (mg)
Ruffles, 1 oz.	150	10	0
Ruffles, Cajun Spice, 1 oz.	150	10	0
Ruffles, Sour Cream & Onion, 1 oz.	150	9	na
PRETZELS			
Enriched flour, 2¼-in. sticks, 10 pretzels	10	tr	0
Enriched flour, twisted, dutch, 1 pretzel	65	1	0
Enriched flour, twisted, thin, 10 pretzels	240	2	0
Mister Salty, Dutch, 2 pretzels	110	1	na
Mister Salty, Juniors, 29 pretzels	110	2	na
Mister Salty, Mini, 16 pretzels	110	1	na
Mister Salty, Mini Mix, 23 pretzels	110	1	na
Mister Salty, Rings, 22 pretzels	110	2	na
Mister Salty, Rings, Butter Flavor, 23 pretzels	110	2	na
Mister Salty, Sticks, 1 oz.	110	1	0
Mister Salty, Sticks, Butter Flavor, 90 pretzels	110	1	na
Mister Salty, Twists, 1 oz.	110	2	0
Mister Salty, Veri-Thin, 45 pretzels	110	1	0
RICE CAKES			
Barley & Oats, Quaker Oats, 0.32 oz.	34	0.3	0
Buckwheat, Quaker Oats, 0.32 oz.	35	0.3	0
Corn, Quaker Oats, 0.32 oz.	35	0.3	0
Multi-Grain, Quaker Oats, 0.32 oz.	34	0.4	na
Multi-Grain, Salt-Free, Quaker Oats, 0.32 oz.	35	0.4	0
Plain, Quaker Oats, 0.32 oz.	35	0.3	0
Plain, Unsalted, Quaker Oats, 0.32 oz.	35	0.3	0
Rye, Quaker Oats, 0.32 oz.	34	0.4	0
Sesame, Quaker Oats, 0.32 oz.	35	0.3	0
Sesame, Salt-Free, Quaker Oats, 0.32 oz.	35	0.3	0
Wheat, Quaker Oats, 0.32 oz.	34	0.3	0
MISCELLANEOUS			
Cheez Balls, Planters, 1 oz.	160	11	5
Cheez Curls, Planters, 1 oz.	160	11	5
Doo Dads, Cheddar 'n Herb, ½ cup	140	6	na
Doo Dads, Original, ½ cup	140	6	na
Doo Dads, Zesty Cheese, ½ cup	140	6	na
Sour Cream & Onion Puffs, Planters, 1 oz.	160	10	0

Soup

FOOD/PORTION SIZE	CAL	FAT (g)	CHOL (mg)
Bean with bacon, canned, condensed, prepared with = volume of water, 1 cup	170	6	3
Beef broth bouillon consume, canned, condensed, prepared with = volume of water, 1 cup	15	1	tr
Beef noodle, canned, condensed, prepared with = volume of water, 1 cup	85	3	5
Bouillon, dehydrated, unprepared, 1 packet	15	1	1
Chicken, cream of, canned, condensed, prepared with = volume of milk, 1 cup	190	11	27
Chicken, cream of, canned, condensed, prepared with = volume of water, 1 cup	115	7	10
Chicken, Lemon, Lipton Lite Cup-A-Soup, 6 oz.	45	1	na
Chicken noodle, canned, condensed, prepared with = volume of water, 1 cup	75	2	7
Chicken noodle, dehydrated, prepared with water, 1 packet	40	1	2
Chicken rice, canned, condensed, prepared with = volume of water, 1 cup	60	2	7
Clam chowder, Manhattan, canned, condensed, prepared with = volume of water, 1 cup	80	2	2
Clam chowder, New England, canned, condensed, prepared with = volume of milk, 1 cup	165	7	22
Minestrone, canned, condensed, prepared with = volume of water, 1 cup	80	3	2
Mushroom, cream of, canned, condensed, prepared with = volume of milk, 1 cup	205	14	20
Mushroom, cream of, canned, condensed, prepared with = volume of water, 1 cup	130	9	2
Onion, dehydrated, prepared with water, 1 packet	20	tr	0
Pea, green, canned, condensed, prepared with = volume of water, 1 cup	165	3	0
Tomato, canned, condensed, prepared with = volume of milk, 1 cup	160	6	17
Tomato, canned, condensed, prepared with = volume of water, 1 cup	85	2	0

FOOD/PORTION SIZE	CAL	FAT (g)	CHOL (mg)
Tomato & Herb, Lipton Lite Cup-A-Soup, 6 oz.	70	1	na
Tomato vegetable, dehydrated, prepared with water, 1 packet	40	1	0
Vegetable beef, canned, condensed, prepared with = volume of water, 1 cup	80	2	5
Vegetable, Oriental, Lipton Lite Cup-A-Soup, 6 oz.	30	1	na
Vegetarian, canned, condensed, prepared with = volume of water, 1 cup	70	2	0

Vegetables

FOOD/PORTION SIZE	CAL	FAT (g)	CHOL (mg)
ALFALFA			
Seeds, sprouted, raw, 1 cup	10	tr	0
ARTICHOKES			
Globe or French, cooked drained, 1 artichoke	55	tr	0
Hearts, Birds Eye Deluxe Vegetables, 3 oz.	30	0	0
Jerusalem, red, sliced, 1 cup	115	tr	0
ASPARAGUS			
Canned, spears, 4 spears	10	tr	0
Cuts, Birds Eye Regular Vegetables, 3.3 oz.	25	0	0
Cuts & tips, cooked, drained, from raw, 1 cup	45	1	0
Cuts & tips, from frozen, 1 cup	50	1	0
Spears, Birds Eye Regular Vegetables, 3.3 oz.	25	0	0
Spears, cooked, drained, from raw, 4 spears	15	tr	0
Spears from frozen, 4 spears	15	tr	0
BAMBOO SHOOTS			
Canned, drained, 1 cup	25	1	0
BEANS			
Baby Lima, Birds Eye Regular Vegetables, 3.3 oz.	130	0	0
Fordhook Lima, Birds Eye Regular Vegetables, 3.3 oz.	100	0	0

FOOD/PORTION SIZE	CAL	FAT (g)	CHOL (mg)
Green, Cut, Birds Eye Regular Vegetables, 3 oz.	25	0	0
Green, French Cut, Birds Eye Deluxe, 3 oz.	25	0	0
Green, Italian, Birds Eye Regular Vegetables, 3 oz.	30	0	0
Green, Whole, Birds Eye Deluxe Vegetables, 3 oz.	25	0	0
Sprouts, (mung), cooked, drained, 1 cup	25	tr	0
BEETS			
Canned, drained, solids, diced or sliced, 1 cup	55	tr	0
Cooked, drained, diced or sliced, 1 cup	55	tr	0
Cooked, drained, whole, 2 beets	30	tr	0
Greens, leaves and stems, cooked, drained, 1 cup	40	tr	0
BROCCOLI			
Baby Sprouts, Birds Eye Deluxe Vegetables, 3.3 oz.	30	0	0
Chopped, Birds Eye Regular Vegetables, 3.3 oz.	25	0	0
Cooked, drained, from frozen, 1 piece (4½-5 in. long)	10	tr	0
Cooked, drained, from frozen, chopped, 1 cup	50	tr	0
Cuts, Birds Eye Regular Vegetables, 3.3 oz.	25	0	0
Florets, Birds Eye Deluxe Vegetables, 3.3 oz.	25	0	0
Spears from raw, cooked, drained, 1 cup, (½-in. pieces)	45	tr	0
Raw, 1 spear	40	1	0
Spear, medium from raw, cooked, drained, 1 spear	50	1	0
Spears, Birds Eye Regular Vegetables, 3.3 oz.	25	0	0
BRUSSELS SPROUTS			
Birds Eye Regular Vegetables, 3.3 oz.	35	0	0
Cooked, drained, from frozen, 1 cup	65	1	0
Cooked, drained, from raw, 1 cup	60	1	0
CABBAGE			
Chinese pak-choi, cooked, drained, 1 cup	20	tr	0
Chinese pe-tsai, raw, 1-in. pieces, 1 cup	10	tr	0
Common varieties, coarsely shredded or sliced, 1 cup	15	tr	0

FOOD/PORTION SIZE	CAL	FAT (g)	CHOL (mg)
Common varieties, cooked, drained, 1 cup	30	tr	0
Red, raw, coarsely shredded or sliced, 1 cup	20	tr	0
Savoy, raw, coarsely shredded or sliced, 1 cup	20	tr	0
CARROTS			
Baby, Whole, Birds Eye Deluxe Vegetables, 3.3 oz.	40	0	0
Canned, sliced, drained, solids, 1 cup	35	tr	0
Cooked, sliced, drained, from frozen, 1 cup	55	tr	0
Cooked, sliced, drained, from raw, 1 cup	70	tr	0
Raw, without crowns or tips, scraped, grated, 1 cup	45	tr	0
Raw, without crowns or tips, scraped, 1 cup	30	tr	0
CAULIFLOWER			
Birds Eye Regular Vegetables, 3.3 oz.	25	0	0
Cooked, drained, from frozen (flowerets), 1 cup	35	tr	0
Cooked, drained, from raw (flowerets), 1 cup	30	tr	0
Raw (flowerets), 1 cup	25	tr	0
CELERY			
Pascal type, raw, large outer stalk, 1 stalk	5	tr	0
Pascal type, raw, pieces, diced, 1 cup	20	tr	0
COLLARDS			
Cooked, drained, from frozen (chopped), 1 cup	60	1	0
Cooked, drained, from raw (leaves without stems), 1 cup	25	tr	0
CORN			
Big Ears, Cob, Birds Eye Regular Vegetables, 1 ear	160	1	0
Little Ears, Cob, Birds Eye Regular Vegetables, 2 ears	130	1	0
On the Cob, Birds Eye Regular Vegetables, 1 ear	120	1	0
Sweet, Birds Eye Regular Vegetables, 3.3 oz.	80	1	0
Sweet, canned, cream style, 1 cup	185	1	0
Sweet, cooked, drained, from frozen, 1 ear (3½ in.)	60	tr	0

FOOD/PORTION SIZE	CAL	FAT (g)	CHOL (mg)
Sweet, cooked, drained, from raw, 1 ear (5 × 1¾ in.)	85	1	0
Sweet, cooked, drained, kernels, 1 cup	135	tr	0
Sweet, vacuum packed, whole kernel, 1 cup	165	1	0
Tender, Sweet, Birds Eye Deluxe Vegetables, 3.3 oz.	80	1	0

CUCUMBER

Peeled slices ⅛-in. thick, (large 2⅛-in. diameter, small 1¾-in. diameter), 6 large or 8 small	5	tr	0

EGGPLANT

Cooked, steamed, 1 cup	25	tr	0

ENDIVE

Curly (including escarole), raw, small pieces, 1 cup	10	tr	0

GREENS

Dandelion, cooked, drained, 1 cup	5	1	0
Mustard, without stems and midribs, cooked, drained, 1 cup	20	tr	0
Turnip, cooked, drained from frozen (chopped), 1 cup	50	1	0
Turnip, cooked, drained from raw (leaves & stems), 1 cup	30	tr	0

KALE

Cooked, drained from frozen, chopped, 1 cup	40	1	0
Cooked, drained, from raw, chopped, 1 cup	40	1	0

KHOLRABE

Thickened bulb-like stem, cooked, drained, diced, 1 cup	50	tr	0

LETTUCE

Looseleaf (bunching varieties including romain or cos), chopped or shredded, 1 cup	10	tr	0
Butterhead, as Boston types, raw, 1 head (5-in. diameter)	20	tr	0
Butterhead, as Boston types, raw, leaves, 1 outer or 2 inner leaves	tr	tr	0
Crisphead, as iceberg, raw, ¼ of head, 1 wedge	20	tr	0

FOOD/PORTION SIZE	CAL	FAT (g)	CHOL (mg)
Crisphead, as iceberg, raw, head (6-in. diameter), 1 head	70	1	0
Crisphead, as iceberg, raw, pieces, chopped, shredded, 1 cup	5	tr	0

MIXED VEGETABLES

Baby Carrots, Peas, Pearl Onions, Birds Eye Deluxe Vegetables, 3.3 oz.	50	0	0
Bavarian Green Beans Spaetzle, Birds Eye International Recipe, 3.3 oz.	110	6	10
Broccoli, Baby Carrots, Water Chestnuts, Birds Eye Farm Fresh Mix, 3.2 oz.	35	0	0
Broccoli, Carrots, Pasta, Birds Eye Combination Vegetables, 3.3 oz.	90	4	0
Broccoli, Cauliflower, Carrot, Birds Eye Farm Fresh Mix, 3.2 oz.	25	0	0
Broccoli, Corn, Red Pepper, Birds Eye Farm Fresh Mix, 3.2 oz.	50	0	0
Broccoli, Green Beans, Pearl Onions, Red Peppers, Birds Eye Farm Fresh Mix, 3.2 oz.	25	0	0
Broccoli, Red Peppers, Bamboo Shoots, and Straw Mushrooms, Birds Eye Farm Fresh Mix, 3.2 oz.	25	0	0
Brussels Sprouts, Cauliflower, Carrots, Birds Eye Farm Fresh Mix, 3.2 oz.	30	0	0
Cauliflower, Baby Carrots, Snow Pea Pods, Birds Eye Farm Fresh Mix, 3.2 oz.	30	0	0
Chinese Style, Birds Eye International Recipe, 3.3 oz.	80	5	0
Chinese Style, Birds Eye Stir-Fry Vegetables, 3.3 oz.	35	0	0
Chow Mein Style, Birds Eye International Recipe, 3.3 oz.	90	4	0
Corn, Green Beans, Pasta, Birds Eye Combination Vegetables, 3.3 oz.	110	5	0
Green Beans, French, Toasted Almond, Birds Eye Combination Vegetables, 3 oz.	50	2	0
Green Peas, Pearl Onions, Birds Eye Combination Vegetables, 3.3 oz.	70	0	0
Italian Style, Birds Eye International Recipe, 3.3 oz.	110	7	0
Japanese Style, Birds Eye International Recipe, 3.3 oz.	100	6	0

FOOD/PORTION SIZE	CAL	FAT (g)	CHOL (mg)
Japanese Style, Birds Eye Stir-Fry Vegetables, 3.3 oz.	30	0	0
Mandarin Style, Birds Eye International Recipe, 3.3 oz.	90	4	0
Mixed Vegetables, Birds Eye Regular Vegetables, 3.3 oz.	60	0	0
New England Style Vegetables, Birds Eye International Style, 3.3 oz.	130	7	0
Pasta Primavera Style, Birds Eye International Recipe, 3.3 oz.	120	5	5
Rice, Green Peas, Mushrooms, Birds Eye Combination Vegetables, 2.3 oz.	110	0	0
San Francisco Style, Birds Eye International Style, 3.3 oz.	100	5	0
Vegetables, mixed, canned, drained, solids, 1 cup	75	tr	0
Vegetables, mixed, frozen, cooked, drained, 1 cup	105	tr	0

MIXED VEGETABLES WITH SAUCE

FOOD/PORTION SIZE	CAL	FAT (g)	CHOL (mg)
Broccoli, Cauliflower, Carrot, Cheese Sauce, Birds Eye Cheese Sauce Combination Vegetables, 5 oz.	100	5	5
Broccoli, Cauliflower, Creamy Italian Cheese Sauce, Birds Eye Cheese Sauce Combination Vegetables, 4.5 oz.	90	6	15
Green Peas, Potatoes, Cream Sauce, Bird's Eye Combination Vegetables, 2.6 oz.	130	6	0
Mixed Vegetables with Onion Sauce, Birds Eye Combination Vegetables, 2.6 oz.	100	5	0
Peas, Pearl Onion, Cheese Sauce, Birds Eye Cheese Sauce Combination Vegetables, 5 oz.	140	5	0

MUSHROOMS

FOOD/PORTION SIZE	CAL	FAT (g)	CHOL (mg)
Cooked, drained, 1 cup	40	1	0
Canned, drained, solids, 1 cup	35	tr	0
Raw, sliced or chopped, 1 cup	20	tr	0

OKRA

FOOD/PORTION SIZE	CAL	FAT (g)	CHOL (mg)
Pods, 3 × 5/8 in., cooked, 8 pods	25	tr	0

ONIONS

FOOD/PORTION SIZE	CAL	FAT (g)	CHOL (mg)
Cooked, (whole or sliced), drained, 1 cup	60	tr	0
Small, Whole, Birds Eye Regular Vegetables, 4 oz.	40	0	0
Raw, chopped, 1 cup	55	tr	0
Raw, sliced, 1 cup	40	tr	0
Rings, breaded par-fried, frozen, prepared, 2 rings	80	5	0
Spring, raw, bulb (3/8-in. diameter) and white portion of top, 6 onions	10	tr	0

PARSLEY

FOOD/PORTION SIZE	CAL	FAT (g)	CHOL (mg)
Freeze-dried, 1 tbsp.	tr	tr	0
Raw, 10 sprigs	5	tr	0

PARSNIPS

FOOD/PORTION SIZE	CAL	FAT (g)	CHOL (mg)
Cooked, (diced or 2-in. lengths), drained, 1 cup	125	tr	0

PEAS

FOOD/PORTION SIZE	CAL	FAT (g)	CHOL (mg)
Black-eyed, immature seeds, cooked, drained, from frozen, 1 cup	225	1	0
Black-eyed, immature seeds, cooked, drained, from raw, 1 cup	180	1	0
Frozen, cooked, drained, 1 cup	125	tr	0
Green, Birds Eye Regular Vegetables, 3.3 oz.	80	0	0
Green, canned, drained, solids, 1 cup	115	1	0
Pods, edible, cooked, drained, 1 cup	65	tr	0
Tender Tiny, Birds Eye Deluxe Vegetables, 3.3 oz.	60	0	0

PEPPERS

FOOD/PORTION SIZE	CAL	FAT (g)	CHOL (mg)
Hot chili, raw, 1 pepper	20	tr	0
Sweet, (about 5 per lb., whole) stem and seeds removed, 1 pepper	20	tr	0
Sweet, (about 5 per lb., whole) stem and seeds removed, cooked, drained, 1 pepper	15	tr	0

PICKLES

FOOD/PORTION SIZE	CAL	FAT (g)	CHOL (mg)
Cucumber, dill, medium whole, 1 pickle (3 3/4-in. long, 1 1/4-in. diameter)	5	tr	0
Cucumber, fresh-pack slices, 2 slices (1 1/2-in. diameter, 1/4-in. thick)	10	tr	0
Cucumber, sweet gherkin, small, 1 pickle (whole, about 2 1/2-in long, 3/4-in. diameter)	20	tr	0

FOOD/PORTION SIZE	CAL	FAT (g)	CHOL (mg)
POTATOES			
Baked (about 2 per lb. raw), flesh only, 1 potato	145	tr	0
Baked (about 2 per lb. raw), with skin, 1 potato	220	tr	0
Boiled (about 3 per lb. raw), peeled after boiling, 1 potato	120	tr	0
Boiled (about 3 per lb. raw), peeled before boiling, 1 potato	115	tr	0
French fry strip (2- to 3½-in. long), fried in vegetable oil, 10 strips	160	8	0
French fried strip (2- to 3½-in. long), oven heated, 10 strips	110	4	0
Sweet, candied, 2½ × 2-in. piece, 1 piece	145	3	8
Sweet, canned, solid packed, mashed, 1 cup	260	1	0
Sweet, cooked (baked in skin), 1 potato	115	tr	0
Sweet, cooked (boiled without skin), 1 potato	160	tr	0
Sweet, vacuum pack, 1 piece, 2¾ × 1 in.	35	tr	0
POTATO PRODUCTS			
Au gratin, prepared from dry mix, 1 cup	230	10	12
Au gratin, prepared from home recipe, 1 cup	325	19	26
Hashed brown, prepared from frozen, 1 cup	340	18	0
Mashed, prepared from home recipe, milk added, 1 cup	160	1	4
Mashed, prepared from home recipe, milk and margarine added, 1 cup	225	9	4
Potato salad, prepared with mayo, 1 cup	360	21	170
Prepared from dehydrated flakes (without milk), water, milk, butter, salt added, 1 cup	235	12	29
Scalloped, prepared from dry milk mix, 1 cup	230	11	27
Scalloped, prepared from home recipe, 1 cup	210	9	29
PUMPKIN			
Canned, 1 cup	85	1	0
Cooked, from raw, mashed, 1 cup	50	tr	0
RADISHES			
Raw, stem ends and rootlets cut off, 4 radishes	5	tr	0

FOOD/PORTION SIZE	CAL	FAT (g)	CHOL (mg)
SAUERKRAUT			
Canned, solids and liquid, 1 cup	45	tr	0
SEAWEED			
Kelp, raw, 1 oz.	10	tr	0
Spirulina, dried, 1 oz.	80	2	0
SPINACH			
Canned, drained solids, 1 cup	50	1	0
Chopped, Birds Eye Regular Vegetables, 3.3 oz.	20	0	0
Cooked, drained, from frozen, leaf, 1 cup	55	tr	0
Cooked, drained, from raw, 1 cup	40	tr	0
Raw, chopped, 1 cup	10	tr	0
Souffle, 1 cup	220	18	184
Whole Leaf, Birds Eye Regular Vegetables, 3.3 oz.	20	0	0
SQUASH			
Summer (all varieties), cooked, sliced, drained, 1 cup	35	1	0
Winter (all varieties), cooked, baked, cubed, 1 cup	80	1	0
Winter, cooked, Birds Eye Regular Vegetables, 4 oz.	45	0	0
TOMATOES			
Canned, solids and liquid, 1 cup	50	1	0
Juice, canned, 1 cup	40	tr	0
Paste, canned, 1 cup	220	2	0
Puree, canned, 1 cup	105	tr	0
Raw, 2⅗-in. diameter (3 per 12-oz. pkg.), 1 tomato	25	tr	0
Sauce, canned, 1 cup	75	tr	0
TURNIPS			
Cooked, diced, 1 cup	30	tr	0
VEGETABLES WITH SAUCE			
Broccoli with Cheese Sauce, Birds Eye Cheese Sauce Combination Vegetables, 5 oz.	120	6	5
Broccoli with Creamy Italian Cheese Sauce, Birds Eye Cheese Sauce Combination Vegetables, 4.5 oz.	90	6	15
Brussels Sprouts with Cheese Sauce, Birds Eye Cheese Sauce Combination Vegetables, 4.5 oz.	110	6	5

FOOD/PORTION SIZE	CAL	FAT (g)	CHOL (mg)
Cauliflower with Cheese Sauce, Birds Eye Cheese Sauce Combination Vegetables, 5 oz.	110	6	5
Green Peas with Cream Sauce, Birds Eye Combination Vegetables, 2.6 oz.	120	6	0
Onions, Small, with Cream Sauce, Birds Eye Combination Vegetables, 3 oz.	110	6	0
Spinach, Creamed, Birds Eye Combination Vegetables, 3 oz.	60	4	0

Yogurt

FOOD/PORTION SIZE	CAL	FAT (g)	CHOL (mg)
Banana, Dannon, 1 cup	240	3	na
Blueberry, Dannon, 1 cup	240	3	na

FOOD/PORTION SIZE	CAL	FAT (g)	CHOL (mg)
Blueberry, Dannon Fresh Flavors, 1 cup	200	4	0
Blueberry, Lite n' Lively, 5 oz.	150	1	10
Blueberry, Yoplait, 6 oz.	190	3	na
Cherry, Yoplait 150, 6 oz.	150	0	5
Fruit-flavors, added milk solids, made with lowfat milk, 8 oz.	230	2	10
Plain, added milk solids, made with lowfat milk, 8 oz.	145	4	14
Plain, added milk solids, made with nonfat milk, 8 oz.	125	tr	4
Plain, Dannon, 1 cup	140	4	na
Plain, without added milk solids, with whole milk, 8 oz.	140	7	29
Raspberry, Dannon Fresh Flavors, 1 cup	200	4	na
Red Raspberry, Lite n' Lively, 5 oz.	140	2	10
Strawberry-Banana, Yoplait, 6 oz.	190	3	na
Strawberry, Dannon Fresh Flavors, 1 cup	200	4	na
Strawberry, Lite n' Lively, 5 oz.	150	2	10
Strawberry, Yoplait 150, 6 oz.	150	0	5
Vanilla, Dannon, 1 cup	200	3	na
Vanilla, Yoplait 150, 6 oz.	150	0	5

Index